Healthy Sleep Habits, Happy Child

Also by Marc Weissbluth, M.D.
Crybabies

Healthy Sleep Habits, Happy Child

Marc Weissbluth, M.D.

Fawcett Columbine • New York

This book is dedicated to my wife, Linda.

Contents

Introduction

Why won't my child sleep better? Where does he get all his energy? He really never seems tired; he just goes and goes and goes until he crashes. I'm burned out and I know he must be exhausted. Of course, he never slept well, even when he was a baby. He was up at all hours during the night, every night. Naps? Forget them. Sure, he took catnaps, but only in my arms or in the car. I just thought it was normal because no baby wants to sleep with so many interesting things going on around him. Anyway, I didn't want to hear all that crying when he didn't want to sleep. But now he's two, and I'm getting tired of those constant bedtime battles. There are times when I wish he would simply just settle down and be less wild.

Sound familiar?

All kids occasionally are firecrackers when things are not going their way. But why do some kids have much shorter fuses than others?

Healthy Sleep Habits, Happy Child will explain how fatigue caused by poor quality sleep makes some children pop off more often or explode with more force than others. It also will explain how chronic fatigue can reduce your child's ability to succeed in school. This book will show you how you can nurture, enhance, and maintain calm and alert behavior in your child by instilling good sleep habits.

I will lead you on a tour through the shadows of your child's night and shine my flashlight on the most frustrating nocturnal problems which can disrupt sleep. As with any other tour, please start at the first signpost, Chapter 1. If you start in the middle, you may miss a signpost and get lost.

The first leg of our journey covers terrain that may not be familiar to even experienced parents; "How Children Sleep" describes healthy sleep, disturbed sleep, sleep problems, and common myths about sleeping. This part covers some sad territory that has not been explored previously: the harmful effects of disturbed sleep when everyone in the family suffers from fatigue. In the second part of our journey we learn "How Parents Can Help Their Children Establish Healthy Sleep Habits: From Birth to Adolescence," an age specific guide to understanding sleep patterns and solving common sleep problems in your child. Finally we explore "Other Sleep Disturbances and Concerns." When we finish our tour, you will be able to direct your own child toward healthy sleep habits.

What do I mean by healthy sleep?

Do you know how to get a good night's sleep and feel rested? I think I do. But sometimes I go to bed too early, sometimes too late. And I'm supposed to know a lot about sleeping! The truth is that no one really knows exactly how to program good sleep to always feel rested. In fact, we're really in the "Dark Ages" when it comes to understanding how sleep works. Interestingly enough, deep, dark caves were the homes for adult volunteers in early sleep studies. This was done to eliminate day/night time cues so that researchers could study how sleep affects our body and our feelings. Of course, sleep researchers now use specially designed laboratories and trick clocks that run faster or slower than "real" time to figure out how our biological rhythms or "internal clocks" work when external time cues are removed. Studies also have been performed on shift workers and Air Force pilots who often cross time zones and suffer from jet-lag syndrome to observe how time differences affect sleep patterns.

But children's sleep habits have not been studied in such detail. Obviously, it's a bigger problem if a bomber crew carrying nuclear weapons is inattentive due to lack of sleep or if their vigilance is impaired from jet-lag syndrome than if a child has fatigue-driven temper tantrums. If it's your child, however, you might disagree!

I have studied both healthy and disturbed sleep in thousands of children as Director of the Sleep Disorders Center at the Children's Memorial Hospital in Chicago. I have helped hundreds of families understand how their children's sleep habits are directly connected to how well they behave and how well they succeed in school. Based on this research, my general pediatric practice spanning more than 14 years, and life with my own four sons, I have discovered that there is hope for bleary-eyed parents. In fact, both you and your child can benefit from this knowledge. I personally benefited from my sleep research because I used to think that naps were a waste of time. I reluctantly withdrew from midday activities on weekends to nap; it was a disorderly retreat. I began to feel guilty: Shouldn't I be spending time with my boys? How was I going to get all those chores done? This attitude often made me combatively irritable from accumulated sleeplessness. Now I think my whole family benefits when I take the naps that I need.

The following chapters will explain everything sleep researchers currently know about what constitutes healthy sleep. I will troubleshoot typical problems and help you modify your child's sleep habits so that all of you can enjoy those wonderful silent nights.

PART I

How Children Sleep

CHAPTER 1

Why Healthy Sleep Is So Important

Healthy sleep appears to come so easily and naturally to our newborn babies. Effortlessly, they fall asleep and stay asleep. Their sleep patterns, however, shift and evolve as the brain matures during the first few weeks and months. Such changes may result in "day/night confusion"—long sleep periods during the day and long wakeful periods at night—which is bothersome, but which is only a problem of timing. The young infant still does not have difficulty falling asleep or staying asleep. After several weeks of age, though, natural sleep rhythms and patterns can be shaped by parents into sleep habits.

It comes as a surprise to many parents that the development of healthy sleep habits is *not* automatic. In fact, parents can and do help or hinder the development of healthy sleep habits. Of course, children will spontaneously "fall asleep" when totally exhausted—"crashing" is a biological necessity! But this is unhealthy, because the extreme fatigue often identified by "wired" behavior immediately preceding the crash, interferes with normal social interactions and even learning.

As you will discover as you read this book, when children learn to sleep well, they also learn to maintain "optimal" wakefulness. This notion of optimal wakefulness or optimal alertness is important, because we often tend to think simplistically of being either awake or asleep. But there are more than two states; there are gradations in sleep and wakefulness. Just as there are differing levels of being asleep (from deep sleep to natural arousals), there are differing levels of wakefulness (from being "wide awake" to being groggy).

The importance of optimal wakefulness cannot be overemphasized. If your child does not get all the sleep he needs, he may seem either drowsy or hyperalert. If either state lasts for a long time, the results are the same: a child with a difficult mood and hard-to-control behavior, certainly not one who is ready and able to enjoy himself or get the most out of the myriad of learning experiences placed before him.

With our busy lifestyles, how can we keep track of nap schedules and regular bedtime hours? Is it really true that I can harm my baby by giving him love at night when he cries out for me? How can I be sure that sleep is really that important?

These are questions that many parents ask me. Parents will often refer to something they have read to support different ideas, and will conclude by saying that since this whole issue is "so controversial," they would rather let matters stay as they are. If you think your child is not sleeping well and if you disagree with the suggestions that follow in this book, ask yourself, how long should you wait for improvement to occur? Three months? Three years? If you are following the opinion of a professional who says you must spend more time with your child at night to make him feel more "secure," ask that professional, when will I know we are on the right track? Don't wait forever. After all, if you are losing money by consistently following the advice of a stockbroker who tells you to be patient, it is reasonable to ask yourself: "How long should I wait before some improvement should occur before switching financial advisors?" If you are thinking of switching pediatricians, consider what Dr. Charles E. Sundell, who was then the physician in charge of the Children's Department at the Prince of Wales's General Hospital in England, wrote in 1922: "Success in the treatment of sleeplessness in infants is a good standard by which to estimate the patience and skill of the practitioner."

He also wrote, "A sleepless baby is a reproach to his guardians, and convicts them of some failure in their guardianship." So don't think that worrying about sleeplessness is just a contemporary issue. In fact, Aulus Cornelius Celsus wrote in A.D. 130 that "infants and children who are still of tender age (may be) attacked by . . . wakefulness at night." Sleeplessness in our children and worrying about sleeplessness have been around for a long time!

The truth is that modern research regarding sleep/wake states only confirms what careful practitioners, such as Dr. Sundell, observed over 60 years ago. He wrote:

The temptation to postpone the time for a baby's sleep, so that he may be admired by some relative or friend who is late in arriving, or so that his nurse may finish some work on which she may be engaged, must be strongly resisted. A sleepy child who is kept awake exhausts his nervous energy very quickly in *peevish restlessness*, and when preparations are at last made for his sleep *he may be too weary to settle down* . . .

Regularity of habits is one of the sheet-anchors by which the barque of an infant's health is secured. The re-establishment of a regular routine, after even a short break, frequently calls for *patient perseverance* on the part of the nurse, but though the child may protest vigorously for several nights, *absolute firmness seldom fails to procure the desired result.* [emphasis added]

Each baby is unique. It's a little like snowflakes, or even roulette . . . except there are no losers, only winners. The obvious ways in which babies are born with individual traits include the amounts of physical activity, durations of sleep, and crying. But babies also differ in more subtle ways—some are much more regular than others. The more regular babies are easier to "read"; they seem to have their own schedules for feeding and sleeping. These babies also tend to cry less and sleep more. Don't blame yourself if you happen to have an irregular baby who cries a lot. It's only luck, although social customs may affect how you feel about it.

In societies where the mother holds the baby close all the time and her breasts are always available for nursing and soothing, there are still great differences among babies in terms of fussiness and crying. The mother compensates by naturally increasing the amount of rhythmic, rocking motions or nursing. She may not even expect the baby to sleep alone, away from her body. As she grows up, the child might share the bed with her parents for a long time. This is not necessarily good or bad, it's just *different* from the expectations of most Western, middle-class families.

So not only do babies sleep differently, but every society's expectations condition parents' feelings. Remember that there are no socially "right" or "wrong" ways, or "natural" versus unnatural styles of raising children. Less-developed societies are not necessarily more "natural" and thus "healthier" in their child-rearing practices. After all, strychnine and cow's milk are equally "natural," but have altogether different effects when ingested.

How much we are bothered by infant crying or poor sleep habits might partially reflect what we have absorbed from our society's and our own family's expectations about how to be "good" parents. Do we want to carry our baby all the time, 24 hours a day, or do we want to put the baby down sometimes to sleep? If we are greatly bothered by his crying or our guilt about not being "good" parents, this may interfere with our developing a sense of competence as parents; we may feel that we cannot later influence sleep patterns in our child. Unfortunately, this can set the stage for future sleep problems.

Sleep problems not only disrupt a child's nights—they disrupt his *days* too, (a) by making him less mentally alert, more inattentive, unable to concentrate, or easily distracted, and (b) by making him more physically impulsive, hyperactive, or alternatively lazy. But when our children sleep well, they are optimally awake and optimally alert to learn and to grow up with charm, humor, and love. When parents are too irregular, inconsistent, or oversolicitous, when mothers or fathers are overly absorbed in their children, when marital problems are left unresolved, the resulting sleep problems converge in the final condition: excessive nighttime wakefulness and crying.

Please do not simply assume that children must pass through different "stages" at different ages that inevitably create sleep problems . . . just as acne occurs during adolescence.

The bad news is that *parents* create sleep problems. The good news is that parents can prevent sleep problems as well as correct any sleep problems that develop.

Parents who favor a more gradual approach than mine to correcting unhealthy sleep habits often complain of frequent "relapses"—or worse. By worse, I mean that the initial impression of success and the subsequent relapse occurred only in the minds of the parents. For instance, some parents have described to me definite improvement gradually developing over many days; at follow-up a few months later they say everything is wonderful. But at a follow-up several months after that, they say that there was never any improvement at all. Upon reminding them that they had previously described improvement, they state that maybe things had only seemed to be a little better at that time.

The truth is that some parents swing back and forth between firmness and permissiveness so often, they cannot make any cure stick. They often confuse their wishful thinking with the child's actual behavior. This is why a sleep diary, which I will explain later, can be an important tool to help you document what you really are doing and how your child is really responding. After all, short-term "successes" might only reflect brief periods when your child crashes at night from chronic exhaustion. Or the actual improvement in sleep habits may be so marginal, that the normal disruptions of vacations, trips, illnesses, or other irregularities constantly buffet the still-tired child and cause repeated "relapses" of night waking or fighting sleep.

In contrast, parents who accomplish an abrupt retraining program—the "cold turkey" approach—to improve sleep habits see immediate and dramatic improvement without any lasting ill effects. These children have fewer relapses and recover faster and more completely from natural disruptions of sleep routines. Seeing a cure really "stick" for a while gives you the courage to keep a tighter control over sleep patterns and to repeat the process again, if needed.

I cannot overemphasize how important it is for parents to start early to help their child learn to sleep well. When you start early, there are no long bouts of crying; no problems with sleeping develop. The process of falling asleep unassisted is a skill—and as with any other skill, it is easier to teach good habits first than it is to correct bad habits later. Also, as with any other skill, success comes only after a period of practice.

The stories about Michelle, Nicholas, and David, among the many other personal accounts in this book contributed by a variety of caring, thoughtful parents, should add extra incentive to teach healthy sleep habits early or to make a change to correct your child's sleep problems right now—so you can all get on with the best part of having children . . . *enjoying* them! Some parents may need professional help to establish reasonable, orderly home routines, to iron out conflicts between parents, or to help the older child with a well-established sleep problem learn to sleep better by himself. To maintain healthy sleep for your young child, please have the courage to be firm, without guilt or fear that she will resent you or love you less. In fact, the very best prescription I can give to create a loving home is a well-rested child with well-rested parents.

> There never was a
> Child so lovely but his
> Mother was glad to see him asleep.
> —Ralph Waldo Emerson

What a *difference* healthy sleep can make in our children!

CHAPTER 2

Healthy Sleep

Are your child's sleep patterns healthy? There are four elements of healthy sleep for children:

1. Sleep duration
2. Naps
3. Sleep consolidation
4. Sleep schedule

When these four items are in proper balance, then children get the rest they need. Let's take a look at all four.

Sleep Duration

If you don't sleep long enough you feel tired. This sounds very simple and obvious, but how much sleep really is enough? And how can you tell if *your* child is getting enough sleep?

Under 3 or 4 months of age, infants' sleep patterns seem mostly to reflect the child's developing brain. During these first few weeks, in fact, sleep durations equal sleep needs, since infant behavior and sleep duration are mostly influenced by biologic factors at this stage. But after about 3 or 4 months, perhaps even about 6 weeks, parenting practices can influence sleep duration and, consequently, behavior. In fact, as I will discuss later in more detail, I think that parents can promote more charming, calm, alert behaviors by becoming sensitive to their growing child's need to sleep and by maintaining healthy sleep habits for them.

Newborns and Young Infants

During their first few days, newborns sleep about 16 to 17 hours total, although their longest single sleep period is only 4 to 5 hours. It makes no difference whether your baby is breastfed or bottle fed or whether it's a boy or a girl.

PRACTICAL POINT

Nursing mothers often misinterpret these first several days of sweet infant slumber as weakness, and worry unnecessarily that long sleep periods deprive their baby of adequate breast milk. Weight checks with your doctor will reassure you that all is well.

Between 1 week and 4 months, the total daily sleep duration drifts down from 16.5 to 15 hours, while the longest single sleep period—usually the night—increases from 4 to 9 hours. We know from several studies that this development reflects neurological maturation and is *not* related to the start of feeding solid foods.

Some newborns and infants under the age of 4 months sleep much longer and others much shorter. During the first few months, trust nature that your baby is getting sufficient sleep. But if your baby cries too much or has colic, you might assist Mother Nature by trying the helpful hints described in Chapter 4 on crybabies.

PRACTICAL POINT

When they are 1 or 2 weeks old, many infants have several-hour periods of increasingly alert, wakeful, gassy, and fussy behavior until about 6 weeks of age, after which they start to calm down. This increasingly irritable and wakeful state is often misinterpreted as resulting from maternal anxiety or insufficient or "bad" breast milk. Nonsense! The culprit is a temporarily uninhibited nervous system which causes excessive arousal. Relax; this developmental phase will pass as the baby's brain matures. It's not your fault.

Young infants are very portable. You can take them anywhere you want and when they want to sleep, they will. I remember when, as a medical student at Stanford University, I was playing tennis with my wife one day and my first child was sleeping in an infant seat near the fence. A huge dump truck came crashing down this narrow street making an awful racket. We ran over to our son only to be surprised that he remained sweetly asleep. After about 4 months of age, he— like all children—became interested in barking dogs, wind in the trees, clouds, and many curious things, all of which could and did disturb his sleep.

Under about 3 or 4 months of age, most infants, like my son, are not much disturbed by their environment when it comes to sleeping. When their body says sleep, they sleep. When their body says wake up, they awaken—even when it's not convenient for their parents! This is true whether they are fed on demand or according to a regular schedule. It also is true when they are continuously fed intravenously because of birth defects of the intestines. Hunger, in fact, seems to have little to do with how babies sleep.

Furthermore, infants brought up in constant light conditions evolve normal sleep patterns just as babies brought up in homes where lights are turned on and off routinely. Another bit of evidence to suggest that environment has little effect on sleep patterns under 3 to 4 months of age is that infants born prematurely tend to mature in their sleep development just as babies born on time. This means that biologic sleep/wake development in our brain does not speed up in those premies who are exposed to more social stimulation.

What we can conclude, therefore, is that, for infants under 3 or 4 months of age, you should try to flow with the child's need to sleep and not try to enforce rigidly or expect predictable sleep schedules. However, some babies do develop regular sleep/wake rhythms quite early, say at about 6 to 8 weeks. These babies tend to be very mild, cry very little, and sleep for long periods of time. Consider yourself blessed, if you are one of these lucky parents.

Older Infants and Children

As children age, the amount of time that they sleep tends to decrease. Figures 1 through 3 describe how much total sleep, daytime sleep, and night sleep occur at different ages for older children. The bottom curve in each graph means that 10% of children sleep less than shown, while the top curve means that 90% of children sleep less than shown for each age. These curves were generated by my own research using data collected from 2,019 children who were mostly white, middle-class residents of northern Illinois and northern Indiana in 1980. These graphs can help you tell whether your child's sleep is above the 90th percentile or below the 10th percentile. (Other studies have used only the 50th percentile or average values and do not tell you whether your child's brief sleep duration is slightly below average or extremely below average.) Interestingly, the results of studies of similar social classes in 1911 in California and in 1927 in Minnesota, also involving thousands of children, were identical to those in my study. In addition, studies in England in 1910 and Japan in 1925 showed identical sleep curves for average durations.

So it seems that despite cultural and ethnic differences, social changes, and such modern inventions as television which shape our contemporary lifestyles, the age-specific durations of sleep are firmly and universally rooted in our children's developing biology.

After about four months, I think that parents can influence sleep durations, and as you will see, sleep durations for these older infants and toddlers are especially important.

I recently studied 60 healthy children in my pediatric practice at 5 months of age and then again at 36 months. At 5 months of age, the infants who were cooing, smiling, adaptable, regular, and who approached curiously toward unfamiliar things or people slept longer than infants with opposite characteristics. These easy and calm infants slept about 3.5 hours during the day and 12.0 hours at night, or 15.5 hours total. Infants who were fussy, crying, irritable, hard to handle,

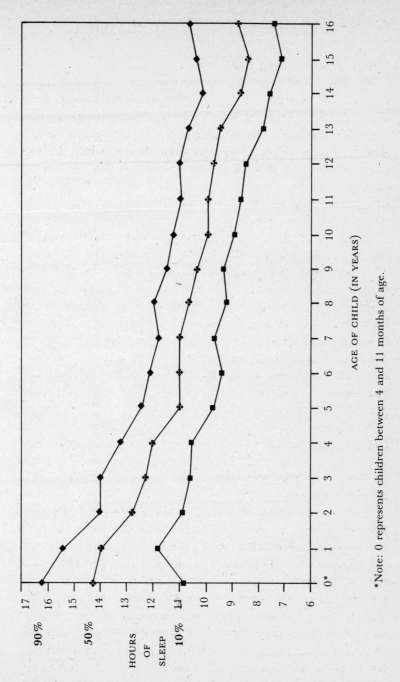

*Note: 0 represents children between 4 and 11 months of age.

FIGURE 1: HOURS OF TOTAL SLEEP BY AGE FOR GIVEN PERCENTILES

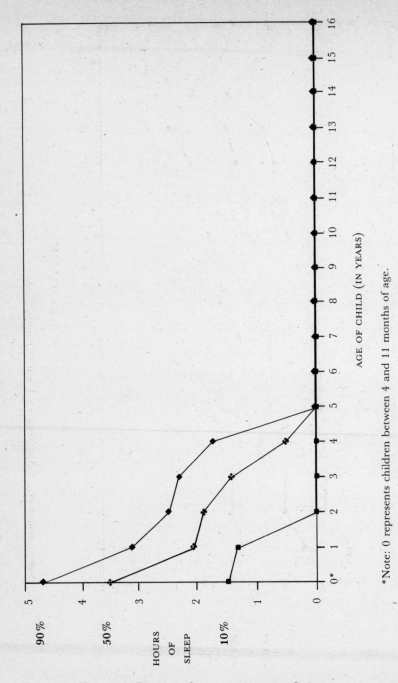

FIGURE 2: HOURS OF DAYTIME SLEEP BY AGE FOR GIVEN
PERCENTILES

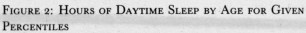

*Note: 0 represents children between 4 and 11 months of age.

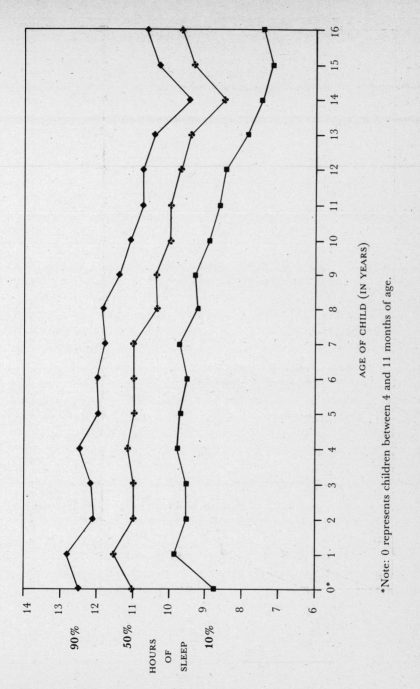

*Note: 0 represents children between 4 and 11 months of age.

Figure 3: Hours of Night Sleep by Age for Given Percentiles

irregular, and more withdrawn slept almost 3 hours less overall, almost a 20% difference (3.0 hours during the day and 9.5 hours at night, or 12.5 hours total).

In addition, for all the 5-month-olds studied, persistence or attention span was the trait most highly associated with daytime sleep or nap duration. *In other words, children who slept longer during the day had longer attention spans.*

As I will discuss in a later chapter, infants who sleep more during the day are better able to learn from their environment, because they have a better developed ability to maintain focused or sustained attention. Like a dry sponge in water, they soak up information about their surroundings. They learn simply from looking at the clouds and trees, touching, feeling, smelling, hearing, and watching their mother's and father's faces. Infants who sleep less in the daytime appear more fitful and socially demanding, and they are less able to entertain or amuse themselves. Toys and objects are less interesting to these more tired children.

By 3 years of age, the easier-to-manage children in my study who were mild, positive in mood, adaptable, and approaching towards unfamiliar people slept 12.5 hours total. The difficult-to-manage children who were intense, more negative, slowly adaptable, and withdrawing slept about 1.5 hours less, almost the equivalent of a daytime nap.

An important conclusion is that the 3-year-olds who nap are more adaptable than those who do not. But napping did not affect the length of sleep at night. Comparing nappers and nonnappers, night sleep duration was 10.5 hours in both groups. Those who napped, however, slept about 2.0 hours during the day, so their total sleep was 12.5 hours. Therefore, it simply is not true that children who miss naps will tend to "make up" for it by sleeping more at night. In fact, the sleep they miss is gone forever.

PRACTICAL POINT

Missing a nap here and there probably will cause no harm. But if this becomes a routine, you can expect your child to sink further and further behind in his sleep and to become increasingly difficult to handle in this over-fatigued state.

SLEEP DURATIONS OF THREE-YEAR-OLD CHILDREN

		Sleep Durations (Hours)		
		Day	*Night*	*Total*
Group A	Easy to manage	1.9	10.6	12.5
	Difficult to manage	0.9	10.4	11.2
Group B	Children who do not nap	—	10.5	10.5
	Children who nap	2.0	10.5	12.5

All in all, at age 3, the children who slept more were more fun to be around, more sociable, and less demanding. The children who slept less not only tended to be more socially demanding, bratty, and fussy, but they also behaved somewhat like hyperactive children. Later, I will explain how these fatigued, fussy brats are also more likely to become fat kids.

Looking at our sleep curves again, we see that throughout early and middle childhood, the duration of sleep declines until adolescence, when the curve shown in Figure 1 levels off and then slightly increases. This increase has been noted in other studies and suggests that teenagers need more sleep than preteens. Yet academic demands, social events, and school sports combine during adolescence to pressure teenagers to stay up later and later. This is the time when chronic and cumulative sleep losses begin to take their toll, and can make a normally rough period in life unbearably rocky.

Naps

Having grown up in a highly achievement-oriented society, most American adults tend to think of naps as a waste of time. We tend to view other adults who nap as either lazy, under-motivated, ill, or elderly. In turn, we do not attach much positive benefit to daytime sleep in our infants and young children.

Let me explain why naps are indeed very important for learning or cognitive development in our children.

Naps are not little bits of night sleep randomly intruding upon our children's awake hours. Actually, night sleep, daytime sleep, and daytime wakefulness have rhythms that are partially independent of each other. During the first 3 to 4 months of life, these rhythms develop at different rates, so they may not be in synchrony. Only later do these sleep/wake rhythms become linked with fluctuations in temperature and activity levels.

For example, most of us have experienced drowsiness in the afternoon. This sensation is partially related—but only partially—to how long you have been up and how long you slept the night before. That's because our mental state also fluctuates during the day between "alert" and "drowsy," just as fluctuations occur during the night between "light" and "deep" sleep stages.

Understanding that these rhythms of night sleep, daytime sleep, and daytime wakefulness are somewhat independent leads to two important ideas.

First, under 3 to 4 months of age, when these rhythms are not in synchrony with each other, the baby may be getting opposing messages from different parts of the brain. The sleep rhythm says "deep sleep," but the wake rhythm says "alert" instead of "drowsy." Wakeful but tired, the confused child cries fitfully—we might call this behavior colic.

Second, if these rhythms are somewhat independent, they may have different functions. I think that mothers are right when they say there must be a separate nap god. I believe that *healthy naps* lead to optimal daytime alertness for learning. That is, naps adjust the ''alert''/''drowsy'' control to just the right setting for optimal daytime arousal. Without naps, the child is too drowsy to learn well. Also, when chronically sleep-deprived, the fatigued child becomes fitfully fussy or hyperalert in order to fight sleep and, therefore, cannot learn from his environment.

My recent studies show that most children take either two or three naps at 4 months of age. The third nap, if taken, tends to be brief and in the early evening. But by 6 months of age, the vast majority of children (90%) are taking only two naps; by 9 months of age virtually all children are taking one or two naps. About 15% of children have started taking a single nap by their first birthday, and this percentage increases to 50% by the age of 15 months. By 21 months, most children are taking just a single nap.

The time in the day when the nap occurs is also important. Some studies have suggested that an early nap, occurring in the midmorning hours, is different in quality from the later nap which occurs in the afternoon. There is more active or rapid eye movement (REM) sleep than quiet sleep in the first nap, and this pattern is reversed in the second nap. So naps occurring at different times are different! Even for adults, when you nap earlier in the day the sleep is lighter and less restorative than an afternoon nap which is comprised of more deep sleep. *Long naps occurring at the right times make the child feel rested.* Brief naps or naps occurring out of synchrony with other biologic rhythms are less restful, less restorative.

Children can be taught how to take naps. A nap does not begin and end like an electric light turned on and off. In fact, a nap or night sleep involves three periods of time: the time required for the process called ''falling asleep,'' the sleep period itself, and the time required to ''wake up.'' I will help you teach your children how to ''fall asleep'' in later chapters.

PRACTICAL POINT

Do not expect your baby to nap well outside his crib after 4 months of age. If you don't protect your baby's nap schedules, you can produce nap deprivation.

When children do not nap well, they pay a price. Infants at 4 to 8 months who do not nap well have shorter attention spans or appear less persistent when engaged in activities. By 3 years of age, children who do not nap or who nap very little are often described as nonadaptable or even hyperactive. Adaptability is thought to be a very important trait for school success.

One mother of a nonadaptable child said that every morning she prayed to the nap god to give her a break. In contrast, another mother described her son as a very easy child as long as she had a bed around. He was such a "rack-monster" that she decided he just liked his own company best. Another mother described her son as the "snooze king." Sometimes it appears that the older toddler needs exactly one and a half naps: One nap is insufficient, but two are impossible to achieve. These children are rough around the edges in the late afternoon or early evening, but parents can temporarily and partially compensate by putting the child to bed earlier on some nights. An earlier bedtime hour may become a necessity when your child develops a single nap pattern between 15 and 21 months.

PRACTICAL POINT

When your child does not nap well and you keep him up in the evening, he suffers.

Nonnapping means lost sleep. Over a long period of time, children do not sleep longer at night when their naps are brief. Of course, once in a while—when there is a holiday visit from relatives or a painful ear infection—a child will make up lost daytime sleep with longer night sleep. But day in and day out, you should not expect to satisfy your child's need to sleep by cutting corners on naps and then trying to compensate by putting your child asleep earlier for the night. What you wind up with is a socially demanding brat in the late afternoon or early evening. Or maybe your otherwise sweet child is just rough around the edges at those hours. Either way, your child pays a price for nap deprivation. And so do you.

Spending hours holding your child in your arms or in a rocking chair while he is in a light, twilight sleep also is lost sleep. It's also a waste of your time. Brief sleep during the day, catnaps, "motion" sleep in cars, swing-sleep, light sleep in the stroller at the pool, and naps at the wrong time are poor quality sleep.

Here is an example of how one family learned to appreciate napping.

How Charley's Parents Became Nap Zealots

I am aware that the practice of toting your baby along with you on every occasion is the new social thing. No doubt it stems from the "me" generation's philosophy that a baby should not be allowed to interfere with your lifestyle. So parents everywhere are seen with their infants: in grocery stores, restaurants, the homes of friends . . . and for the unflappable, at cocktail parties, dinner affairs, even cross-country trips. Although some of these examples may appear to be extreme, be advised, new mothers, that the pressure is on to be a "nouvelle" mom.

As with anything in vogue, you have to have the appropriate raw material to make it work. And the fact is, my husband, Tom, and I simply do not have the baby to make this new "porta-kid" trend work for us. Oh, we tried. But it was, and continues to be, completely futile. So we gave it up when Charley was 3 months old.

Charley is now 7 months into his life. From the beginning,

there has been only one of life's necessities that he requires as much as milk, as much as oxygen, and that is sleep. We, in fact, used to shake him when we first brought him home, to make certain that he was alive. The baby slept . . . serious sleep.

In the beginning he would sleep anywhere. After his second month, he would only sleep in his crib. And that's another subject. I maintain that the person(s) who decreed that a child's bed should be "stimulating" and full of colored linens and mobiles did not have a child of his/her own! If I had to do it all over again, I would buy a solid, dark-colored comforter and pads. After Charley's second month, he would spend hours on end trying to pick the red, white, and blue flowers off the sheets. This is no lie. And he would scream unmercifully for us to remove this distraction which was preventing him from needed slumber!

Since his second month, Charley has slept through the night and half of the day. If we disallowed him this necessity, he became a different baby. "Crabby" did not do justice to his fatigue condition. Without this sleep, our peaceful, alert, sweet, and cuddly baby turned into a raging beast. We did this to him, when we denied him sleep . . . not according to our expectations, but according to his own internal requirements.

Charley gives us his cues, simply and clearly. He doesn't cry at first. He mumbles, then grumbles, and finally, if his unaware parents or sitters persist . . . he wails.

At first we couldn't believe he was tired so often. We changed his diapers a thousand times and forcefed bottles. We took him on endless trips in the buggy, and walked him incessantly in the snuggly, trying to calm our "miserable" baby with the rhythm of our heartbeats. Nothing worked. Nothing, that is, until we finally, out of sheer nervous exhaustion, laid him in his bed to sleep.

Charley still naps four to five times during the course of a day. He's also a very happy child. When Tom and I go anywhere, we go alone, leaving our contented, sleeping son in the hands of a competent babysitter. Our friends, especially our childless friends, think we're overprotective. Well, thank God Charley is not their baby. We are no longer concerned about our parental image; uneducated criticism doesn't count. If we cannot find a babysitter, we don't go. We simply would have a better time watching television . . . anything, even doing the laundry, beats the hell out of making your baby and yourselves crazy. And our family is now harmonious, having discovered the secret of sleep.

PRACTICAL POINT

When you maintain a healthy nap schedule and your child sleeps well during the day, jealous friends will accuse you of being overprotective. They'll say, "It's not real life," or "Bring her along so she'll learn to play with other children," or "You're really spoiling her." Suggestion: Change friends or keep your baby's long naps a family secret.

Sleep Consolidation

Consolidated sleep means uninterrupted sleep, sleep that is continuous and not disrupted by awakenings. When awakenings or complete arousals break our slumber, we call it disrupted sleep or sleep fragmentation. Abnormal shifts of sleep rhythms toward lighter sleep, even if we do not awaken completely, also cause sleep fragmentation. Ten hours of consolidated sleep is not the same as 10 hours of fragmented sleep. Doctors, firefighters, and mothers of newborns or sick children who have their sleep interrupted frequently know this very well.

The effects of sleep fragmentation are similar to the effects of reduced total sleep: Daytime sleepiness increases and performance measurably decreases. Adults with fragmented sleep often fight the ill effects of fragmented sleep with extra caffeine. Alcohol unmasks or uncovers the hidden fatigue and makes them "feel tired." However, well-rested preteens who are given the same amount of alcohol do not "feel tired."

PRACTICAL POINT

Let sleeping babies lie! Never awaken a sleeping baby. Destroying sleep continuity is unhealthy.

Protective Arousals

Sometimes our brain causes us to awaken to prevent us from asphyxiating in our sleep. These awakenings, or protective arousals, occur when we have difficulty breathing during sleep, which can be caused by large tonsils or adenoids obstructing the air passage. I will discuss this problem in detail in Chapter 10.

Arousals may also prevent crib death, or Sudden Infant Death Syndrome (SIDS), which kills young infants. This tragedy is thought to be caused by a failure to maintain breathing during sleep or a failure to awaken when breathing starts to become difficult.

Sleep Fragmentation

After several months of age—beyond the age of crib death—frequent arousals are usually harmful, because they destroy sleep continuity. Arousals can be either a complete awakening from light, deep, or rapid eye movement (REM) sleep. Arousals can also be thought of as a quick shift from deep sleep to light sleep without complete awakening.

Figure 4 is a simplified illustration of the cycling from deep sleep to light sleep that normally occurs after about 4 months of age. During partial arousals, we stay in a light sleep state and do not awaken. But during complete arousals, or awakenings, we might become aware that we are looking at the

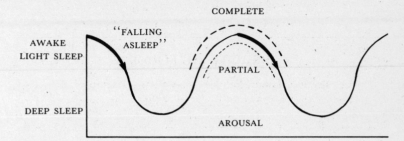

FIGURE 4: AROUSALS DURING SLEEP

clock, rolling over, changing arm positions, or scratching an arm. This awareness is dim and brief, and we return to sleep promptly.

So we see that arousals come in several forms, and depending on which types occur, how many times they happen, and how long they last, we pay a price: increased daytime sleepiness and decreased performance. But some arousals always occur naturally during healthy sleep. Arousals are made by the brain, not the stomach. Please don't confuse arousals from sleep with hunger.

MAJOR POINT

Some arousals from sleep are normal.

It's not just night sleep that can be fragmented. I think that even naps also might be fragmented when parents rely on swing-sleep and motion sleep, or when they allow catnaps in the car or stroller. Holding your dozing child in your arms in a rocking chair during the day also probably prevents good quality day sleep. These naps are too brief or too light to be restorative.

PRACTICAL POINT

Naps less than one hour cannot count as "real" naps. Sometimes, a nap of 45 or 55 minutes may be all he needs, but naps less than 30 minutes don't help your child.

By 4 to 8 months of age, infants should have at least a midmorning and an early afternoon nap, and the total nap duration should be 2 to 4 hours. Night sleep is 10 to 12 hours, with one or no interruptions for feeding. When children do not get healthy, consolidated sleep, we call the problem "night waking." As I will discuss later, the night waking itself is usually due to normally occurring arousals. The real problem is the child's inability to or difficulty in returning to sleep *unassisted*.

PRACTICAL POINT

Some arousals from sleep are normal. Problems occur when children have difficulty returning to sleep by themselves. They have not learned the process of "falling asleep."

Sleep Schedule

Figures 5 and 6 show the times when most children awaken or go to sleep. These graphs are based on data from the same 2,019 children referred to in Figures 1 through 3 (see pages 13–15). Looking at the graphs you can see, for example, that 90% of preschool children, under the age of 6, fall asleep before 9 P.M., and 10% of children between the ages of 2 and 6 fall asleep before 7 P.M.

When sleep/wake schedules are not in synchrony with other biologic rhythms, attentiveness, vigilance, and task performance often are measurably decreased and moods are altered.

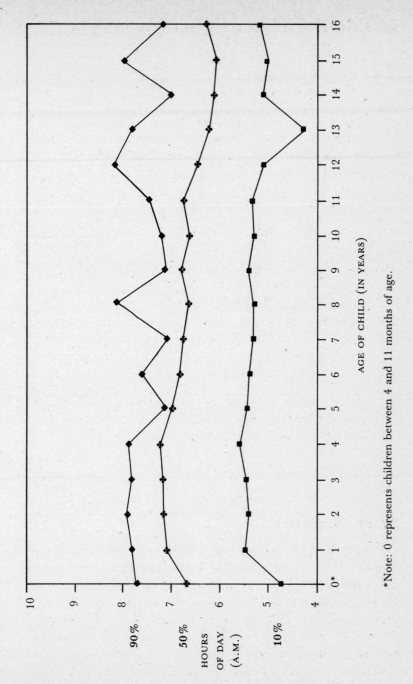

*Note: 0 represents children between 4 and 11 months of age.

FIGURE 5: HOUR AT WHICH CHILDREN ARE AWAKE FOR GIVEN PERCENTILES

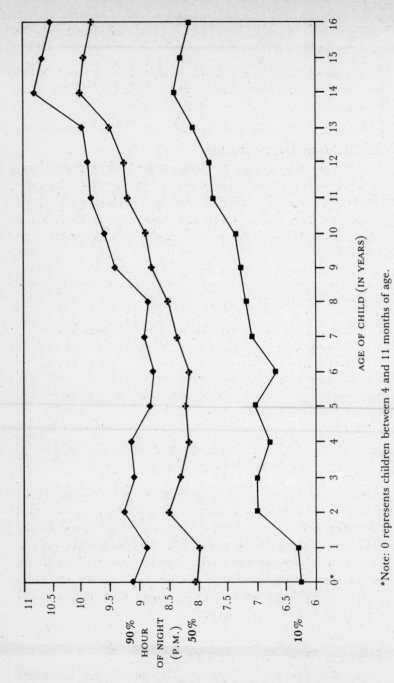

FIGURE 6: HOUR AT WHICH CHILDREN ARE ASLEEP BY GIVEN PERCENTILES

*Note: 0 represents children between 4 and 11 months of age.

Jet-lag syndrome is one example of this, while another is the poor sleep quality some shift workers suffer due to abnormal sleep schedules.

Night Sleep Organization

Before 6 weeks of age, the longest single sleep period, unfortunately, is randomly distributed around the clock. In some babies, this longest sleep may actually be only two to three hours! But by 6 weeks of age, the longest single sleep period will predictably occur in the evening hours and last three to five hours.

PRACTICAL POINT

During these early weeks, you may find breastfeeding too demanding or too frequent, and think that you might want to quit so that you can get some rest. On the other hand, you also may want to continue nursing for your baby's health. Hang in there, and wait until your baby is past 6 weeks of age. Then you, too, will get more night sleep.

After 6 weeks of age, babies sleep longer at night. So do moms! Also, babies start social smiling at their parents, and they then become less fussy or irritable. Life in the family definitely changes after 6 weeks. One exception is the premature baby whose parents might have to wait until about six weeks after the expected date of delivery. Another exception is the colicky baby whose parents might have to wait until their baby is 3 or 4 months old.

Daytime Sleep Organization

At about 3 to 4 months of age, daytime sleep is organized into two or three long naps instead of many brief, irregular ones. Mothers, especially nursing mothers, should learn to nap when their baby naps. You never know what the night will bring, and you might be up a lot then holding, walking, or nursing.

Abnormal sleep schedules usually evolve in infants and young children when parents keep them up too late at night. Parents do this because they (a) enjoy playing with their baby; (b) cannot put the child to sleep, but wait for their child to crash from total exhaustion; or (c) both.

The time when your own child *needs* to go to sleep at night depends on his age, how long his previous nap lasted, and how long his wakeful period was just before the bedtime hour. The time when he *wants* to go to sleep may be altogether different! Obviously, the bedtime hour is not fixed or unchanging. If your child is unusually active in the afternoon or if she misses a good afternoon nap, then she should be put to sleep earlier. This is true even if a parent returning home late from work that night does not see her. Keeping a tired child up to play with a tired parent coming home late from work does no one any good.

Allowing brief naps in the early evening or long late afternoon naps in order to keep a child up late at night will eventually ruin healthy sleep schedules.

PRACTICAL POINT

To establish healthy sleep schedules at 4 to 8 months of age, become your infant's timekeeper. Set his clock on healthy time.

Biological Rhythms

To better understand the importance of maintaining sleep schedules, let's look at how three distinctive biological rhythms develop. Immediately after birth, babies are wakeful, then fall asleep, awaken, and fall asleep a second time over a 10-hour period. These periods of wakefulness are predictable and are not due to hunger, although what causes them is unknown. Thus a partial sleep/wake pattern emerges immediately after birth.

After 1 month of life, body temperature rhythms appear and thereafter influence sleep/wake cycles. Body temperature typically rises during the daytime and drops to lower levels at night. A third pattern is added by 6 months of age when an important hormone, called cortisol, also shows a similar characteristic rhythm, with peak concentrations in the early morning and lowest levels around midnight. This hormone is also related to both mood and performance and will be discussed later in Chapter 3. Interestingly, a part of the cortisol secretion rhythm is related to the sleep/wake rhythm and another part is coupled to the body temperature rhythm. I wish Mother Nature were more simple!

Even at only a few months of age, then, interrelated, internal rhythms already are well developed: sleep/wake pattern, body temperature, and the cortisol hormone level. In adults, it appears that a long night's sleep is most highly dependent on going to sleep at or just after the peak of the temperature cycle. Bedtimes occurring near the lower portion of the temperature cycle result in shorter sleep durations.

Shift work or jet travel in adults, or parental mismanagement in children might cause disorganized sleep. What does disorganized sleep mean?

1. Internal desynchronization
2. Uncoupling of rhythms normally closely linked
3. Shifting rhythms out of phase

Possible consequences of abnormal sleep schedules include fatigue, stress, and elevated cortisol levels. This sets in motion other disturbances of sleep.

REMINDER AGAIN
Never wake a sleeping baby.

I often tell parents to become sensitive to the child's personal sleep signals. This means that you should capture that magic moment when the child is tired, ready to sleep, and easily falls asleep. The magic moment is a slight quieting, a lull in being busy, a slight staring off, a hint of calmness. If you catch this wave of tiredness and put the child to sleep then, there will be no crying. But if you allow him to crash into an overtired state, it will be harder for him to fall asleep, because he is trying to fall asleep out of phase with other biologic rhythms. Timing is most important!

25-Hour Cycles

Although harmonious biologic rhythms promote healthy sleep, random bad days are bound to occur. One explanation for "off" days, when the child's sleep is irregular for no apparent reason, is that our basic biologic clocks have about 25 hours in their cycles, not 24. In other words, without time cues, our free-running sleep/wake rhythms appear to cycle on a 25-hour schedule. As long as we train our children to match sleep/wake rhythms to night and day shifts, problems usually are avoided. Other babies appear to get off schedule every few weeks, and parents then must work to keep them well rested. I suspect that babies, like adults, differ in their individual abilities to adjust their 25-hour biological rhythms to society's 24-hour clocks. Most parents, however, find that the effort to reset baby's clock is worth it because otherwise the child becomes increasingly tired, fatigued, and crabby.

When parents put forth the effort to help the child get needed sleep, the better rested the child becomes, the easier it becomes for the child to accept sleep, to expect to sleep, to take long naps, and to go to sleep by herself. Some parents always have to endure days of disruption following trips, illnesses, or immunizations because irregularity of schedules due to traveling or pain upsets sleep rhythms.

Here is one family's account.

Susan's Night Waking

Last summer, Susan's night waking had become so frequent that she was basically awake more than she was asleep. We had been instructed by a pediatrician at the parenting class we attend to "meet our child's needs." So we were getting up as frequently as she asked and rocking her back to sleep. This happened three or four times a night and often took 30 to 60 minutes. A part of me wanted to do this. Needless to say, however, after months of this nighttime routine, my husband and I became quite exhausted and began to resent our child. I knew I was in trouble when I would get up and go into the baby's room and yell at her and then begin crying myself because of the conflict of meeting her needs and meeting my own sleep needs. The point I'm trying to make is simply that when a problem like a child's sleep habits gets so out of hand, the parents are partially responsible, too. Finally, on our own, we decided to let her cry it out. By the way, my husband had a much easier time psychologically with letting her cry. He knew it was in her best interest and was able to remain unemotional about it. It took about a week and she cried for about two hours for quite a few of those nights. Finally, it seemed that she had gotten the idea.

Unfortunately, the next week we were scheduled to go away for our summer vacation. We didn't want to cancel our trip, but we knew we were taking a chance on destroying the results of our hard work. We stayed at an inn, and there were no cribs, so we made a sleeping area for Susan in the corner of the room. She'd wake up in the middle of the night and think it was play time.

When we got back from the trip we tried to get into the routine of letting her cry it out, but by that time we didn't have the energy to go through a week of crying baby again. So we fell back into a poor nighttime routine. By the way, Susan was only 11 months at this time. Another month went by and we knew we could not go on. We discussed it with the teacher at our parenting class, and she finally recommended the process of letting Susan cry it out again.

This time it took about five days and she was back to sleeping through the night. This lasted about a month.

Susan received a vaccination shortly after that. I went into her room for only a moment to check up on her one night. Then she began waking each night, and we were into our old routine. We repeated the process yet one more time. I think it took about five nights to get her to sleep through the night. After that, Susan slept through the night regularly for months. She eventually asked to be put down before she was asleep at night rather than being rocked to sleep. She began taking very long naps this spring which seemed slightly strange.

This summer we went on vacation for a week, and Susan slept in a crib in our room. She'd awaken and again think it was play time. It didn't take long for her to get back into her old bad habits. We had hoped we were beyond that, since she had been sleeping through the night for so many months . . . but since our trip she's been up at night practicing long dialogues, and it looks like we'll have to go through this one more time. She's also feeling very needy and clingy. I'm sure it's all interrelated, having to do with separation.

In conclusion, raising a child is not always easy. . . . I guess Susan's sleep problem is one we'll have to live with and may come up from time to time and we'll have to keep working on it.

PRACTICAL POINT

A well-rested baby with a healthy sleep habit awakens with a cheerful, happy attitude. A tired baby awakens grumpy.

Now, let's look at some other aspects of healthy sleep. I am often asked many questions about the family bed, sleep position, and feeding practices.

The Question of the Family Bed

About a third of white urban families frequently sleep together in a family bed for all or part of the night. By itself, this is neither good nor bad. Studies in the United States suggest that the family bed might encourage or lead to a variety of emotional stresses within the child; opposite results were found in studies in Sweden. This probably reflects differences in social attitudes toward nudity, bathing, and sexuality. Think of it as a family style which does not necessarily reflect or cause emotional or psychological problems in parents and children.

But when someone is not getting enough sleep, either parent or child, the family bed can cause potential problems. I suspect this often develops in older toddlers because by the age of 1 to 2 years, sleeping together is often associated with night waking. Now there is a well-established habit, and the child is unwilling to go to or return to his own bed.

So if you want to enjoy a family bed, fine. But understand that your cuddling in bed together will make any future changes in sleep arrangements very difficult to execute. Remember that while it sounds like an easy solution to baby's sleep problems, you may wind up with a 24-hour child even when he gets older.

In contrast, many families use a family bed overnight only during the first few months and then shift baby to her own bed for overnight sleep. But at 5 or 6 A.M., parents still might bring their older infant or child into their bed for a limited period of warm cuddling.

Sleep Position

A common myth held by parents is that *children sleep better on their stomachs*. In fact, a Chinese mother said she knew something was really wrong with her baby, because all Chinese babies slept on their back. She could not understand why her own baby preferred her stomach! She truly worried that stomach sleeping was unhealthy. But the truth is that some babies actually seem to sleep better and fuss or cry less when asleep on their backs. Tradition and social circumstances dictate which sleeping position is selected by most parents. Fortunately, most babies sleep equally well on their side, their back, or their stomach.

A variant of this myth is that when the child rolls over away from the less popular or traditional sleeping position selected by the parents, the parent assumes he has to intervene and roll the child back. Actually, leaving the child alone allows the child to learn to sleep in different positions. If you roll your child back and he instantaneously returns to sleep, obviously there is no problem. On the other hand, going to your child to roll him back can become a game for the infant by 5 months of age. Games should occur at playtimes, not sleeptimes.

Likewise, when the older child pulls herself to a standing position in her crib, parents do not need to "help their child get down." A child might fall down in an awkward heap, but she will not hurt herself. Next time she will think twice about standing up and shaking the crib railings or will be more careful when letting go.

Parents who rush in to roll the baby over or to help a child down run the risk of reinforcing this behavior or encouraging it to be repeated night after night. Children are very crafty and learn quickly how to get parents to give them extra attention.

Solid Foods and Feeding Habits

Do you remember how drowsy you felt after eating all that Thanksgiving turkey? Big meals make us sleepy, so shouldn't solids make babies sleep better? Wrong. Feeding rhythms do not alter the pattern of waking and sleeping.

Sleeping for long periods at night is *not related* to the method of feeding, whether it be breast, bottle, or continuously fed intravenously as for infants with certain intestinal birth defects. This is a fact—if you don't believe it, please look at the eleven studies cited at the end of this book (see pages 256–57). The studies that I think are the most convincing involve comparing the development of sleep/wake rhythms in demand-fed infants with those who are continuously fed intravenously because of birth defects involving their stomachs or intestines. The babies fed on demand cycle between being hungry and being full. The other babies are never allowed to become hungry. The objective recordings in sleep laboratories show that there are no differences between these groups of infants. Other studies involve the introduction of solid foods; they all show that solid food feedings, such as cereal, do not influence sleeping patterns at night. All studies show that the method of feeding (breast vs. bottle or scheduled vs. demand) or the introduction of solids does not affect sleeping. No published research studies have ever shown opposite results.

Some studies, however, have shown that bottlefeeding is more popular for mothers who were more restrictive or less permissive than breastfeeding mothers. Mothers who bottle-feed their babies tended to be more interested in controlling their infant's behavior. Because they can see the number of ounces of formula given at each feeding, they are more likely to perceive night waking in a problem/solution framework and consider the social *wants* of the child instead of nutritional *needs*. In contrast, the nursing mother, perhaps more sensitive to the health benefits of nursing, might respond to night waking more often or more rapidly because she perceives herself primarily responding to her infant's need for nourishment. After a while, of course, the child learns to enjoy this nocturnal social contact. Over time, the baby learns to expect attention when he awakens.

This explains why there is no difference in night waking between breast- and bottlefed infants at 4 months, but by 6 to 12 months, night waking is more of an issue among breastfed babies.

The bottom line is that cereal sticking to babies stomachs

does not fill them up more and make them sleep better. Formula may appear thicker than breast milk, but both contain the same 20 calories per ounce. Giving formula or weaning breastfed babies also will not directly cause longer sleeping at night, although it is possible that attitudes toward breastfeeding may indirectly foster a night-waking habit. Here is one family's account of how breastfeeding and falling asleep led to a night-waking habit.

Maren's Wake-Ups for Breastfeeding

Maren was born July 18, 1984, after an uneventful pregnancy and an easy Lamaze delivery, three days past term.

We were committed to breastfeeding, with no preconceived expectations of its duration. Maren behaved as a normal infant for about two weeks, at which point persistent crying jags began to occur daily. Though we were assured that real colic was worse, we came to refer to these spells as Maren's colic. The inconsolable crying was endured without much complaint. Although they mostly lasted 1 to 2 hours, the worst individual days would include unabated crying spells for 8 to 10 hours. Various experiments were tried to ease the colic suffering, including having Maren sleep with us, having her sleep on a hot water bottle, etc. Predictably, none worked. At 2 months, the colic ended relatively abruptly.

From 2 months on, a very happy, trusting relationship between Maren and me developed. For about 7 months, Maren was fed virtually exclusively on breast milk. From 7 to 10 months, increasing amounts of solid food were introduced at breakfast and lunch. Maren has always been a very happy, bubbly, joyful child. The breastfeeding seemed to contribute to this sunny disposition. Maren's nap patterns were completely normal. Generally, I would sleep with her in the morning. Part of the feeding ritual for these 10 months included twice nightly breastfeedings for Maren, interrupting my sleep.

Massive campaigns were mounted by both sets of grandparents to convince me that breastfeeding needed to end.

These began at 2 months and reached fever pitch around 7. We listened politely. Except for a brief experimental period at around 8 months, no attempts were made to pump my breasts to permit me extra sleep. This was a conscious decision, because direct feeding was easier and more satisfying for mother and baby.

Breastfeeding, in addition to the satisfaction it provided, was an indispensable part of the sleeping ritual. From birth to 11 months, Maren expected to be held, fed, and gently rocked or lulled to sleep in the pleasant company of her mother. At around 9 months, Maren's rapid growth was taking its toll. After nearly a year without a full night's sleep, I was beginning to reach a whole new level of fatigue. There was more solid food in the daytime now.

New attempts were begun to get Maren to sleep without her mother's direct attention. Her father would give her a bottle, rock her, sing to her, etc. Female friends of the family, familiar to Maren, would do the same. Maren was a good sport about these experiments, but preferred my attentions. At 11 months, we agreed it was time to wean Maren to a bottle.

Maren didn't like the plan much. She obviously disliked formula as much as I disliked feeding it to her. For nearly a week she rejected cow's milk. I ended the morning nap breastfeeding ritual first. Juices (orange, apple, pear) in the morning or in car rides helped to improve Maren's familiarity with and affection for bottles. They also allowed my husband, Larry, to feed her while I rested later in the mornings. Putting cow's milk in a special bottle (formed and painted to look like a dog) allowed this unpleasant white stuff to become gradually more acceptable. After a few days, Maren started to respond more favorably to her ''pooch juice'' and the games I created and associated with it.

I experienced some depression with the cessation of breastfeeding. As that special link came to an end, my contribution to Maren's development suddenly seemed more mundane, repetitive, and less satisfying. This depression came on and off for two months. It was a strange feeling, since it was offset at all times by the joy that comes of having a bright, personable, and developing child.

Maren was fully weaned at 11 months. The last feeding to change over was bedtime. But even if she was fed milk at bedtime, Maren continued to wake up once or twice per evening, crying to be fed. The next step was to get her to sleep through the night. We were repeatedly advised to let her cry herself to sleep. The phrase "even for five or six hours" was used, a reminder of colic days. We considered this proposition, but continued to feed Maren warm milk, sing lullabies, and rock her to sleep, once or twice per night. The big question: What was waking her up?

We decided it was mostly habit, and that she just wanted the comfort of our company. A new go-to-sleep ritual was introduced: After much playing and affection, Maren was put to bed alone with her favorite doll, not rocked to sleep. If she woke, warm milk was provided, but Maren was purposely not picked up. Maren cried 10 minutes when left alone the first night, then rested her head on top of her favorite doll and drifted off to sleep. After expecting possibly an hour or more of crying, this was an unbelievable, almost anticlimactic relief to us. After two or three nights of feeding without picking her up, Maren began sleeping through the night.

At the end of month 11, the go-to-sleep ritual is routine. Maren rarely cries at all. Key elements: a big dinner, a bath, gentle play, eight ounces of warm milk, hugs, and her favorite doll. Even a babysitter can do it. At one year, Maren had finally learned to sleep eight hours straight.

Maren is our first child; we hope to have one or two more. Except for the period of mild colic for Maren's first two months, we have never considered her to have any "sleep disorders." The rest of the phases we have gone through seemed to be a constant question of balance: how to balance Maren's satisfaction and her nutritional needs with our basic sleep needs. And as always with young parents, there are other nagging questions: Are we spoiling her? Is she controlling us?

Is the advice of our parents correct or old-fashioned? What is "normal" for other babies?

We consider our experiences unexceptional compared with other parents we know. Perhaps the biggest differences are that we were committed to breastfeeding more completely and longer than most, with all the sacrifice that such a commitment entails. We gave up dating for a year, despite the enjoyment we both derived from going out to dinner, movies, or just quiet evenings together. Relationships with our friends, virtually all of whom were childless, waned. We pushed ourselves nearly to exhaustion.

We did a few things we are sure were right. For us, especially me, we sensed Maren's needs and delivered them unasked. This created an extraordinary self-assurance in Maren, and led to a happy household. Maren seemed to cry less than other children, and to be a bright, curious quick-learner. Other things we are happy about: lots of new games all the time; plenty of visual stimulation; roughhousing motions and playing; exposure to music, texture, any stimulation we could dream up. It all seemed to add to her alertness, her trust for us, and the regularity of her sleeping.

There are also some things we may not have done so well. We may have gone too long before we tried to put Maren to sleep alone. Our parents continuously warned us we were being too indulgent. They may have been right. But then, first-time parents are like that.

The Effects of Healthy Sleep: Sleep Patterns, Intelligence, Learning, and School Performance

Do sleep patterns really affect learning in our children? Yes! Different studies of children at different ages all agree on this point. Focusing on perfectly normal, healthy children, let's consider the data by age groups: infants, preschoolers, and school-aged children.

Infants

A recent study at the University of Connecticut showed that there was a strong association between the amount of time infants were in REM sleep and the amount of time they spent when awake in the behavioral state called "quiet-alert." In the quiet-alert state, babies have open, "bright" eyes, they appear alert and their eyes are scanning, their faces are relaxed, and they do not smile or frown. Their bodies are relatively quiet and inactive. One mother described her 4-month-old who was frequently in this quiet-alert state as a "looker and a thinker." She's right! These infants don't miss a thing. This and another study from Stanford University of sleep development both agreed that environmental factors, not simply brain maturation, are responsible for the proportion of time infants spend in REM sleep. Unfortunately, the exact environmental factors were not identified, but presumably parental handling could influence all of these items: sleep patterns, the proportion of REM sleep, and the amount of time the child is quiet-alert.

Infants who are notoriously *not* quiet-alert are those with colic/difficult temperament. Their fussy behavior may be due to imbalances of internal chemicals such as progesterone or even cortisol. High cortisol concentrations in infants have been shown to be associated with decreased duration of quiet or non-REM sleep. So, even in infants, as in adults, there seem to be connections between internal chemicals, sleep patterns, and behavior when awake. Also, these fussy children tend to be irregular and have short attention spans. Among 2- to 3-month-old infants, one study showed that the more irregular and impersistent the child was, the slower the rates of learning. Looking ahead to Figure 10 (see page 215), you can see how colic/difficult temperament children with brief sleep durations, who are irregular and who have a short attention span, might not learn quickly to fall asleep unassisted when parents remove their soothing efforts. Thus they easily could become sleep-deprived, fatigued, and hyperactive older children. This concept of increased alertness, wakefulness, and irritability due to chemical imbalances will be discussed later in Chapter 3.

One reason I think naps are especially important for infants is because my study of children showed day sleep durations to be most highly associated with persistence or attention span. Infants who took long naps had longer attention spans. They spend more awake time in the quiet-alert state and seem to learn faster. Infants who do not nap well are either drowsy or fitfully fussy and in either case, they do not learn well.

PRACTICAL POINT

Naps promote optimal alertness for learning. Children who nap well appear quiet-alert when awake.

It is a myth that long naps interfere with learning socialization skills or infant stimulation. It's true that "rack-monsters" simply are not available for all the little classes, activities, swim-gym, Mom-Tots, Pop-Tots, or infant stimulating groups that abound today. But is that bad? Do infants suffer by becoming social outcasts? Are they less likely to get into the right preschool which feeds to the right nursery school which feeds to the right private school. No. No. No.

Please do not confuse the quantity of time spent in these scheduled/organized activities with the high-quality social awareness that well-rested children exhibit. The truth is that these infant support groups, especially in cities, often are not important for infants, but instead serve legitimate parental needs by allowing them to meet other parents and escape from their apartment or condominium isolation.

Preschool Children

Three-year-old children who nap well are more adaptable. (Adaptability means the ease with which children adjust to new circumstances.) *Adaptability is the single most important trait for school success*. The briefer the naps, the less adaptable the child. In fact, the major temperament feature of 3-year-old children who do not nap at all is nonadaptability. It is exactly these nonnapping, nonadaptable children who also have more night wakings!

My research also has shown that when easy infants at 5 months of age develop into more crabby, difficult 3-year-old children, they also develop a brief sleep pattern. In contrast, those difficult infants who mellow into easier 3-year-old children develop a long sleep pattern. I think that parents' efforts in helping or hindering regular sleep patterns caused these shifts to occur between 5 months and 3 years of age.

But let's now consider measurable intelligence in older children.

School-Aged Children

In 1925, the father of the Stanford-Binet Intelligence Test, Dr. Lewis M. Terman, published his landmark book, *Genetic Studies of Genius*. He compared approximately 600 children with IQ scores over 140 to a group of almost 2,700 children with IQ scores below 140. For every age examined, the gifted children slept longer!

Two years later, about 5,500 Japanese school children were studied, and those with better grades, slept longer!

These two studies were followed by three others in the early 1930s that did not support the notion that bright children sleep longer. But they did not support the opposite premise either. In fact, they were worthless studies because the numbers of children tested (34, 166, and 42) were too small for a proper survey study.

Even 60 years later, Dr. Terman's study stands apart in design, execution, and thoroughness. Furthermore, a 1983 scientific sleep laboratory study from Canada conclusively proved that Dr. Terman's research was right. This study provided objective, sleep-laboratory evidence that children of superior IQ had greater total sleep time. The Canadian researchers and Dr. Terman even agreed on the sleep duration differences: Brighter children slept about *30 to 40 minutes* longer each night than average children of similar ages.

PRACTICAL POINT

Please don't think that when you *routinely* keep your child up too late—for your own pleasure after work or because you want to avoid bedtime confrontations—or when you cut corners on naps in order to run errands or visit friends it has no lasting effect, simply because it's only for maybe a half hour each day. Once in a while, for a special occasion or reason, OK. But day-in, day-out sleep deprivation at night or for naps as a matter of habit could be very damaging to your child. *Cumulative, chronic sleep losses, even of brief durations, may be harmful for learning.*

Another modern study from the University of Louisville School of Medicine examined a group of identical twins who were selected because one twin slept less than his co-twin. At about 10 years of age, the twin with the long sleep pattern had higher total reading, vocabulary, and comprehension scores than the co-twin with brief sleep patterns.

There are many other studies that show an association between sleeping and school performance, but these involve children with allergies or large adenoids. These problems are discussed in Chapter 10.

CHAPTER 3

Disturbed Sleep

We really do not know how our young children feel when they cannot talk to us; all we can do is observe them and guess their feelings. When they do not sleep well, their behavior changes and presumably they feel differently. I think we should consider carefully how we feel and behave when our sleep is disturbed, so that we can better understand and sympathize with our children.

Daytime sleepiness resulting from disturbed sleep typically causes us to feel a mild itching or burning of the eyes and heavy eyelids. Our limbs feel heavy, too, and we tend to be lethargic. We are less motivated, lose interest easily, and have difficulty concentrating. Our speech slows down, we yawn and rub our eyes. As we get sleepier, our eyes begin to close and we may even catch our head nodding.

But this familiar picture of adult sleep is not usually seen in infants and young children who suffer from disturbed sleep. While it is true that well-rested infants yawn when occasionally overtired, it seems that chronically tired infants do not yawn much, semi-sleep, or nod off. Instead, when most very tired, young kids get sleepy, they get grumpy and excitable. My first son at age 3 coined the perfect word to describe this turned-on state: "upcited" from "upset and excited," as in "Don't make me upcited!," when we admonished him for behaving like a monster.

REMEMBER

When your infant or young child appears wired, . . . he may be tired.

Mood and Performance

Before we look at common sleep problems, let's review how disturbed sleep affects mood and performance.

Two very interesting Australian studies on adults have helped to shed light on childhood "upcited" behavior. A 1971 study showed that the level of activation of the nervous system was associated with personality traits, sleep habits, and activity of the adrenal gland. Poor sleepers were more anxious and had higher levels of those hormones, such as cortisol, which typically rise during stressful situations.

The second study, published in 1984, was complex, but I think its results will better help you to understand your child's behaviors.

Adult volunteers reported their moods on four scales:

1. Tired to rested
2. Sluggish to alert
   SLUGGISH: Having little motion, to feel lazy or lethargic
   ALERT: A watchful promptness for action
3. Irritable to calm
   IRRITABLE: Peevishness, impatience, fretfulness, excitability
   CALM: Undisturbed, unruffled, still
4. Tense to relaxed
   TENSE: Under mental or nervous strain
   RELAXED: Relieved from strain or effort

The first two scales reflect degrees of *arousal*, while the third and fourth scales reflect degrees of *stress*.

The researchers measured four different chemicals (cortisol, noradrenaline, adrenalin, and dopamine) that our bodies make naturally. These powerful chemicals affect our brain and how we feel and are related to the four scales in different ways.

For example, fatigue produces an increase in adrenaline concentrations. That is, when we are tired, our body chemically responds with a burst of adrenaline to give us more drive or energy. We become more aroused, alert, and excitable.

Cortisol concentrations also increase with increasing alertness. Increasing irritability and tenseness—the stress factors—are both associated with increasing concentrations of adrenaline, noradrenaline, and dopamine. Yet the specific chemical patterns or biochemical fingerprints for irritability and tenseness are not the same.

Different chemicals, different feelings.

These studies support the notion that when our overtired child appears wired, wild, "on the edge," excitable, or unable to fall asleep easily or stay asleep, he is this way precisely because of his body's response to being overtired. It's a vicious cycle. Sleep begets sleep, but sleeplessness also begets sleeplessness. When our babies miss the sleep that they *need*, the fatigue causes a physical or chemical change in their bodies. These chemical changes directly affect their behavior and interfere with maintaining the calm-alert wakeful state or blissful sleep. They are fractious because they are overtired.

Other studies also have proven that adults who sleep for brief durations are more anxious. When we study adults who are irritable, tense, poor sleepers and have high concentrations of these hormones, we find the old chicken-egg dilemma. Which came first?

I think an experience familiar to all of us helps solve the dilemma. If we work hard to get an important job done, we can push our bodies with lots of caffeine-laden coffee and cola and very little sleep. At the end of the work project, though, if we suddenly stop to take a vacation, it takes a few days to "unwind" and get rid of our accumulated "nervous energy." We really cannot enjoy low-intensity pleasures, like walking barefoot on the grass or playing quietly with children, because we are "all keyed up." After a few days, we eventually calm down and relax, and can enjoy recreational reading and quiet activities. This tells me that our lifestyle and sleep habits can affect our internal chemical machinery, which in turn causes us to feel certain ways. In one study at Dartmouth College, coronary-prone Type A students had more night wakings than Type B students. A vicious reinforcing cycle could develop whereby the fragmented sleep causes increased arousal, the student feels more energized, and sensing this greater level of energy he works even harder late into the night to achieve more but at the same time loses more sleep.

Babies only 2 to 3 days old also have elevations of their cortisol levels during the period of behavioral distress following circumcision. Infants over 4 months of age and children can push themselves hard fighting sleep to enjoy the pleasure of their parents' company and play. The resulting sleep disturbances might produce fatigue, and the body would naturally respond by turning up those chemicals, such as cortisol, responsible for maintaining alertness and arousal. Perhaps researchers may someday find that different patterns of sleep deprivation (total sleep loss, abnormal schedules, nap deprivation, or sleep fragmentation) produce different patterns of chemical imbalances.

I think the following clinical terms can be used to describe "wired" or "turned-on" children with disturbed sleep.

Here are some terms used by professionals to describe hyperalert children:

Physiologic activation
Neurological arousal
Excessive wakefulness
Emotional reactivity
Heightened sensitivity

Obviously, we all get slightly irritable, short-tempered, and grumpy when we do not get the sleep we need. Jokes and cartoons don't seem very funny when we are tired. But children might be even more sensitive to mild sleep loss, and yet simply appear to be more wild or unmanageable. Perhaps off-the-wall behaviors in children are due to sleep loss that is severe, chronic, and prolonged but not recognized as such by parents.

How often have I heard, "She's so tired, she's running around in circles." A classic paper published in 1922 described this "increased reflex-irritability of a sleepy child."

In dramatic contrast, over and over again, I have seen well-rested children in my practice who spend enormous amounts of time in a state of alert/calmness. They take in everything with wide-open eyes, never missing a thing. They find simple little toys amusing or curious. They never appear bored, although the toy they pick up is one they have played with many times before. Parents of children 4 to 12 months of age can dramatically change their children's behaviors from alert/calm to drowsy/active depending on how much sleep they allow their kids to get.

REMEMBER, AGAIN

A sign of sleeping well is a calm and alert state. Upon awakening, these children are in good cheer and are able to play by themselves.

In infants and young children I think a cause-and-effect relationship exists between disturbed sleep and fitful, fussy behaviors. This means that there is a progressive worsening in a child's mood and performance even when the amount of lost sleep each day or night is constant. So baby becomes increasingly crabby even if the nightly sleep is constantly just a little too brief.

PRACTICAL POINT

A constant small deficit in sleep produces a cumulative reduction of daytime alertness.

As the child develops, the relationship between disturbed sleep and problems of mood and performance becomes less clear because of the increasing complexity of psychological and intellectual function. It is even possible that chronic, disturbed sleep causes children to grow up experiencing excessive daytime sleepiness, low self-esteem, or mild depression. In one study, about 13% of teenagers with disturbed sleep were reported to be like this. They usually took longer than 45 minutes to fall asleep or awoke frequently at night. Some of these teenagers simply may have never learned self-soothing skills to fall asleep easily when they were much younger. As adults, they are described as insomniacs.

One theory of adult insomnia is that it is characterized by an internalization of emotions associated with a heightened or constant state of emotional arousal plus physiological activation which causes disturbed sleep. But distinct differences exist between adult insomniacs whose insomnia started in childhood compared with those whose insomnia started in adult life. The childhood-onset insomniacs took longer to fall asleep and slept less than the adult-onset insomniacs. I think this kind of data tends to support the notion that the failure to establish good sleeping habits in infancy or early childhood may have long-term harmful effects, such as adult insomnia. And, among psychologically unhealthy adults, the more severe the sleep difficulty, the more severe the degree of mental illness.

Let's now review some of the most common sleep problems which can disrupt our children's sleep.

Early Bloomers . . . Who Fade Fast

The easiest sleep problem to deal with is the baby about 3 months of age who had been sleeping well, but now wakes up crying at night and during the day. The parents also may note heightened activity with wild screaming spells. These are regular adaptable, mild infants who matured early but, at 3 months, began to decide they would rather play with their parents than be placed in a dark, quiet, and boring room. Parents who have not had enough experience believe this new night waking represents hunger due to a "growth spurt" or insufficient breast milk.

When these parents begin to focus on establishing a regular daytime nap schedule, when they put these babies in their cribs when they need to sleep, and when they avoid overstimulation, the frequent night waking stops. If the children had developed irritability or fussiness, this disappears, too. More on this in Chapter 5.

<hr>

PRACTICAL POINT

Think of overstimulation not as excessive intensity with which you play with your child but rather too long a duration of baby's normal period of wakefulness. It's not too much of a good thing, it's just being up too long.

<hr>

REMEMBER

The more rested a child is, the more she accepts sleep and expects to sleep.

<hr>

Night Waking

When children wake up frequently at night, we call this a night-waking problem. The truth is that awakening at night or complete arousals are normally occurring events, as discussed in Chapter 2, "Healthy Sleep." Problems arise when the child has difficulty or is unable or unwilling to return to sleep unassisted. The more often these events occur, the longer each separate awakening lasts.

Infants

Brief awakenings in young infants under 4 months of age are acceptable to most parents because these usually are thought to be caused by hunger. For the older child, especially if he had been sleeping overnight previously, night wakings are often thought of as a behavioral problem.

Older Infants

Two separate groups of infants between 4 and 8 months of age seem especially prone to night waking.

The first and larger group—about 20% of infants—includes

those infants who had colic when they were younger. These infants not only awaken more often, but their total sleep time is less. Although boys and girls in this group awaken the same number of times, parents are more likely to state that it is their sons who have a night-waking problem. In fact, boys are handled in a more irregular way than girls when they awaken at night. This was shown in studies using videotapes in dim light in the children's own bedrooms at home. Even when the colic had been successfully treated with a drug during the first few months, by 4 months of age the children still were reported frequently awakening at night.

My conclusion is that some biological disturbances in infants can cause an overaroused, hyperalert, irregular state, full of crying, especially in the late afternoon or early evening. This is commonly called colic. In the past, the crying part of colic has been thought to be the major problem. But while this evening crying diminished at about 3 to 4 months, the wakeful, not sleeping, state may continue and thus be more serious and harmful in the long run.

This is because the parents have the correct impression that regular and consistent parenting does not much affect the colic, and, unfortunately, they give up the effort permanently. They do not know that after 4 months of age, regular and consistent attention to bedtimes and naptimes really does help the older infant sleep better. The parents' failure to develop and maintain healthy sleep patterns in these older postcolic babies then leads to prolonged fussiness driven by chronic fatigue.

The second group of frequent night wakers in the 4- to 8-month-old age group includes the 10% of infants who snore or breathe through their mouths when asleep. This difficulty in breathing during sleep might be due to allergies (see page 204). These infants awaken as frequently as do those with postcolic night waking, but their parents do not label this night waking as a problem. Probably the parents had not worried about night waking because the infants had not suffered from colic. Those infants who snored also had shorter sleep durations than other infants. As in many sleep disturbances, when one element of healthy sleep is disrupted, other elements are disturbed. I will discuss why snoring is more than an acoustical annoyance in Chapter 10, as well.

A third frequent cause of night waking in this age group is sometimes associated with abnormal sleep schedules. Going to bed too late and getting up too late seem to set the stage for frequent night waking. One child I cared for took two to two and a half hours of soothing, rocking, or holding before she would go to sleep, and then would usually awaken three to four times each night, sometimes as often as 10 times. This prolonged period to put a child to sleep is called increased latency. It's also called a waste of parents' time because the off/on twilight sleep for the child during the rocking, walking, and hugging represents lost, good quality sleep.

PRACTICAL POINT

Fatigue causes increased arousal. Therefore, the more tired your child is, the harder it is for him to fall asleep, stay asleep, or both.

One consequence of increased arousal, which is discussed in more detail later, is that disturbed sleep produces more wakeful, irritable, and active behaviors in children. Also, these children often have increased physical activity when asleep. Although all babies can have gross movements involving the entire body or localized movements or twitches involving only one limb, these are brief motions lasting only a second or less. But chronically fatigued babies who are overly aroused move around more in a restless, squirmy, crawly fashion when sleeping. It seems that their motor is always running at a higher speed, awake or asleep. Later, I will explain how you can reduce your child's idle speed by making sure that he gets the sleep he needs.

What is disturbed sleep?

Abnormal sleep schedules (going to bed too late,
  sleeping too late in the morning, napping at wrong
  times)
Brief sleep durations (not enough sleep overall)
Sleep fragmentation (waking up too often)
Nap deprivation (no naps or brief naps)
Prolonged latency to sleep (taking a long time to fall
  asleep)
Active sleep (lots of tossing and turning)

Night waking is not caused by:

Too much sugar in diet
Hypoglycemia at night
Zinc deficiencies
Pinworms

Night waking also is not caused by teething, contrary to
popular belief. If you ask parents what happens when teething
occurs, the answer is . . . everything! All illnesses, fevers, and
ear infections that happen to occur around the time a tooth
erupts are blamed on teething. Throughout medical history,
doctors used the diagnosis "teething problems" as a smoke-
screen to hide their ignorance. In fact, at the turn of the cen-
tury, 5% of deaths in children in England was attributed to
teething.

A proper study of problems caused by eruption of teeth was
performed in Finland in 1969. Based on daily visits and testing
of 233 children between the ages of 4 and 30 months, it concluded that teething does not cause fevers, elevated white blood
cell counts, or inflammation. And most importantly, teething
did not cause night waking.

Night waking between the ages of 6 and 18 months is more
likely due to nap deprivation, overstimulation, or abnormal
sleep schedules—not teething.

PRACTICAL POINT

Putting your baby to bed, allowing the child to hold a
bottle of milk or juice or resting the bottle on a pillow,
will cause "baby bottle cavities." Protect your child's
teeth. Hold your baby in your arms when you give a
bottle.

Growing pains also do not cause night waking. One study
examined 2,178 children between 6 and 19 years of age and
found that 16% complained of severe pain localized deep in
the arms or legs. Usually the pain was deep in the thighs,
behind the knees, or in the calves. The pain usually occurred
late in the afternoon or in the evenings.

But when the growth rates of these affected children were
compared to children without pain, there was no difference.
In other words, growing pains do not occur during periods of
rapid growth! Blaming night waking on growing pains is a
handy excuse. But the rubbing, massaging, hot water bottles,
or other forms of parental soothing at night is really serving
the emotional needs of the parent or child and not reducing
organic pain.

Night waking may be caused by:

Fever
Painful Ear Infections

Older Children

In one study of children between 1 and 2 years old, about
20% woke up five or more times a week, while in another
study of 3-year-old children, 26% woke up at least three times
a week. Unfortunately, you simply cannot assume that difficulties returning to sleep unassisted will magically go away.
Returning to sleep unassisted is a learned skill; you should
expect problems to persist in your child until she learns how
to soothe herself back to sleep without your help.

Also, in the study of 1- and 2-year-old children, those who

woke up frequently were much more likely to have an injury such as a broken bone or a cut requiring medical attention than those who slept through—while only 17% of good sleepers had injuries, 40% of the night wakers were injured! Chapter 11 will discuss further the connection between injuries and disturbed sleep.

The majority of children between the ages of 1 and 5 have a bedtime routine less than 30 minutes long, go to sleep with the lights off, and fall asleep in about 30 minutes after lights out. Night waking occurs in the older children in this group once a week; only a few awaken once a night. If your child's pattern between the ages of 1 and 5 is substantially different, consider the possibility that your child is among the 20% of children in this group with disturbed sleep. If so, then you might also later notice the excessive daytime sleepiness which has been observed in about 5% to 10% of children between the ages of 5 and 14 years.

Excessive Daytime Sleepiness

Superficially, we tend to think of being either awake or asleep. But just as there are gradations between light sleep and deep sleep, there are gradations of wakefulness. Task performance, attentiveness, vigilance, and mood may be influenced by the degree of daytime wakefulness. When we do not feel very awake during the day, we say that we feel "sleepy." Excessive daytime sleepiness or impaired daytime alertness is a result of disturbed sleep.

The Stanford Sleepiness Scale is a self-rating instrument developed at Stanford University to describe the different stages or levels of daytime sleepiness. Obviously, children who are depressed or irritable due to sleep deprivation will have high numerical ratings.

LEVEL	DESCRIPTION
1	Feeling active and vital; alert; wide awake
2	Functioning at a high level, but not at peak; still able to concentrate

3   Relaxed; awake; not at full alertness, responsive
4   A little foggy; not at peak; let down
5   Fogginess; beginning to lost interest in remaining awake; slowed down
6   Sleepiness; preferring to be lying down; fighting sleep; woozy
7   Almost in reverie; sleep onset soon; lost struggle to remain awake

Young children and infants, of course, cannot tell us how they feel, but watch their behaviors. Does your child behave as though he were active, alert, vital, wide awake or is he fighting sleep, woozy?

This chapter and the two previous chapters describe the terms "healthy sleep" and "disturbed sleep." Obviously, sleeping is not an automatically regulated process such as the control of body temperature. Sleeping is more like feeding. There are many different ways parents feed their children, but all children need a certain number of calories to grow. If the food that is provided is insufficient or unbalanced, then this unhealthy diet interferes with the growth and development of the child. This is equally true for unhealthy sleep patterns.

CHAPTER 4

How Crybabies Become Crabby Kids: Colicky Baby and the Postcolic Child

If your child suffered from colic during infancy—and 20% of all babies suffer from this mysterious condition—then you'll be most interested in learning how your crybaby's colicky first months could have set the stage for unhealthy sleep habits. This chapter will be of interest to you even if your baby never had colic, though, because *all* babies experience unexplained fussiness and crying in their first weeks of life—no matter what your ethnic group, no matter what birthing method brought her into the world, no matter if your lifestyle is that of jetsetter or stay-at-home.

All parents, too, tend to use the same techniques and strategies to successfully weather those first few months of life with the baby, whether fair sailing for the most part or storm-tossed by colicky waves of crying. Sleep problems arise when some parents don't change their techniques for coping with crying and fussiness at bedtimes and naptimes after about 3 or 4 months of age, after their babies have become more settled. That's when unhealthy sleep habits and their resulting problems begin.

> ### PRACTICAL POINT
>
> Parenting "tricks of the trade" effective for infants under
> 3 or 4 months of age may create bad sleep and naptime
> habits in older babies.

Let's take a brief look at why parents adopt certain strategies for comforting crying infants, and particularly for colicky babies.

Some Babies Cry a Little, Some Cry a Lot

All babies cry or fuss at times without explanation. Wet diapers, hunger, vomiting, cramped positions, chilling or overheating, bright lights, loud noises, or loss of equilibrium are *not* the cause. We learned earlier that one of every five infants experiences this unexplained fussiness severely enough to be called colicky. And while all babies can develop poor sleep habits due to parental mismanagement, colicky babies are even more at risk of developing unhealthy sleep as older children. I'll explain why just a little later on.

How can you tell if your baby's fussy, crying spells merit the term "colic," and mark him as more at risk? If those periods of unexplained crying follow this checklist, then he probably experiences what researchers call colic:

1. Crying spells started at about 2 weeks of age and did *not* dramatically decrease in intensity after about 6 weeks.
2. Spells lasted three or more hours a day and occurred more than three days a week for more than three weeks.
3. Most attacks started between 5 P.M. and 8 P.M. and ended by midnight.
4. Crying spells generally tapered off at about 3 to 4 months of age.

It would be helpful to add the "cause" of colic to this checklist, but, unfortunately, no generally acceptable reason has been found. In fact, we know a great deal more about what doesn't cause colic. Researchers have ruled out gastrointestinal or allergic causes, as well as maternal anxiety or maternal diet, in the case of breastfed infants. Instead, we now believe colic may be set off by one or more physiological disturbances, such as disordered breathing during sleep, sleeping patterns that are not in synchrony with other body rhythms, or abnormal levels of naturally occurring substances (such as prostaglandins or progesterone). Most likely, colic is related to these physiological factors, as well as to a baby's measurable temperament characteristics.

In many studies published in reputable medical journals, "colic" is really not defined. Crying only after meals is discussed, or results are based only on parents' hazy memories years after the event. False conclusions from such studies include the following: colic is caused by parental smoking, colic occurs more often among breastfed babies, or colic is more common among higher social classes.

What is important here is the impact that unexplained crying has on the development of healthy or unhealthy sleep habits. Unexplained crying, whether moderate or severe as with colicky babies, can undermine parents' self-confidence and set the stage for future sleep problems. Here is one vivid personal account.

A Father Remembers Colic: Or, Is the French Foreign Legion Accepting Applications?

Sleep? Hmmm . . . Oh, yes! I remember that! We used to do that frequently before Michelle was born.

Two years and another baby later, I still replay Michelle's birth in my mind at least daily. I joked in the delivery room that the newborn was "ugh-lie," but it was just a ruse to help me hold back the tears. A healthy, normal baby! The demons of the past nine months disappeared in a flash.

The first few days were spectacular. While my wife and baby recovered in the hospital from a long, tough, toxemic labor, I played the role of red-eyed, tired-but-ecstatic new father to the hilt. I showed up at work the next day, ostensibly to guard against using up a vacation day, but actually to show off the Polaroid pictures that I had carried home with me in the wee hours of that postpartum morning to avoid waiting an ungodly 24 hours for the 35-millimeter prints to be developed.

Everything was perfect. I was getting the house in shape, making the phone calls, bringing goodies to the hospital. Nursing was starting off fine for my wife, Sharon, and our new baby was peaceful and thriving.

The false security even lasted through the first few days Sharon and Michelle were home. Michelle would wake up about every three or four hours, and with a tiny, delicate cry, let us know that it was time to nurse again. We marveled at the fact that no matter how soft the cry or what room it came from we could always hear it. Isn't parenthood amazing? And as Michelle nursed, she would usually doze off again. When Sharon was finished, she'd put the baby back in her crib, and we would just stare down at her, enjoying the peaceful sight of our sleeping baby.

Just as Michelle crossed the boundary into her second week of life, the scene started to change. Same little cry. Same nursing routine. But then, when the nursing stopped, a new cry would start. This one was different. Louder. More agitated. More demanding. I rather enjoyed it at first. It gave me a role. I could pick her up, and with a few minutes of rocking and patting, the crying would stop. It was my first fleeting sense of competence as a father.

But the crying grew worse and worse. Five minutes of rocking were replaced by hour-long midnight jaunts in the stroller. On rainy nights, I'd carry her around the kitchen-to-dining-room-to-living-room-to-kitchen circuit so many times, that I actually started to vary my route for fear of imbedding a path in the carpet. The left shoulder of every T-shirt I owned had spit-up stains on it. I switched to the football carry: holding Michelle face down with my hand on her tummy and my fingers supporting her chin, I would swing from my hips, back-and-forth, back-and-forth, back-and-forth. At 3 A.M., I would strap on the Snugli and set off for another trek with my frantic daughter.

Each of these stratagies worked for a short time. But Michelle had become a motion junkie. Absent motion, she would shriek and scream violently and tirelessly, literally for hours at a time. She would become hoarse, but even that failed to deter her.

Everyone we knew had a theory, and even some people we had only just met in the supermarket checkout line. All the advice was offered freely and generously, but never without the subliminal undercurrent that the real problem was our incompetence as parents. The baby was nursing too much. She wasn't getting enough food from nursing, give her formula. Mix some cereal in with the formula. Wait four hours between feedings. Put her on a schedule. Relax, she senses your stress. And on and on and on. There was no end to the advice, all of it contradictory, much of it accusatory, and none of it helpful.

Michelle got worse and worse. And we got more and more tired, more and more frazzled, and more and more testy. Then we got the swing.

The swing was one of those wind-up numbers where you place the baby in the seat, turn the crank 50 times, and the seat swings back and forth with a mechanical click as it reaches the apex of each direction.

The swing was the true definition of a mixed blessing. While it was in action, clicking away, Michelle was quiet and often fell asleep. But within two minutes after the final click, Michelle would stir, stretch her arms, fill her lungs, and scream.

One good crank would last about 20 minutes. So we organized our lives into neat, 20-minute intervals, always trying to catch the sound of lessening momentum so we could crank *it* up before Michelle got cranked up. And it worked.

It worked so well that Michelle would accept no substitute. Unless she was hungry, there was no longer any time that we could hold our child without her screaming. All of our fears, all of the subliminal messages we had received, were coming true. We were rotten parents. A mechanical swing could calm our child, but we could not. We hated the swing, but we dared not, could not, put it away.

Dr. Weissbluth gave us a copy of what was then just a manuscript for his forthcoming book, *Crybabies*. Sharon and I each devoured the book in one sitting. One section was particularly important and encouraging to us. It was a bell-shaped curve. Along the bottom, horizontal axis were the first 12 weeks of life. Along the vertical axis was the amount of what was laughingly called "unexplained fussiness." "Unexplained fussiness" is medical jargon for unending, sharp, fierce shrieks that push parents to the edge of insanity.

The point is this: All newborn babies cry a lot. A portion of that crying is for no good reason, as far as we in the grown-up world can tell. If you normalize the daily variations in the amount of this crying, what you find is that it keeps going up for the first six weeks of life, then gradually falls off over the next six weeks. Then it's gone.

We weren't sure it was true, but we decided to delay our mutual suicide pact for 12 weeks to see if it was. As Michelle reached her eighth week of life, we started to notice a strange phenomenon: There were brief periods of time when she was awake and not crying! And those periods of calm were starting to increase! *We were believers.*

While this father's story may sound extreme, it actually is typical of the lengths parents will go to help their babies through their crying spells. Although many remedies have been suggested for colic, including catnip or herbal tea, papaya juice, peppermint drops, heartbeat or womb recordings, hot water bottles, or trying new baby formulas, only three maneuvers have been found that do calm fussiness and crying:

1. Rhythmic motions: Using rocking chairs, swings, cribs with springs attached to the casters, cradles, carriages and strollers. Walking, taking ceiling tours, using your baby for curling exercises to strengthen biceps, and taking car rides. Rocking waterbeds are good, and studies have shown that they stimulate and regulate breathing. Maybe all rhythmic

rocking soothes babies by encouraging regular breathing, thus taking away the need for the baby to ''make'' colic in order to breathe well.

2. Sucking: At breast, bottle, fist, wrist, thumb, or pacifier.
3. Swaddling: Wrapping in blankets, snuggling, cuddling, and nestling, like a Chinese eggroll. After a few weeks, this maneuver is often less effective.

You should avoid trying gimmick after gimmick because you will only feel more frustrated or helpless as the crying continues. You may also feel resentment or anger since your child, unlike your friend's child, doesn't seem to respond as well to home remedies.

PRACTICAL POINT

Feelings of anger toward your crying child are frightening—and normal. You can love your baby and hate her crying spells. All parents sometimes have contradictory feelings toward their baby.

Please take breaks when your baby is crying. Because the breaks will enable you to better nurture your baby, it's a smart strategy for baby care, not a selfish idea for parent care.

You may have the impression that during the first few months you are not influencing your colicky child's behavior very much. Consider this to be a rehearsal. Your hugs, kisses, and loving kindness are expressing the way you feel and practicing showering affection on your baby, even when he's crying. This loving attention is important for both you and your baby.

However, this unceasing attention showered on your crybaby, whether colicky or just occasionally fussy, during the first few months *can* have complications, if you maintain this strategy of intervention for the older, postcolic child at bedtime and naptimes. Thus, after the colic passes, the older child is never left alone at sleep times and is deprived of the opportunity to develop self-soothing skills. These children never learn to fall asleep unassisted. The resultant sleep fragmentation/sleep deprivation in the child, driven by intermittent positive parental reinforcement, leads to fatigue-driven fussiness long after the biologic factors which had caused colic are resolved.

What Happens When Baby Does Not Stop Crying?

When the excessive crying and fussiness of your baby's first few months have passed and baby seems more settled, what next? After about 4 months of age, most parents have learned to differentiate between their child's *need* for consolidated sleep and their child's *preference* for soothing, pleasurable company at night. Most parents can learn to appreciate that prolonged, uninterrupted sleep is a health habit which they can influence; they can quickly learn to stop reinforcing night wakings and irregular nap schedules that rob kids of needed rest. A "social" weaning process from the pleasure of Mom's or Dad's or caretaker's company at nap and bedtimes is underway. As one young mother said, "I see, I should now forget the company she [the baby] wants."

But parents of postcolic children still have a few challenges to face. That's because children who have had colic appear more likely to develop difficult temperament, shorter sleep durations, and more frequent night wakings between 4 and 8 months of age than other babies. My research also has shown that parents of postcolic kids are more likely to view frequent, instead of prolonged, night wakings as a problem. Furthermore, boys are more likely than girls to be labeled by their parents as having a night-waking problem. Let's see how these patterns could have emerged.

Temperament differences among babies were described by Dr. Alexander Thomas and his associates in a study based on both their own careful observations and parent interviews. Dr.

Thomas noted interrelations among four temperament characteristics: mood, intensity, adaptability, and approach/withdrawal. Infants who were moody, intense, slowly adaptable, and withdrawing in Dr. Thomas's study also were rated as *irregular* in all bodily functions. Thus they were diagnosed as having "difficult" temperaments because they were difficult for parents to manage! We don't know why these particular traits cluster together. But we do know that infants with "easy" temperaments had opposite characteristics. In Dr. Thomas's study, four additional temperament characteristics were described: persistence, activity, distractibility, and threshold. (Threshold means how sensitive or insensitive the child appears to changes in lighting or noises.) These four temperament characteristics were not part of either the easy or difficult temperament clusters.

Infants who have had colic during the first few months are significantly more likely to develop a difficult temperament at 4 months of age than are noncolicky babies. This progression occurs even when colic is successfully treated with dicyclomine hydrochloride, a prescribed drug which is no longer used to treat colic. Since careful studies show that maternal emotional or personality factors do not directly lead to the development of colic and because the difficult temperament develops even when the colicky crying is abolished, it seems that congenital factors (i.e., factors present at birth) and not parental behaviors lead initially to colic and subsequently to difficult temperaments.

PRACTICAL POINT

Babies are "born" with colic. Parents don't give their infants colic through poor handling.

Congenital factors may be inherited, such as skin color, or acquired prenatally, such as birth defects from maternal drugs taken during pregnancy. We know that congenital factors do influence a baby's degree of irritability, sociability, emotionality, breathing control, and even sleep patterns. Much of our knowledge regarding these biological differences comes from comparing fraternal and identical twins.

One congenital factor recently investigated was plasma progesterone concentrations. Progesterone is a hormone that can, along with its byproducts, depress the central nervous system. Progesterone can even be used as an anesthetic agent. Progesterone might have calming, sleep-inducing properties by dulling the brain in normal infants. A possible mechanism for the quieting, calming, sleep-inducing, and anesthetic effects of progesterone is the reduction of another potent chemical in the brain, called dopamine. Progesterone is also capable of suppressing or inhibiting rhythmic, jerking movements in experimental animals. In newborn infants, this hormone is derived mostly from the placenta, but levels of progesterone fall dramatically by the fifth day of life. Thereafter, progesterone is made by the newborn, probably in the adrenal gland. In fact, these high progesterone concentrations derived from the placenta might account for the delayed onset of unexplained crying or colic until after the first week of life.

If congenital factors indeed are the cause of colic/difficult temperament, perhaps this condition might serve some biologically useful functions. "Colic" historically has implied inadequate maternal soothing skills, while "difficult" temperament has a Western middle-class negative implication, suggesting that a child has a problem requiring treatment. Western middle-class mothers tend to view crying as "difficult" behavior, because it forces the mother to spend more time with her baby. The crying child is more socially demanding, because he demands more attention and stimulation and he provides less self-entertainment. In a Western setting, the crying child might be quieted by too much feeding, and the result can be overfeeding or obesity. However, in a study in an East African village where drought conditions were causing starvation of many infants, the temperamentally difficult infants were more likely to be among the survivors. In other words, the squeaky wheel gets oiled.

Similarly, more intense infants temperamentally were observed to have fewer breathing pauses and less irregular breathing during sleep, and thus, they might be at a lower risk for Sudden Infant Death Syndrome (SIDS). It's possible that the pumping breathing, increased muscle tone, and jerky movements occurring during a colic spell occur during a storm of one particular type of REM sleep, called phasic REM sleep, and that this storm really represents the baby's struggle against a deep, dangerous sleep period. We do know that infants who almost die from SIDS tend to have brief night sleep durations, and that infants who are temperamentally more active, intense, and stimulus-sensitive have better breathing quality during sleep (see Figure 7).

Therefore, colic or difficult temperament might confer some biologically adaptive or protective advantage to some infants in some settings. Usually, however, after four months, many of these crying infants in Western, middle-class families proceed to develop sleep disturbances instead of developing healthy sleep habits.

Here's how child development specialist Laya Frischer described a postcolicky baby.

Jane at Age 4 Months

Jane was difficult and unpredictable, with less than average sleep and cuddling and more than average crying. Observations over five weeks revealed an extremely sensitive infant. For a period of time, she could not tolerate touches on her abdomen. Swaddling helps a little, and the rhythmic swing movement gives her some relief. If these things fail, the parents walk her around. Sometimes these efforts quiet her fussiness, but at other times it escalates to panic crying. Jane seems to have no capacity to console herself, and very little capacity to be consoled by usual methods of touch. The pacifier has

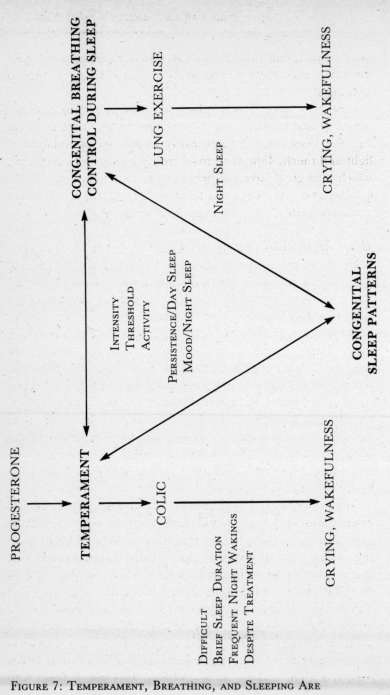

FIGURE 7: TEMPERAMENT, BREATHING, AND SLEEPING ARE
CONNECTED IN BABIES

been helpful, but not always successful. Jane does not have good state regulation. *She can be in a panic cry state when she seems to be asleep.*

Jane goes from sleep to distress in seconds. She becomes overtired and cannot sleep, which contributes to her irritability. She does not habituate easily to sensory stimulation of light and touch. Jane requires a very protective environment, which puts great stress on her parents, particularly her mother. Her cries are very hard to read; her parents feel that she is unpredictable, and often uncommunicative.

Brief Sleep and Night Wakings

In one of my studies, infants at 4 months of age who had had colic slept hours less than infants who had not. Similarly, infants diagnosed as having a difficult temperament slept less than those with an easy temperament. Persistence, or attention span, was the infant temperament characteristic most highly correlated with *day* sleep duration, while mood was the infant temperament characteristic most highly correlated with night and *total* sleep, as shown in Figure 7. Thus those infants who slept less during the day had shorter attention spans, while those with less total sleep had more negative moods, fussiness, or crying. What this means is that a postcolic baby who is not getting enough sleep overall and is missing naps has a shorter attention span and is going to be difficult to control.

In another study I performed, I showed that a past history of colic was associated significantly with the parents' affirmative answer to the question that they considered night waking to be a current problem. Specifically, parents stated that the number of awakenings each night was a major problem in 76% of infants, while the duration of each awakening was a major problem in 8%. Both the number and the duration were problems in 16% of the infants. Although there were no significant group differences in the number of night wakings based on the infant's sex, parents of boys more often reported night waking as a problem. Overall, infants who had had colic awoke twice as often as those who had not had colic.

But here is a continuation of the story of Michelle, who had extreme unexplained fussiness or colic.

A Father Remembers Colic: Or, Is the French Foreign Legion Accepting Applications? (continued)

Of course, nothing kids do ever conforms entirely to what the books say. Getting Michelle settled down to sleep remained a long, drawn-out ritual well past her 12th week. And getting her to sleep through the night was still an impossible dream. We were still tired (especially Sharon, who had gone back to work but still nursed her at night and expressed milk for her during the day), but we were no longer frantic and frazzled. We had regained a sense of time, a sense of day and night. We no longer felt like miserable failures at the baby business.

We let it ride until Michelle reached 5 months. Then, after another series of consultations with our doctor, we decided to aggressively manage Michelle's sleep patterns, so both we and she could get some meaningful rest.

The theory was that Michelle was waking up at night at various times just as we all do. But instead of turning over and going back to sleep, she was demanding food and attention from us. She no longer needed the food, and the attention was robbing both her and us of a satisfying night's sleep.

The first rule was no more middle-of-the-night feedings. And because of that, we decided that Sharon should not go to the baby at all during the night, since the sight and smell of her would be too tempting for Michelle. When she cried, I would go in and rock, cuddle, sing, or swing . . . whatever it took to get her back to sleep.

After a few nights of this routine, we discovered that Michelle had not lapsed into malnutrition, had not stopped growing, and had not faded away into nothingness. We were ready to move on to the next step. For the next few nights, I did my entire moonlit song and dance number, but I didn't pick Michelle up. And sure enough, she continued to survive.

The next phase was no more talking. Now when I was summoned to her room for a soiree, I would just lean over her crib and pat her on the back until she was fast asleep. In fact, anything short of a full five minutes would lead to a revival meeting shortly thereafter.

A few days later we held our final strategic planning session with our pediatrician. The moment of truth was upon us. He suggested that we make the room as dark as possible, put Michelle in her bed, and not open the door until morning. He recommended that Sharon spend the night with a friend, and promised us that this final step would not take more than three nights of prolonged screaming. Very encouraging.

Sharon decided to gut it out with me. When the designated time approached, we started the bedtime ritual. Then we put Michelle in her crib, turned, marched out of the room, and shut the door. The crying started immediately. But it only lasted 10 minutes. Ten minutes! That was it.

Neither of us slept well that night. We kept craning our necks and straining our ears to hear the cries. But there were none. And when daylight came, we rushed into Michelle's room—and, lo and behold, she was fine.

And that was it. Ten tough minutes and the three of us were free from this five-month ordeal. As the days passed, we noticed some very positive side effects. Just like us, Michelle was becoming much more pleasant and fun now that she was well rested. She was thriving, and we were loving it. Life has resumed.

One more thing. The swing is gone. One evening, after we had put Michelle to bed for the night, we dismantled the thing, brought it down to the basement, and opened a bottle of champagne. We never used the swing again, and I'm extremely pleased to say that it is no longer in our possession. It served us well, but I still cringe every time I hear a click.

Are Poor Sleep Habits Congenital?

The observation that brief and interrupted sleep often follows colic might suggest that some congenital, biologic factors lead initially to colic, and that they are still affecting baby. This is supported by the observation at the age of 4 months that despite successful drug therapy which eliminated or reduced crying, brief sleep periods were still the norm. In addition, some, but not all, postcolic infants continue to behave as if they had heightened activity levels and excessive sensitivity to environmental stimuli, as with the case of Jane.

Here is another story from my own experience: When my first son had colic, I had to keep the crib railing up and locked in place, because the "clunk" of the spring lock would always awaken him. This made it awkward for me to place him in his crib, but fortunately I was limber from college gymnastics. For my wife, it was an impossible situation until we got a sturdy stool for her to stand on—but it still hurt our backs!

Interestingly, these two temperament characteristics (high activity and low threshold) are not part of the diagnostic criteria for babies with or without colic who fall into the "difficult" temperament category. But some of these postcolic infants were exquisitely sensitive to irregularities of their nap or night sleep schedule. Disruptions of regular routines due to painful ear infections or holidays and trips subsequently caused extreme resistance to falling asleep and frequent night waking lasting up to several days after the disruptive event. These prolonged recovery periods might reflect easily disorganized internal biologic rhythms caused by enduring congenital imbalances in arousal/inhibition or sleep/wake control mechanisms.

Crabology and Momitis

Some postcolic kids have boundless energy. "She crawls like lightning" was how one mother described her baby. These babies are constantly on the move. They would rather crawl up mom's chest to perch on her shoulder than sit quietly in her lap. But once having reached the shoulder, they immediately want to get down and check out that dust ball or some equally exciting object off in the corner. They appear easily bored and stimulus-sensitive, especially to rough mechanical noises, such as a vacuum cleaner, hair dryer, or coffee-bean grinder. It's as if they have a heightened level of arousal, activity, and curiosity. When tired, they are always crabby, socially demanding, needing mommy's presence and wanting to be held all the time. They also are quick to fuss when mom leaves the room for only a minute. But, when they are well rested, it's a different story.

When well rested, these same babies appear to have boundless curiosity, actively seeking opportunities to learn to touch or to taste. Maybe these are very intelligent children who are so alert, curious, and bright, they have difficulty in controlling their impulses to explore or investigate the world. No data supports the conclusion that postcolic kids in general are more intelligent, but there may be a small number who are so exceptionally bright that they gave birth to this myth. One study of infants published in 1964 connected increased crying induced by snapping a rubber band on the sole of the foot at age 4 to 10 days to increased intelligence at age 3 years. Whether this artificial crying and its link with intelligence can be generalized to colic crying is an open question.

Beating the "Crybaby Syndrome"

When you become your child's timekeeper and program her sleep schedules, she will be able to sleep day and night on a regular clock schedule. For most parents, this is a relatively easy adjustment to make. But for postcolic infants, expect to put forth great effort to be regular and consistent. Your effort to keep your child well rested will be rewarded by a calmer, happier, more even-tempered child. One family thanked me when they were finally able to permanently decrab their baby and they responded to their active explorer by saying, "The 'other' baby is back!"

But without your effort to maintain sleep schedules, your child will have a tendency to sleep irregularly and become unmanageably wild, screaming out of control with the slightest frustration, and spend most of the day engaged in crabby, demanding, impatient behaviors. The majority of postcolic infants do not fit this extreme picture, but they do require more parental control to establish healthy sleep schedules compared to noncolicky infants. Thus, it appears that after about 4 months of age, poor sleep habits are learned, not congenital.

PRACTICAL POINT

For all post-colic infants after 4 months of age, my clinical observations are that frequent night wakings may be eliminated and the sleep durations lengthened if, and only if, parents establish and maintain regular sleep schedules for their child.

It appears that most postcolic sleep problems are caused less by a primary biologic disturbance of sleep/wake regulation, but rather by a secondary failure of parents to establish regular sleep patterns when the colic dissipates at about 4 months of age. Both obvious and subtle reasons can be cited as to why parents have difficulty in enforcing sleep schedules when colic ends.

Three months of crying sometimes adversely and permanently shape parenting styles. The inconsolable infant behavior triggers in some parents a perception that their baby is out of their control. They observe no obvious benefit to their colicky child when they try to be regular according to clock times or to be consistent in bedtime routines. Naturally, they then assume that this handling will not help their postcolic child either. Unfortunately, they do not observe the transition at age 4 months from *need-based*, colicky crying to *contingency-based*, fatigue-driven crying.

Alternatively, some parents may unintentionally and permanently become inconsistent and irregular in their responses to their infant, simply because of their own fatigue. The constant, complex, and prolonged efforts they used to soothe or calm their colicky baby are continued. But these ultimately lead to an overindulgent, oversolicitous approach to sleep scheduling when the colic has passed. Their nurturing at night, for example, becomes stimulating overattentiveness. In responding to their child's every cry, the parents inadvertently deprive their child of the opportunity to learn how to fall asleep unassisted. The child then fails to learn this important, self-soothing skill, which she will need for her entire life.

In addition, my studies have shown that when daytime sleep is interrupted, the same consequences occur. The nap-deprived infant develops a short attention span. Remember, other studies have shown that the difficult child is irregular. It is exactly these two temperament traits, short attention span and irregularity, that have been shown to interfere with a child's ability to learn—unfortunately, beginning with learning how to fall asleep without their parents' help.

Effective behavioral therapy to establish healthy postcolic sleep patterns by teaching the child how to fall asleep and stay asleep may or may not be acceptable to you, depending on your ability to perceive and respond to the sleep needs of your infant. A variety of ways to achieve healthy sleep will be discussed in detail in the chapters that follow.

Other parents, usually mothers, have extreme difficulty separating from their child, especially at night, as discussed in Chapter 12. They may have some difficulty themselves being alone at night because their husband's work requires frequent or prolonged absences or because nights have always been lonely times. They perceive every cry as a need for nurturing. These are wonderful mothers, but they may be *too* good. According to this view, the infant is robbed of desire, because his every need is anticipated and met before it is experienced. The infant is left with undischarged aggression. The mother unintentionally thwarts the development of her child's capacity to be alone; she interferes with this developmental process in which the mother's role of soothing and nurturing is taken over by the child. The mother blocks attempts of her infant to provide substitutes (such as thumb sucking or pacifiers) for her physical presence.

These parents perpetuate brief and fragmented sleep patterns in their children. Their infants become, according to Dr. Ogden, a child psychiatrist, "addicted to the actual physical presence of the mother and [can]not sleep unless they are being held. These infants are unable to provide themselves an internal environment for sleep." Although the *child* has disturbed sleep, here the focus of the problem and its solution is on the *parent*.

Colic certainly does not cause the parents to have difficulty in separating from their child! But it is more than a sufficient stimulus to cause them to regress toward the least adaptive level of adjustment. The result is severe, enduring sleep disturbance in the child. In this setting, simplistic suggestions to help the child sleep better often fail to motivate a change in how the parents approach the problem. Thus, while it is the wakeful child who may be brought for professional help, it is often the parent who has the unappreciated problem.

Colic is the most obvious example of extreme crying but please remember that any painfully overtired infant or child might cry. In some nonindustrial societies, this may occur rarely because the child is always held in a papoose device or cloth carrier. But these mothers do not drive cars, wear watches, or keep many daily appointments. Also, there is less intense environmental stimulation so that the baby might sleep well outdoors when the mother is planting rice or cooking. Our lifestyles are different.

Our goal is to avoid the overtired state just as we would

want to avoid an overhungry state. Whether overhungry or overtired, the child expresses his discomfort by crying, but crying is not the real problem. Allowing your child to become overtired is the problem and the way to avoid it is to focus your attention on timing. Timing means that you try to plan ahead. You anticipate when your child will become slightly tired and that is when you soothe him and then place him in his crib. If your child's sensation or tiredness and your soothing efforts occur at the same time, then the result will be peaceful slumber for your child.

Timing is not always easy because we may have very busy lifestyles or our baby is colicky. But timing is very important to establishing healthy sleep habits.

PART II

How Parents Can Help Their Children Establish Healthy Sleep Habits: From Infancy to Adolescence

CHAPTER 5

Months 1 to 4

Every newborn baby is unique. The closer we look, the more we see differences between babies. Some of these differences reflect inborn traits and are called genetic differences. But other congenital differences which are not inherited are due to whether the baby was born at 37 versus 42 weeks of gestation or whether the mother smoked or drank large amounts of alcohol during her pregnancy. All of these differences in smiling, sucking, sleeping, and physical activity combine to make a baby an individual. This chapter will describe the individual sleeping patterns in our babies and how these patterns change as our babies grow.

Newborn: The First Week

While recovering from labor and delivery or the aftereffects of anesthesia, you may begin to experience new feelings of uncertainty, inadequacy, or anxiety. After all, Parentcraft 101 probably was not one of your high school or college courses. Unfortunately, hospital schedules can serve to underline these feelings. In hospitals without total "rooming in," an artificial time schedule is imposed on baby care activities. This is determined by changes of nursing shifts, visiting hours, and measurements of vital signs, not by your baby's whim.

But as soon as you arrive home, please disregard the clock and feed your baby whenever she seems hungry; change her when she wets; and let her sleep when she needs to sleep. Full-term babies sleep a lot during the first several days. They also eat very little and often lose weight. This is all very natural and should not alarm you. Don't confuse sweetness with weakness.

PRACTICAL POINT

Your baby has no circadian rhythms or internal biological clocks yet, so you can't set baby to clock time.

Presumably this calm, quiet period during the first days is somehow synchronized with the need for a few days to pass before breast milk comes in. Babies sleep a lot, 15 to 18 hours, but usually in short stretches of 2 to 4 hours. These sleep periods do not follow a pattern of day or night transitions. So get your own rest whenever you are able.

HELPFUL HINTS

Unplug your phone when nursing.
Unplug your phone when napping.
Unplug your phone when your husband is with you.
Consider a relief bottle (one bottle a day of water, formula, or expressed breast milk) if you are nursing.

Weeks 2 to 4

All babies are a little hard to "read" during these first few weeks. Most activities such as feeding, changing diapers, and soothing to sleep occur at irregular times. Try not to expect a scheduled baby, because the baby's needs for food, cuddling, and sleeping occur erratically and unpredictably. When your baby needs to be fed, feed him; when he needs to have his diapers changed, change him; and when he needs to sleep, allow him to sleep.

What do I mean by "allow him to sleep"? Try to provide a calm, quiet place for your baby if he sleeps better this way. Many babies are very portable at this age and seem to sleep well anywhere. You're lucky if your baby is like this, and you're even luckier if your baby is one of the few that has long night sleep periods. Most babies don't sleep for long periods at night.

Studies have shown that for babies a few weeks old, the longest single sleep period may be only three to four hours and it can occur at any time. Colicky babies may not even have single sleep periods that are this long; premature babies may have longer sleep periods.

Parentcraft strategies such as changes in the amount of light or noise don't appear to greatly influence babies' sleep patterns now. In fact, specific styles or methods of burping, changing, or feeding do not seem to really affect the baby. Try not to think of doing things *to* the baby or *for* the baby. Instead, take time to enjoy doing things *with* your baby. Do that which gives both of you pleasure: holding, cuddling, talking and listening, walking, bathing, and sleeping together.

A change will occur in all babies during these first few weeks, and you should prepare for it. When your baby is about to fall asleep or just about to wake up, a sudden single jerk or massive twitch of his entire body may occur. Sometimes the eyes appear to roll upward when the drowsy baby drifts into a deeper sleep. This is normal behavior during sleep/wake transitions. Also, all babies become somewhat more alert, wakeful, and aroused as their brain develops. You may notice more restless movements, such as shuddering, quivering, tremulousness, shaking or jerking, twisting or turning, and hiccoughs. There may be moments when your sweet little baby appears impatient, distressed, or agitated . . . for no identifiable reason. This is normal newborn behavior.

During these spells of unexplainable restlessness, the baby may swallow air and become gassy. Often he appears to be in pain. Sometimes he cries and you can't figure out why. The crying baby may be hungry or just fussy. This is confusing to all mothers.

All in all, you may now not have the baby you dreamed of having. She cries too much, sleeps too little, and spits up on you whenever you forget to cover your shoulder with a towel. Here are some concrete steps you can take to make it easier for everyone:

1. Take your naps during the day whenever your baby is sleeping.
2. Unplug all phones in the house.
3. Go out, without baby, for breaks: a walk, a coffee date, a movie.
4. Plan for or arrange for blocks of a few hours of private time to take care of yourself.
5. Do whatever comes naturally to soothe your baby; don't worry about spoiling your baby or creating bad habits.
6. Use swings, pacifiers, or anything else that provides rhythmic, rocking motions or sucking.

If you find that your baby sleeps well everywhere and whenever she is tired, enjoy your freedom while you can. A time will come when you will be less able to visit friends, shop, or go to exercise classes, because your baby will need a consistent sleep environment.

Q: I've heard that my baby should not sleep in the bassinet in my room or in my bed with me. It will spoil him.

A: Nonsense. For feeding or nursing, it makes it easier for both of you if your baby is close. When your baby is older, say 3 or 4 months, both of you may sleep better if your baby is not in your room. Anyway, the number of night feedings by then is usually none or one.

Weeks 5 to 8

At about 6 weeks of age, or six weeks after the expected date of delivery for premies, your baby will start to return your social smiles.

If you are lucky to have a calm baby who appears to have regular sleep periods, prepare yourself for changes resulting from your child's increased social maturation. The social smiles herald the onset of increased social awareness, and it may come to pass that your baby will now start to fight sleep for the social pleasure of your company. This is natural!

PRACTICAL POINT

Try to meet your baby's needs. If he's hungry, feed him. If he's tired, sleep him.

In addition to the onset of social smiling at about 6 weeks of age, night sleep becomes organized so that the longest sleep period predictably and regularly occurs in the evening hours. This sleep period is now about four to six hours long. (If your baby has colic, the longest sleep period might be less than this.) Your baby will start to settle down more and more, too. She will become more interested in objects such as mobiles, toys, and playing games, and her repertoire of emotional expressions will dramatically increase.

Yet many parents find this time particularly frustrating, since many babies reach a peak of fussy/wakefulness at about 6 weeks. Your baby may irritate and exhaust you. She may give up napping altogether, and to make matters worse, when awake she may appear to be grumbling all day. You may feel battered at the end of each day; you may be at your wit's end. This, too, is natural. Being annoyed with your baby does not make you a "bad" parent. Just understand why you're annoyed. Remember, your baby's immature nervous system lacks inhibitory control. The brain will develop inhibitory capabilities as it matures, but this takes time; things will settle down after 6 weeks of age.

Here is an account of one mother's first eight weeks.

My First Bath in Eight Weeks

Today my baby girl, my first (and probably only) child, Allyson, is 8 weeks old. I celebrated by taking a relaxing bath—my first uninterrupted bath since her birth. Of course, she woke up just as I was toweling off, but I have learned to be grateful for all small pleasures.

Allyson doesn't sleep much, and when she's awake she's usually either crying or nursing. It's been a little better the past week, but she still sleeps very little: six to eight hours at night and two to four hours during the day. And since I can't bear to hear her cry, that means she spends most of her time on my breast where, mercifully, she can always be soothed. I feel as if I've merged with the brown corduroy chair where I nurse her.

Lately she's good for a couple of 10- to 20-minute "play periods" (on the floor—on her back and me leaning over her, or on the changing table while I change her diaper). I can't hold her and play with her; she's always squirming to get at my breast. So, anyway, she's on my breast 10 to 12 hours a day. As my gay hairdresser said when I related all this to him: "Well, honey, I guess you can kiss *one* erogenous zone good-bye." How true. The first week my nipples bled (I did my Lamaze breathing during nursing), then they kind of scabbed over, and now not even during her most violent writhing spells do I feel a thing. When she twists her head with my nipple in her mouth, my nipple just stretches like a rubber band. No problem. (By the way, hydrocortisone ointment saved my life.)

Given Allyson's behavior (constant crying or "fussiness" and constant desire to nurse, or at least "hang out" at my breast), I naturally concluded that my baby was starving, that I did not have enough milk for her. If I did have enough, surely she would fall asleep and *stay* asleep. Obviously, I thought, she was waking after a few minutes or half an hour because she was hungry. A weighing at the doctor's, where I learned that she was in the 75th percentile for growth (at 3 weeks) did not reassure me. I remembered after the weighing that she had drunk about 8 to 10 ounces of formula on the way to the doctor's office. It was the only way to keep her quiet in the cab and in the doctor's waiting room, so I thought this must have misrepresented her true weight. I continued to worry . . . and nurse around the clock.

This brings up another worrisome aspect of Allyson's behavior. She would gulp down any bottle anyone would give her. She once drank 10 ounces of formula immediately after having sucked at my breasts for 45 minutes. Of course, a few days later I conducted an "experiment" and let her drink about the same amount of formula, then put her to my breast—where she sucked away for about an hour.

At one time I thought she just had a great need to suck, but she spits out any pacifier my husband and I have tried to give her (and we've tried every kind in existence). I was again left with the conclusion that my breast milk supply was insufficient, and that the only way my baby could satisfy her hunger was to nurse almost constantly, until she finally slept from pure exhaustion.

Throughout all this, I received a steady stream of "advice" from friends and relatives about how my baby was obviously hungry and how I should put her on the bottle immediately. Also it was suggested that I: (1) start the baby on some cereal to help fill her up; (2) stop smoking; it was probably ruining my milk; (3) handle the baby more gently; (4) bounce and jiggle the baby more to help her pass the gas that she had in such abundance; (5) get a lambskin for her to sleep on (we did; it gave her a rash on the side of her face she slept on) (6) RELAX; the baby was probably picking up on my freaked-out vibes; (7) take her to this place where infant massage was taught (I didn't; someone said they turned out the lights there and burned incense and I already went through that in the sixties in college, thank-you-very-much); (8) stop drinking milk and eating cheese and put the baby on soy formula for the three to five bottles she was getting each week, and; (9) buy a swing so the rocking motion could help soothe her. Well, we got the swing when Allyson was 3 weeks old, and she hated it at first. But we got her used to it a minute at a time, and now at 2 months, she's good for up to 20 minutes. She even fell asleep in it twice!

Anyway, most of the above advice was heaped on me all at once by the many relatives who gathered in my hometown when Allyson was a month old for my mother's funeral. How I survived my mother's unexpected death, my anxiety about my baby's behavior (which at that time was unexplained), the fatigue, the hormonal changes *plus* all this unwanted advice—I'll never know. Why I did not abandon breastfeeding I will never know. I came close at the 6-week mark, but my doctor encouraged me to persevere just a few more weeks, and I did.

A second trip to my hometown when Allyson was 6 weeks old convinced me that I needed to discuss my baby's behavior at length with the doctor. A new batch of relatives who were actually staying in the house with me could not believe how much she cried or how much I nursed. They assured me that this was not normal, that something was definitely wrong, and I should see a doctor.

I had, of course, talked previously to the doctor by phone. The first phone call was made to him at home on a Sunday afternoon, the first full day I was home from the hospital with the baby. Allyson had been very sleepy in the hospital, but awoke at dawn the first day home screaming. The doctor told me all babies had fussy periods and that it would get better. A week later, I called to tell him how much time I spent nursing to calm her, and again I was told it would get better. In the meantime he suggested the hydrocortisone ointment, which really helped my nipples heal fast. When she was three weeks old, I called again. That's when the doctor had me bring her in for a weighing, at which time he pronounced her to be a normal, healthy baby with some bad fussy spells that would eventually pass. I started to think I was a real wimp for being upset about what all mothers must go through, so I decided to grit my teeth and wait it out. At my doctor's suggestion, I hired a nurse to take care of the baby three afternoons a week so I could get out of the house, and that helped tremendously.

At this point I started reading some of the most popular books about babies—Dr. Spock's and one by Penelope Leach called *Your Baby & Child*. Nothing in either book seemed to explain my baby's behavior or to offer help. If my baby was "normal" and "healthy," then I should be able to read about similar behavior in these well-known books, right? My baby cried and could be consoled only by nursing. She would doze at my breast after an hour or two of sucking, only to awake within minutes to start the cycle all over again, until—after anywhere from 6 to 18 hours—she would fall asleep for three to six hours; she would then wake up crying and start all over again.

So what does Dr. Spock have to say about all this? I found this: "What do you do if . . . she wakes as soon as you put her to bed or a little later?" Good question, Dr. Spock! That's what I want to know! Basically, he says "let her fuss for a while if you can stand it" (I couldn't) or, he says, feed her again, "if you must," because "the chances are that the baby will outgrow this inconvenient pattern in a few weeks no matter how you handle it." This gave me great hope until a "few weeks" went by, then several more, with no change. So much for help from Dr. Spock.

What advice does Ms. Leach have to offer? My baby could not fall asleep and, once asleep, could not seem to stay asleep. Therefore, my baby was sleeping only about 8 to 12 hours a day. Well, Ms. Leach devotes a couple of pages to what she describes as "the wakeful baby," a category in which I figured my baby certainly belonged. She says: "A really wakeful baby may never sleep for more than 12 hours and may seldom do that sleeping in stretches of more than 2 hours at a time." When I first read those words I remember how excited I got that someone, somewhere, had heard of a baby like mine. I read on. In her "Living With It" section, she advised: "Start by reminding yourself that he would sleep if he needed to" (which I've since learned is absolute poppycock; I guess she hasn't seen the bags under my baby's eyes). She continues: "Find different ways of keeping the baby company. Perhaps his carriage could come into the kitchen . . . get into the habit of stopping for quick chats as you move around." *WHAT??* Stop for quick CHATS for heaven's sake? How does one CHAT with a wailing, writhing infant? The book made me furious, and still does. What nonsense.

I was not looking in the index under "colic" in either of these books, because the doctor had assured me when I took the baby in for her weighing at 3 weeks of age that she could not be diagnosed as having colic. This is probably because she was too young and he felt that crying which could be called colic should be present for more than 3 weeks.

Weeks 3 through 7—when I didn't know what was wrong or why I was so upset by Allyson crying, when I kept hearing it was "normal"—were absolute hell. I "lost it" only three times, though. Once was one Sunday when my husband left to play golf all day and Allyson was particularly wild. I found myself shaking her bassinet and screaming "SHUT UP" into her little helpless, screaming face. (Of course, I then immediately picked her up and nursed, convulsed with guilt.) Another time was at the funeral home for my mother's visitation. I had Allyson camouflaged sucking at my left breast, so she would not scream and disturb everyone else. All I could think of was that I wanted to get away from my baby so I could sob and grieve for my mother ALONE. I couldn't, so I got somewhat hysterical, which I'm sure was interpreted by everyone else there as my way of grieving. Little did they know how angry I felt toward this little baby glued to my chest.

The third time was in the doctor's office on the day I finally went in for a consultation. Allyson was 7 weeks old, and I was convinced I had something other than the normal "fussy" baby. In the waiting room my reserves of strength were nearly exhausted by a woman who asked me where my child was. (It was a pediatrician's office, after all.) When I told her I was there just to talk to the doctor about my child's excessive crying, she said something about how I must be a first-time mother, and said I was probably the "nervous type" and my baby sensed this. She also said she worked in a hospital maternity ward and asked me what kind of formula I used when not breastfeeding. When I said "Enfamil" she acted like "A-ha!" She said she swore that when the babies in the hospital nursery were given Similac they were much calmer than when they were given Enfamil. I did my best to ignore her, but then, at about the same time, two women with babies walked into the waiting room. One baby was 18 days old, the other looked about Allyson's age. Both women were holding their babies in their arms quite calmly waiting to be seen by the doctor. Their babies seemed content to be held. They weren't asleep; they were just lying there, kind of moving their heads around and looking. It hit me that in the nearly two months since my baby was born (with the exception of the two and a half days in the hospital and part of the first day at home), I had *never* been able to simply hold my baby like that. I repeat (and I am NOT exaggerating): I had *never* been able to simply cuddle my baby, unless she was nursing. I started to cry right there in the waiting room, and couldn't stop.

When I talked with the doctor, he said it did seem my baby was "colicky," and I took his book home to read. Finally, I found descriptions by other mothers of babies like mine! I was not alone. I came to understand how sleeping problems, like those of my baby, are probably related to colic, and how although my baby appears to be hungry, she really isn't. I also learned how there's nothing that I can do for my baby that I'm not already doing, and so I might as well turn some of my energy around and start taking care of myself. Truly, I believe that in the case of a colicky baby, who in most cases cannot be treated for her condition, it is the MOTHER who needs "treatment" or help, and to this end I suggest:

1. Get out of the house an hour or two a day, MINIMUM.
2. When out of the house, try to get some physical exercise to burn off the tension.
3. Don't feel guilty about doing anything that makes you feel good. (In my case, it's smoking, which I resumed after cutting down to practically nothing during pregnancy.)
4. Socialize as much as possible outside the home, but for God's sake stay away from people when you're with your baby. Discourage visitors. You don't need the inevitable nonsense advice; it will just make you more anxious and confused.
5. Keep a diary or log of your baby's sleeping/feeding habits. One day, when you're especially tired you'll find yourself thinking in despair that your baby's behavior is getting much worse, but when you look at your log you'll find this is probably not the case—it's just *you* who are more fatigued than the day before, and things are looking bleaker.

6. When the baby is asleep, go to sleep yourself, unless you're doing something for your own peace of mind. Sleep is so important. I'm convinced that only women who have had babies, doctors on call, and possibly victims of Viet Cong sleep deprivation torture can understand how lack of deep, long sleep periods can make you do and say things you couldn't possibly have thought you were capable of.

Well, there's hope, I guess. Baby Allyson is slowly getting better. My husband and I have adapted somewhat. I continue to put her to my breast whenever she needs consoling, which is most of the time. During her several catnaps, I put her down and rush around the house doing whatever it is that needs doing with two hands (grating cheese for spaghetti for dinner, making the bed, taking a shower, etc.). Then, while she is nursing on my left breast during the day, I do everything I can with my right hand (browning the meat for spaghetti, dusting, brushing my teeth, even going to the bathroom). It's a challenge for me to have the house picked up, myself looking presentable, and something started for dinner by the time my husband comes home from work. It's kind of a game I play with myself, getting everything done that needs doing during the day. It is important to me that I feel I have accomplished something, however mundane, besides feeding my baby and changing her diapers. That's how I keep myself going. My husband has been great. He cuts my meat for me at dinner, for example, so I can eat with my right hand while she's nursing on my left side. That way we can both eat in peace, without having to hear her heartbreaking wails.

And things are getting better. Last night (I saved the best news for last) Allyson woke up from a three-hour nap, nursed calmly, and wasn't fussy for several hours afterward. She didn't go back to sleep, but she didn't cry either. Later that evening she slipped back into her old ways, but I got to HOLD her and play with her for over an hour; then she stayed calm in the swing for a while.

And I got my bath this morning.

If you are lucky to have an easy baby, at 5 to 6 weeks you may have already noticed sleep patterns becoming somewhat regular. You can try to help your baby become more regular by putting her down to sleep after about two hours of wakefulness when she appears tired. If she cries for 5, 10, 20 minutes, it will do her no harm and sometimes she may drift off to sleep. If not, console her and try again at other times. Try to become sensitive to her need to sleep. The novelty of external stimulating noises, voices, lights, and vibrations will more and more disrupt her sleep, so try to have her in her crib when she needs to sleep. Go slowly and be flexible.

Here is an account from one mother who needed to get her child's sleep more scheduled before she went back to work. Trying her methods with a more irregular, fussy child probably wouldn't work at this early age and shouldn't be tried. But an easy baby often responds quickly to sleep-training strategies at around age 6 weeks.

My Maternity Leave Would Soon Be Over

When Ron and I interviewed and selected our pediatrician before David was born, we left his office comfortable with the care we felt our child would receive. Although we knew the doctor had a special interest in sleep disorders, we never dreamed we would be faced with a baby whose internal clock thought day was night and night was day.

Oh, it didn't happen right away. In fact, the first few weeks were spent nursing and changing diapers in between David's naps. He was blissful, and I tried not to worry every time he did something new and different. Looking back at those first weeks, Dr. Weissbluth must have really chuckled at some of the questions I asked him. (Thankfully, he didn't.) My embarrassment has lessened after talking to some of my friends and hearing some of the questions they have asked their doctors.

At the same time I was beginning to relax and feel, yes, everything was going along normally. David became more alert; Ron and I knew it was a great step in his development. We looked forward to his periods of wakefulness as a time to interact with him. But a pattern began to develop. David didn't want to go to bed at night.

At first, we were happy to have David's company for the evening. But the stretch of hours became longer and longer and it was obvious to us that David was not as happy as we were to be awake. We began to try everything. The bouncy seat, the rocking infant seat, the swing. The swing worked. Perhaps too well. David slept in the swing, all propped up with rolled diapers. Then, when it was time for bed, David cried.

So I nursed him, rocked him, walked with him, gave him to Ron to be walked, tried to nurse again, tried the pacifier, walked some more. And on and on into the night. We took David for rides in the car and that usually helped. And we called the doctor.

The doctor listened to what we were going through and assured us that, first of all, this was normal for some babies. He suggested putting David in his Snuggli and going for a walk, taking rides in the car, and being loving and patient with our baby. David was really too young to go through sleep training at 6 weeks. Most babies respond to training at 3 or 4 months, he told us. So, Ron and I resigned ourselves to some more of the same. Luckily, Ron was a night owl and I was an early bird. He stayed up with David most nights, waking me for nursings when necessary (about every two hours). It helped, too, that Ron did most of his work out of the house. I relied on him and he on me and we shared all the tasks (except, of course, nursing). Even though our friends shared their stories of sleepless nights with us, we really understood we were not alone the night Ron was taking David for a ride in the car at 2 A.M., pulled up to a stoplight, and turned to see a woman in the car next to him with a baby strapped into a car seat, also trying to get her baby to sleep. Ron had visions of sleepy parents at stoplights all over the world, trying to get their babies to sleep.

At the doctor's suggestion we tried to keep David up a little

longer during his daytime wakings, hoping that we could turn
his little inner clock around. But David would not cooperate.
Just as he refused to go to bed at night, he wouldn't keep
awake for anything during the day. We felt we were losing the
battle. I can remember some nights standing over his crib,
crying in exhaustion. Too tired and angry to hold him, just
needing a break. I think the anger was the most difficult emo-
tion all this sleeplessness brought out. How could I be angry
at this little, helpless baby that I loved so much? It took a
while (and a lot of guilt) before I realized that it was OK to
be angry as long as you don't take it out on the baby.

David was now 2 months old and I began to panic. My
maternity leave would soon be over. I could barely stand up
most of the time, I was so tired. I also wanted to continue to
nurse David whenever I would be home. I knew we had to do
something before I went back to work. So we called Dr. Weissbluth and made an appointment to see him.

First, the doctor checked over David's physical condition.
He was in perfect health. Then we talked. Dr. Weissbluth
explained we would have to make some changes in the way
we handled David's sleep periods. David was to have a quiet,
darkened room when sleeping. No more night light, music,
etc. Naps should last at least 45 minutes to 1 hour. If David
got up sooner, we were to leave him until he got the rest he
needed. Instead of letting David stay up late, we were to put
him in bed between 7 and 9 P.M. No rides in cars, strollers,
or swings, where sleep occurred for a short time. David
needed to learn that rest came in his crib. The doctor explained that sleep from motion was not restorative, which
was what David needed now. And then the hard part. When
we put David down for the night we were not to go to him
if he began to cry, only if he had at least 45 minutes to 1
hour of sleep and he was scheduled to be fed. Older babies
can turn around in about three days, the doctor explained.
If after three days there was no improvement, we should
abandon the training for a few weeks and try when David
was older. We were assured that three days of crying himself

to sleep would in no way harm our baby, but for it to go on any longer without improvement would be unfair, to David and to us.

We decided to start that next Monday, since Sunday was Mother's Day and I knew that while we were ready to begin, the grandmothers would rebel if we limited David's time with them. Early on Monday I called the doctor to make sure I had his instructions straight. (Turns out I didn't, but I didn't know that until Tuesday.) We agreed that I would call the doctor daily for the next few days to report on David's progress. Ron and I took a deep breath and braced ourselves for the days to follow.

Poor David. That first day I woke him after he napped for an hour instead of letting him sleep for as long as he wanted. The doctor later explained you should never wake a sleeping baby. The baby will know when to wake up. But in spite of my mistake, the day went quite well, that is until that night. For some reason, the night before David had fallen asleep on his own at 7:00 P.M. and had slept through the night. I hoped that he would repeat the cycle and that somehow, as if by magic, he would have straightened himself out. Wrong. That night Ron had to work late and out of the house. I nursed David at 9 P.M. and by 9:30 he was asleep in my arms. I tiptoed him into bed and crept back to the living room and turned on the intercom. It was quiet until 9:45 when I heard David sucking his fingers. I thought, OK, he'll get back to sleep soon, but at 10:00 the crying began. David cried until 12:30. Two and a half hours. For every cry I heard I shared his frustration, anger, and seeming pain. And I was angry. At David, the doctor, myself, and Ron, who unfortunately wasn't there to keep me going. Finally, David slept—until 6:45 the next morning, when I woke him to nurse.

The morning wakeup was planned and agreed to with Dr. Weissbluth. The idea was to get David to wake before I left for work so that I could nurse him. David seemed fine. I was exhausted. It was really an emotional night. I was having doubts about proceeding with the remaining two days, but my morning call to the doctor gave me one more day's courage. He assured me that, first of all, my one-hour nap wakeups did not ruin anything. He was encouraged that David slept through the night and told me that the two and a half hours of crying was normal during a training program.

So Tuesday, I let David wake himself up. I found out that the poor little thing had really been cheated out of some sleep the day before. He took two- to three and a half-hour naps that day, but his schedule was rather loose. At 8:30 that night when he woke up I fed, bathed, and played with him until he had one last nursing and I put him in bed, although he was not asleep at 10:50. This time he cried from 10:50 until 11:15. Only 25 minutes? Could it be this easy? I was very encouraged. Weeks of David's inability to get to sleep at night seemed to be at an end. Even Dr. Weissbluth seemed surprised at David's progress. Once again, he slept through the night.

Although we were still unsuccessful at getting David to bed early, the periods of crying himself to sleep were getting shorter. On day three he cried 21 minutes and not another peep until the next morning.

Just when Ron and I began to let out our breaths, David put us back in our places. Day 4 David cried for nearly an hour and a half. My spirits dropped. Was it just a temporary setback or were the last three days just a fluke? When I called the doctor that next morning he told me to continue the training. David will have some off days, he explained. The great strides we had taken over the past few days were important and showed that David could and would accept some training. We may not yet get perfection, but our success should not be denied.

David had his good days when he would only cry for 5 to 10 minutes, and then his bad days when the crying would go on for up to 45 minutes. Ron and I were really beginning to understand David's needs and wants. We found that if we responded too quickly, assuming he wanted to nurse, he became irritable and difficult to feed. Those were the nights the crying seemed to go on forever. Thank goodness Ron was around to keep me from running at David's every whimper. The poor thing would have never gotten any sleep.

We continued to check in with Dr. Weissbluth, but less frequently. At the end of our third week of sleep training David, Ron, and I really had our acts together. Ron and I could tell when David was ready to call it a day, and we didn't push him to stay up any later than he wanted. David had developed an unusual way of confirming his need for sleep. When we put him in bed, he would lay his little head down, put his fingers in his mouth, and suck his way to sleep. If he began to cry, he refound his fingers and would pacify himself back to sleep. At 8 months, he still lets us know he's tired by putting his fingers in his mouth.

When Ron and I started the sleep training we kept a log of David's wakings and sleepings. We still do. Not because he's still in training. We've established reasonable bedtimes and sleeping patterns. But with my return to work and Ron's busy schedule, we are better able to understand David's moods and hunger patterns when the sitter lets us know what's gone on during the day.

Do we regret having trained David at such an early age? Well, Ron and I realize that his training took a bit longer because he was so young. And I wish that I had been able to take a bit more time off from work to be with David, but that just wasn't possible. No, we have no regrets. David became a happier baby. By putting some structure in his day, he became more relaxed and in return, so did we.

As we have seen, every baby behaves differently during these first few months. Your own baby most likely will fall somewhere in between the "easy" baby and the colicky infant. And even if your baby has been "easy," this may well be a period in which she "forgets" what she has learned.

The "Easy" Baby . . . Who Stops Being Easy

These are placid, easy-to-manage infants who are quiet angels during most nights. Sure, they may have a fussy period in the evening, but it's not too long, intense, or hard to deal with. They appear to sleep well anywhere and anytime during the day and quite regularly at night. In fact, the early development of regular, long night sleep periods—starting well before age 6 weeks—is a characteristic feature. These kids are very portable and parents bask in their sunny dispositions, particularly when social smiling begins at about the 6-week mark.

But shortly later, dark clouds may gather. The baby starts to have some new grumbling or crabbiness that does not occur only in the evening, like the classic "sundown" syndrome. In fact, the quiet evenings might now be punctured by new, "painful" cries suggesting an illness. Or it might now take longer than before to put the baby to sleep. What has happened to your sound-sleeping baby?

Irregularity of sleep schedules and nap deprivation are the chief culprits. Now is the time to become ever more sensitive to your child's need to sleep.

After about 6 weeks of age, the best strategy is to try to synchronize your caretaking activities with your baby's own rhythms. You should try to reestablish healthy sleep habits by removing the disruptive effects of external noises, lights, or vibrations. Although it may be inconvenient for you, try to have your baby home in her crib after no more than two hours of wakefulness. Consider this two-hour interval of wakefulness to be a rough guide to help organize the day into naps and wakeful activities.

Be Careful, But . . .
No Set Schedules
No Rigid Rules

Two hours of wakefulness is about the maximum time that most babies can stay awake without becoming overtired. Sometimes a baby may need to go to sleep after being up for only one hour. Often this brief wakeful period occurs early in the morning. Try to soothe him to sleep before he becomes overtired: before he behaves slightly crabby, irritable, pulls his hair, or bats at his ears. Expect this type of behavior to develop within a two-hour interval of wakefulness if he is not put to sleep when tired. Please do not mistake this two-hour guide to mean that your child should be up for two hours and then down for two hours. Rather, two hours is the time interval during which you should expect to put your baby to sleep.

Expect your tired child to protest sometimes when you put her down to sleep. This is natural, because she prefers the pleasure of your soothing comfort to being in a dark, quiet, boring room.

Keep in mind the distinction between a protest cry and a sad cry. You are leaving your baby alone to let her learn to soothe herself to sleep—you are not abandoning her.

Q: How long should I let her cry?

A: Start with 5, 10, or 20 minutes. Try to make a decision whether your child is tired based on (a) your child's behavior, (b) the time of day, and (c) the interval of wakefulness—how long she has been up.

When you have decided she is tired, put her down to sleep— even if she doesn't want to sleep. Sometimes she'll fall asleep and sometimes she won't. When she doesn't, pick her up, soothe and comfort her, and then at some future time, try again. You may try again after several minutes or you may decide not to try again for several days. If your baby cries hard for 3 minutes and quietly for 3 minutes and then sleeps for an hour, he would have lost that good hour nap if you had not left him alone for 6 minutes.

Remember, this baby had once been a good sleeper and

now is fighting sleep for the pleasure of your company. At those times when she needs to sleep but wants to play with you, your playing with her is robbing her of sleep.

Keep a log or diary as you go through these trials to see if any trend of improvement occurs. Here's an account from Allyson's mother, who helped her baby make a dramatic—and permanent—improvement in her sleep habits at this time.

Allyson's Sleep Log

DAY #56: Allyson woke up from an afternoon nap, and I thought she was ill—she was so *calm*! No jerky movements and agitated behavior, which I guess I'd assumed was just "normal" for her. About this time, though, she still cried a lot when not nursing, and she still had trouble falling asleep.

DAY #58: Went to doctor for 2-month checkup and discussed "training" her to sleep by letting Allyson cry again. The rule was not to pick her up during the day when she fussed. Instead, I would comfort her in crib (stroking head, kissing her, patting her back, etc.). I would put her down after she had been up two to three hours and was getting really tired and would not pick her up for two hours (the minimum I figured she should be in her crib sleeping). At night, however, if she cried I *always* picked her up and nursed her. I thought she might really be hungry then—plus she never had terrible problems sleeping at night—it was the daytime when she needed help getting to sleep.

DAY #59: Let her fuss one hour—and she went to sleep for three and a half hours (5:45 to 9:00 P.M.).

DAY #60: Allyson fussed all morning and wouldn't sleep, but I kept her in her crib 10:15 to 12:00 A.M., staying with her most of the time. Got her up to nurse at 12:00. That night she got up at 2:30 A.M.—for the first time in several weeks. I nursed her until 3:00 A.M. and then put her down. She fussed off and on until 4:00 A.M., when she went to sleep.

DAY #61: Some problem getting her down for morning nap,

but I kept her in crib. Again, she woke at night at an unusual time—12:30 A.M. I nursed her 12:30 to 1:30 (she seemed hungry); then she whimpered until 3:30 A.M.

DAY #62: Same problem—no sleep in morning. However, she slept through the night (9:30 P.M. to 5:10 A.M.!!!).

DAY #63: Breakthrough! She went to sleep for 45 minutes in A.M. and took a really long nap in the afternoon (12:45 to 5:00). But she woke in the middle of the night again (3:20 A.M.). She went back to sleep at 4:30 A.M. and slept until 8:30 A.M. *She was happy in her crib*—no screaming as I changed her diaper, which was new behavior!

Careful records show that up to Day 59, the total sleep duration per 24 hours was about 6 to 12 hours. After Day 63, the total sleep duration was always longer—12 to 17 hours. The four-day "training" really helped the child sleep longer.

DAY #64: Two wonderful things happened: First, Allyson took a morning nap (10:45 A.M. to 1:30 P.M.). *AND* when I put her down for the night with her eyes *wide open* she did not fuss at all. I quickly left the room and heard *no* crying. She slept 8:35 P.M. to 5:05 A.M.

DAY #65: No morning nap. Cried four minutes when putting her down for evening.

DAY #66: Morning nap 9:30 to 10:45! Cried one minute after putting down for evening.

DAYS #67–69: Same as #66.

DAY #70: Took morning nap again. Fussed 10 minutes at bedtime. Woke at 3:30 A.M. but went back to sleep when husband gave pacifier.

DAY #71: Took short morning nap!

DAYS #72–86: The morning nap habit "sticks." Also, Allyson is much "happier" in general. She almost always sleeps through the night. She is much more regular in her habits. For example, she begins taking a catnap in her swing in the kitchen for 30 to 45 minutes at nearly the same time every day.

DAYS #87–96: Allyson is just about perfect. If she starts to fuss, I know she is hungry, wet, or tired. If she's tired, I simply put her in her crib and *within two minutes* she is asleep. It is a miracle!

(We had a slight problem with naps when I was breaking in the new caretaker. Allyson starting waking up again—testing the new person??—but I was there and would not let the caretaker pick her up. After fussing 10 to 15 minutes before naptime and waking up midnap for three or four days, this problem also disappeared.)

Colicky Infants

The other "extreme" in behavior for babies up to 3 or 4 months of age is colicky infants. These are intense, difficult-to-manage infants who tend to be very wakeful during the day, irregular when they do sleep, or stimulus-sensitive. Colicky babies behave this way for three to five months, and unlike Allyson, often a portion of their crying is inconsolable. Because of their irregularity and alert/aroused state, it doesn't make sense to try to schedule their sleep. They are hard to read. Most parents have difficulty telling whether they are hungry, fussy, or plain tired. So leaving them alone is confusing to everyone. The following hints and the information in Chapter 4 will help you get through the rugged first few months.

Helpful Hints for Parents of Colicky Kids

Pamper yourself; remember, this is smart for the baby—not selfish for you. You will better be able to nurture your baby.

> Forget errands, chores, housework.
> Unplug the phone.
> Don't listen to your baby's sleeping sounds.
> Nap when baby sleeps.
> Hire help for housework or breaks when baby is most
>   bothersome.
> Plan pleasurable, brief outings without baby
>   (swimming, shopping, movies).

Hints to Help Soothe Colicky and Noncolicky Babies

Definitely Helps Soothe:

Rhythmic rocking
Sucking: A pacifier on a very short ribbon can be
 attached to a pillow cover or pajama top so that it
 won't be lost. The ribbon must be short so that it
 cannot go around the child's neck.

Questionably Helps Soothe:

Lambskin rug
Warm water bottle placed on abdomen
Heartbeat sounds in teddy bear
Low-volume recording of vacuum cleaner or running
 water
Removal of stimulating toys from crib or bright night
 light
Placing a soft blanket in baby's clenched fist
Putting the child's head against a soft crib bumper or
 laying a cloth diaper over the head like a scarf

Crying should not be thought of as a test for you. Don't feel that you are creating a crying habit, because of your prolonged, complex, soothing efforts. Your first test to help your baby sleep will come later, when the colic subsides at 3 to 4 months of age.

You can't treat colic with smiles, but there will be less crying in a home where there is a lot of social smiling. Practice smiling; smile broadly, open your eyes wide, regard your child with a nodding up and down, say "good boy" or "good girl" . . . do all of these things, especially when your baby calms down or smiles at you.

PRACTICAL POINT

Don't save your smiles until colic ends.

Here's an account from David's mother who noted colicky behavior between the third and eleventh week.

His "Crying (and Awake) Button" Got Stuck in the ON Position

"David is such a great baby, I can't hardly believe it!" I heard myself say to Dr. Weissbluth, David's pediatrician. It was David's fourteenth-week birthday. "Well, if you hadn't kept a log," he replied, "you wouldn't remember how awful things were." Quite frankly, even if I hadn't kept one I certainly would never forget how terrible things were, and not just with the baby. It is now 16 weeks since the baby arrived, approximately four months, and my life is actually resembling something of what it once was.

David, our first baby, was born in spring, five days early, and because I had pre-eclampsia, he was a tad on the small side at 4 pounds 13 ounces. His doctor described him as robust but lean and quite healthy. The baby seemed awfully scrawny to me and sounded like a hungry kitten when he cried. I could detect his cry from all the others as the nurses wheeled babies down the corridor for feedings. Even before I became pregnant, I had decided that I would try breastfeeding. Consequently, David spent very little time in the nursery and almost all his time in my bed. The delivery was a textbook one, much to my surprise—no drugs, fast delivery, no birth trauma, everything in its place, and eyes wide open. David nursed well right away, didn't seem sleepy, and never really slept for more than an hour or so. That should have tipped me off!

The first two weeks were quite exciting, although David did appear hungry very often, every two hours or so. I was told that breastfed babies do eat more frequently than bottlefed ones, but I hadn't expected it to be that often. David slept close to my bed, usually remaining there most of the night. Although he did awaken every two hours for nursing, he was basically a model baby. My husband and I felt very fortunate. On our first dinner alone after the first two and a half weeks we discussed our good fortune. As Larry said, "Aren't we lucky we don't have one of those colicky babies you hear so much about?" Ah yes, I agreed.

Exactly three days later, at the beginning of David's third week on planet Earth, his "crying button" got stuck in the ON position and remained that way for what would turn out to be the longest eight weeks of my life! He cried and shrieked until his face would be red—nonstop from 3:00 in the afternoon until 9:00 each morning. I called his pediatrician constantly as well as everyone else I knew who has, or ever had, a baby. Friends who had infants would offer all manner of suggestions:

> Maybe it's your milk;
> Maybe he's hungry;
> Give him formula;
> He sounds like he has cramps;
> You're spoiling him, put him in his own room;
> Let him cry, it's good for his lungs;
> You're nervous, he can tell;
> Get a second opinion;
> Give him some water, etc., etc., etc.

These suggestions were always followed with the comment, "Well, all I can say is *my* baby slept through the night by the time he was 4 weeks old!"

Well, that confirmed it to me. God was punishing me! I remember *nothing* of June or July; the months that I had planned to take wonderful walks in the park with the baby were spent in a haze. Doing one thing a day was a major accomplishment. Grocery shopping was really an event. I was constantly on the verge of tears. It then occurred to me that perhaps I was having a classic case of postpartum depression. In retrospect, all I was having was a very bad time and severe fatigue.

The baby and I would stagger into Dr. W's office for periodic weight checks. David was gaining remarkably for a breastfed baby. "Of course, you have enough milk," the doctor tried to reassure me. I couldn't believe there was nothing wrong with the baby; I thought Dr. W was missing something. Sitting in the waiting room of the office, I would stare at the other mothers and find it impossible to believe them when they said they were enjoying their newborns. They're lying, I know it, I thought. This is one big conspiracy and I'm failing at motherhood. It's been 6 weeks and he has already cried for half his life.

Larry and I took shifts at night holding the baby on our chests and rocking him. We probably walked 10 miles a night up and down our hallway. The second we would put him down, even if he had fallen asleep, he would shriek. He NEVER slept. When he did close his eyes, he dozed. What a nightmare. Dr. Weissbluth assured me almost daily that David would probably stop by about 12 weeks. I felt very irritable after my phone calls. We're doing everything he says to do and David is still crying! What if he never stops and never sleeps, I thought, always on the verge of panic.

It was now 10 weeks into the game. I was furious when Larry was even 15 minutes late coming home from the office. After calling David's doctor I would call my husband at the office at least every hour and was frantic if he was on another line or at a meeting. I was angry, constantly. Getting dinner together was a major accomplishment as we each took turns holding the baby. He no longer would permit us to put him in the Snuggli. We used our babysitter three days a week; I tried to take naps on those days, but found it difficult to nap since I was so agitated. The baby cried very little on those days, but Dorothy held him and rocked him nonstop from the moment she walked in until she was ready to leave. He would begin to scream again at 3:00 P.M. as she left. I knew that on the days Dorothy sat with him, David was really just resting up for another marathon session.

At Larry's suggestion, we braved going out to dinner with the baby and another couple. A noisy Mexican restaurant was my choice, although I really rather would have stayed home. I knew what would happen and I was right. I sat with the baby under my shirt where he sucked nonstop for two hours. It was a horrible dinner, and I was not only exhausted but furious with my husband for wanting to do it.

We began trying to give David supplementary bottles at night just in case his waking was from hunger. David held the bottle in his mouth and occasionally took 1 ounce. It made NO difference. We were both drained and finally agreed that if this didn't diminish by the end of the week, we would hire a nurse to come stay at night for one week so that we could get some relief.

By this point it was the eleventh week. Saturday night I got into bed for my usual one hour of sleep. I might also add that I was going through my second episode of mastitis. My life is falling apart, I thought, as I tossed and turned, listening to the baby screaming and wailing two minutes after I had nursed him. Larry walked back and forth in the downstairs hallway. Who could sleep with that? The baby stopped crying, and I finally convinced my husband to put him in the crib and come to bed. Larry had planned to stay up all night bringing David to me for feedings only so that perhaps I might get some rest. We were terrified it would start all over again. Finally at midnight, 20 minutes passed and all was quiet. Larry came to me. We both collapsed in exhaustion.

At 5:30 A.M., I awoke with a start. It was getting light outside and the house was quiet. Squinting at the clock and then at my wristwatch, I confirmed that it truly was 5:30. Why hadn't Larry brought the baby to me as we had agreed? I was upset and very uncomfortably full of milk. I rolled over and saw my husband still asleep.

Crib death, I thought.

I panicked—if Larry is next to me and the house is quiet,

the baby might be dead. I charged down the hallway toward his room. There he was, snoring slightly, eyes closed. That means he's asleep. Was it really possible? He hadn't even had any formula. At 8:00 he finally woke up after we had watched the clock.

Sunday was a repeat, so was Monday, Tuesday, and Wednesday. Thursday David slept even longer, and on Friday I called Dr. Weissbluth to tell him the news with my new anxiety. "What if this is temporary and he starts up again?" It never happened. David is now a "regular" baby. By his 12th week he was sleeping from 7:30 P.M. until 8:00 A.M., and sometimes even longer. He takes two real naps a day and rarely, if ever, cries, only if he's tired.

In retrospect, the only encouragement that did not increase my depression came from David's doctor and other mothers with colicky babies. David is such great fun and so good natured that everyone who meets him now cannot believe that he was ever not so great!

Months 3 to 4

Let's consider the ways in which your child has changed. The increased smiles, coos, giggles, laughs, and squeals light up your life. Your child is now a more social creature. She is sleeping better at night, but naps may still be brief and irregular.

Become sensitive to her need to sleep and try to distinguish her need to sleep from her wanting to play with you. She would naturally prefer the pleasure of your company than be left alone in a dark, quiet bedroom. Therefore, she will fight off sleep to keep you around.

In addition to your presence providing pleasurable stimulation, your baby's curiosity about all the new and exciting parts of her expanding world will disrupt her sleep. How interesting it must be for an infant to observe the clouds in the sky, the trees moving in the wind, the noise of barking dogs, or the rhythms of adult chatter.

Become sensitive to the difference in quality between brief, interrupted sleep and prolonged, consolidated naps. Your child is becoming less portable. As her biologic rhythms evolve for day sleep, your general goal is to *synchronize your caretaking activities with her biologic needs*. This is no different from being sensitive to her need to be fed or changed.

When your baby needs to sleep, try to have her in an environment where she will sleep well. As she continues to grow, you probably will notice that she sleeps poorly outside of her crib.

PRACTICAL POINT

The crying baby may be hungry or just fussy.
OR
The crying baby may be TIRED.

I have examined many children who cried with such intensity and persistence that their mothers were sure that they were sick. During their crying or fussing, they may swallow air and become very gassy. It is tempting to assume that their formula doesn't agree with them or that they have an intestinal disease—but only at night? These children were healthy, but tired. Not only did they cry hard and long when awake, they also cried loud and often during sleep-wake transitions.

Most of these children are tired from not napping well. They are not napping well because they're getting too much outside stimulation, too much handling, or too much irregular handling.

What is a good sleep strategy for your child at this age? As with the easy 6- to 8-week-old, plan to put your child somewhere semi-quiet or quiet to nap after she's been awake for about two hours.

Q: After I put my child to sleep after about two hours of wakefulness, how long should he sleep?

A: At this point, the naps may be short or long without any particular pattern. This variability occurs because that part of the brain which establishes regular naps has not yet fully developed. Watch for signs of tiredness to help you decide whether a particular nap was long enough.

The two-hour limit is an approximation. Often there is a magic moment of tiredness when the baby will go to sleep easily. She is tired then, but not overtired. After you go past two hours, expect fatigue to set in. When the baby is up too long she will tend to become overstimulated, overaroused, irritable, or peevish. Please don't blame changes in weather—it's never too hot or too cold to sleep well.

Many parents misunderstand what overstimulation means. A child becomes overstimulated when the duration of wakeful intervals is too long. Overstimulation does not mean that you are too intense in your playfulness.

Become Your Child's Timekeeper

Watch the clock during the day and expect your baby to need to sleep after about two hours of wakefulness. Use whatever soothing method or wind-down routine works best to comfort and calm your baby. This may include a scheduled feeding, nonnutritive "recreational" nursing, swings, rocking chairs, and pacifiers.

After awhile, you may notice a partial routine or a rough pattern of when your child's day sleep is best. It may then come to pass that based on (a) your child's behavior, (b) the time of day, and (c) the duration of wakefulness, you reasonably conclude that your child *needs* to sleep. However, she may *want* to play with you. Please try to distinguish between your child's needs and your child's wants. Have the confidence to be sensitive to her need to sleep and leave her alone a little to let her sleep. How long do you leave her alone? Maybe 5, 10, or 20 minutes.

No rules. No regulations. No rigid schedules.

Simply test her once in a while to see whether she goes to sleep after 5 to 20 minutes of protest crying. If this approach fails, pick her up, soothe her, comfort her, and either play with her or try again then or later on.

This lack of rigid scheduling is appropriate for children a few months old who are biologically immature but later, inconsistency will produce unhealthy sleep habits. Be flexible, but also become sensitive to your child's need to sleep.

You are giving her the opportunity to develop *self-soothing* skills. She is being allowed to learn how to fall asleep unassisted. Some children learn this faster than others, so don't worry if your child seems always to cry up to your designated time. Perhaps she was too young. Try again another time.

Always going to your child when your child needs to sleep, robs him of sleep. Never even letting your child cry might reflect a confusion in your mind between the healthy notion of allowing your child to be alone sometimes and your own fear that he will feel abandoned.

Here's an account from the mother of a 12-week-old infant.

It Goes Against Human Nature

To leave a baby crying and not pick it up goes against human nature. However, after three days of teaching Katie to sleep, and having to listen to her crying and being helpless— her hysteria was almost completely solved!

It started at just 12 weeks. Katie was so fatigued, she would cry for hours, screaming completely out of control, scratching her head, pulling her ears. Holding her didn't help, so it wasn't hard not to pick her up—she screamed anyway.

Instituting a new day schedule was easy. As soon as she started getting cranky, I rushed her to her crib to sleep. She would watch her mobile, and then sleep for hours at a time. The first week she was so tired, that she only stayed up 30 to 50 minutes at a time and slept three to four hours in between. The key for me was to get her down before she got *really* upset.

The afternoon was when she was awake the longest, and then it was hard getting her to sleep at night. The first few

nights under our new regime were the worst. Positive reinforcement from my doctor was important then. I had to hear
several times that this "cure" was the best thing to do.

The first night under our new strategy, my husband lay on
the floor in her room (I guess to make sure she didn't choke)
while I sat crying in our living room. Finally after 45 minutes
Katie was *quiet*! Hurray! Each night she cried less and less,
and I handled it better and better. After a week, hysteria was
gone! Sure she cried, a little, sometimes, but now she was on
a schedule. She napped two or three times a day, 2 to 4 hours
at a time, and slept 12 to 15 hours a night. Sleeping promotes
more sleep, and makes it easier to fall asleep. It's a Catch-22.

Writing down the sleep patterns helped, too. For one week,
I kept track of every time I put her down and every time I
picked her up from her nap. At the end of the week, I noticed
a distinct pattern. She fell into it herself!

CHAPTER 6

Months 4 to 12

Our goal is to establish healthy sleep habits, so we don't want to get sidetracked by overly worrying about crying. When your 2-year-old cries because he doesn't want his diaper changed or your 1-year-old cries because he wants juice instead of milk, you don't let the crying prevent you from doing what is best for him. Establishing healthy sleep habits does not mean that there will always be a lot of crying. But there may be some protest crying; if you find this to be unacceptable at age 4 months, please reconsider this chapter when your baby is 9 or 10 months old.

Months 4 to 8

As months 3 to 4 blend into months 4 to 8, behavior does not change sharply. But nonetheless, a distinct shift occurs at about age 4 months. Increased sociability permits more playfulness and gamelike interactions between you and your infant. Your child may roll over, sit well, imitate your voice with babbling, or respond quickly to your quiet sounds. This increased social interaction certainly makes having a baby more fun.

Infants really do enjoy your company; they thrive in response to your laughter and smiles. However, your baby is not like an empty vessel which you can fill with love, warmth, hugs, kisses, and soothing until it is full, thus leading to satisfaction, blissful contentment, or undemanding repose. The more you entertain her, the more she will want to be amused. So it is natural and reasonable to expect your baby to protest when you stop playing with her. In fact, the more you play with your child, the more she will come to expect that this is the natural order of things. Nothing is wrong with this, except that there are times when you have to dress your baby or leave her alone, and she will probably resist the partial restraint or curtailment of fun and games. Or you might have to dress yourself!

Leaving your baby alone protesting for more fun with you while you get dressed is not the same thing as abandonment.

Leaving your baby alone protesting for more fun when your baby needs to sleep is not neglect. You have become sensitive to your child's need to sleep, and he is now old enough to set his clock at a healthy sleep time. Our goal is to synchronize our caretaking activities with his needs: his need to be fed, to be kept warm, to be played with, and to sleep.

Let's look at Figure 8. As discussed previously, the four elements of healthy sleep are (1) the duration of night sleep, (2) the schedule of night sleep or the time when sleep begins, (3) consolidated versus fragmented sleep, and (4) naps.

This circle graph is a navigational aid for parents to help them understand sleep-wake rhythms. Although I designed this graph, I did not create this any more than a map maker creates the shape or location of an island. Please note that there are no clock hours during the day. Also, the shorter suggested nap durations and wakeful periods are for the younger infants, the longer periods are for the older infants.

How to Teach Your Baby to Sleep or to Protect His Sleep Schedule

You are now about to learn how to help your child learn to sleep well and to protect a naturally developed healthy sleep pattern.

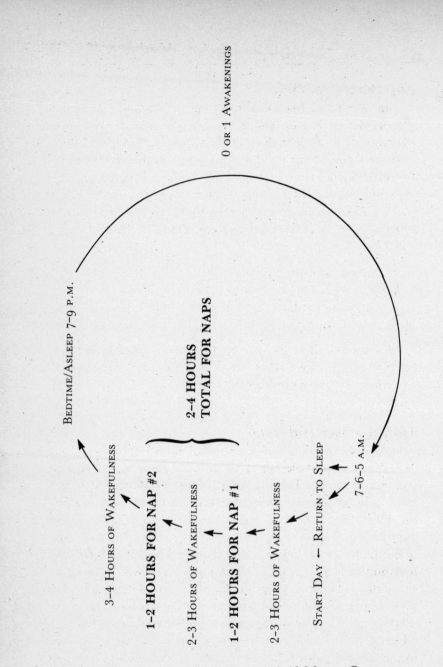

0 OR 1 AWAKENINGS

BEDTIME/ASLEEP 7–9 P.M.

2–4 HOURS
TOTAL FOR NAPS

3–4 HOURS OF WAKEFULNESS

1–2 HOURS FOR NAP #2

2–3 HOURS OF WAKEFULNESS

1–2 HOURS FOR NAP #1

2–3 HOURS OF WAKEFULNESS

START DAY — RETURN TO SLEEP

7–6–5 A.M.

FIGURE 8: HEALTHY SLEEP SCHEDULE FOR 4–12-MONTH-OLD INFANTS

The Wake-Up Time

Some babies tend to either wake up early at 5 to 6 A.M. and after a brief feeding or diaper change, return to sleep. This is a continuation of night sleep. This is not a nap. Other babies wake up later to start the day. The wake-up time seems to be an independent, neurological alarm clock in these young infants that is somewhat independent of that part of the brain which puts them to sleep or keeps them asleep. In fact, you *cannot* change the wake-up time by:

1. Keeping your baby up later.
2. Feeding solids before bedtime.
3. Awakening your baby for a feeding before you go to sleep.

Item number 3 seems insensitive, anyway. How would you feel if someone woke you from a deep sleep and started to feed you when you were not hungry?

Morning Wakeful Time

Focus now on the intervals of wakefulness. After about two hours for 4-month-olds or three hours for 8-month-olds, put your baby down in her crib for a midmorning nap. Actually, some easy babies or babies born early may be able to stay up for only 1 hour at 4 months of age. Plan a wind-down or naptime ritual of up to 30 minutes. You decide what you want to do: bath, bottle, breastfeed, lullaby, massage . . . but limit it. Hours of holding your baby only produce a light or twilight sleep state, which is poor quality sleep. At the end of your predetermined naptime ritual, whether your baby is asleep or awake, put her in her crib. As one mother commented to me, "I cannot tell you what a *liberating experience* it was to be able to put my baby down in her crib before she fell asleep in my arms."

The baby may now cry a little, a lot, or none at all.

The temperamentally easy child cries very little, and the routine is repeated for an early afternoon nap.

The temperamentally more difficult child, who may have also been a very fussy or colicky infant, might now cry a lot. The premie may cry a lot also, and the following approach might be delayed until four months after the expected date of delivery.

Midmorning Nap #1

We will consider a sleep period to be a restorative nap if it is about an hour or longer. Maybe 40 to 45 minutes is sometimes enough, but most babies in this age range sleep at least a solid hour. Certainly sleep periods under 30 minutes should not count as naps.

Once you have determined that your baby is going to take a nap, and you are enforcing a nap time, then leave your baby completely alone to allow your baby to (1) learn to fall asleep unassisted, and (2) return to sleep unassisted until he has slept about an hour in an uninterrupted fashion.

You are responding sensitively to his need to sleep by not providing too much attention. You are decisive in establishing a routine because you are upholding his right to sleep. Be calm and firm. You should be consistent because *consistency helps your baby learn rapidly*.

Your baby will pick up on your calm/firm attitude and will learn quickly not to expect the pleasure of your company at this naptime. You are not abandoning your child in her moment of need; you give her all the attention she needs when she is awake. But now, she needs to be alone to sleep.

Naturally, she may protest and cry.

Q: How long do I let my baby cry?

A: Until she sleeps uninterruptedly for about an hour.

Q: Even if she cries for one or two hours?

A: Yes, even three to four hours.

Q: Even if she cries through her usual midday meal?

A: Yes.

Q: What's wrong if I quickly check my baby when she first cries and I give her her pacifier or roll her back to her stomach? She always immediately stops crying and returns to sleep.

A: "Checking" for soothing at about 4 months of age may not interfere with naps or night sleep in some infants. But please be careful, because eventually all babies learn to turn these brief visits into prolonged playtimes. This learning process may develop slower if it is the fathers who do the checking and provide minimal intervention.

When the child has slept for about an hour and awakens, check the clock.

Midday Wakeful Time

Expect your baby to be ready for another nap after two to three hours of wakefulness. In general, avoid long excursions which might lead to mini-snoozes in the car or park.

Early-Afternoon Nap #2

This nap should usually begin before 3 P.M. Please remember, this is an outline of a reasonable, healthy sleep pattern, not a set of rigid rules to blindly enforce. There is nothing magic about 3 P.M. or any other time in this sleep schedule. You'll have to make some adjustments to fit your own individual lifestyle and family arrangements.

If the duration of crying and sleeping associated with the midmorning nap puts you way past 3 P.M. or if your child has prolonged crying starting before 3 P.M. at the onset of the early-afternoon nap and is continuing well past 3 P.M., then to get things going . . . forget this nap. And put your baby down for the night early at 5, 6, or 7 P.M. It's important to protect a reasonable bedtime hour.

If your baby naps well in the afternoon, again it should be about an hour or more, then go out afterwards and enjoy this longer period of wakefulness.

PRACTICAL POINT

Never wake a sleeping baby.

Afternoon Wakeful Time

This is the time to go on longer excursions, errands, or shopping trips. Many mothers will give their baby solid foods during this time. Exercise classes and outings to the park may be longer during this wakeful period.

Between 4 and 6 months of age, some children are taking a third brief nap in the late afternoon or early evening. This third nap is inconsistent and usually disappears by age 9 months.

Q: How long should my child nap?

A: You should ask yourself, does my child appear tired?

If your baby is tired late in the afternoon or early in the evening, this *might* indicate insufficient naps. A possible solution is simply to put your child to bed earlier at night. Keeping a baby up past his time of tiredness, produces fatigue, lost sleep, and sleep deprivation, and will ultimately lead to resisting falling asleep or night waking. This especially may be a problem when a working parent or parents come home late feeling guilty about being away from the family so long. A nonsolution after about 6 months of age is to encourage a third, brief nap around 5, 6, or 7 P.M. What happens here is that the baby gets his body recharged enough so that he is better able to fight off nighttime drowsiness, and the bedtime hour starts to migrate closer and closer to midnight. This leads to an abnormal sleep schedule, and the result is the equivalent of sleep deprivation. If the third nap does not interfere with an early bed-time hour, especially under about 6 months, there is no reason to eliminate it.

PRACTICAL POINT

One parent who keeps baby up past the child's natural time to sleep may be using this "play time" with the child to avoid unpleasant "private time" with the other parent.

Bedtime/Asleep

Remember, you are establishing an orderly home routine and enforcing a bedtime hour. You are not forcing your child to sleep. When your child seems tired and needs to sleep, you will establish his bedtime routine . . . whether he likes it or not. This may be the first time, but it is certainly not the last time you will ignore your child's protests. At some future time you will teach other health habits such as hand washing or tooth brushing. You will protect his physical safety by not allowing unreasonable risks involving playground equipment. You won't let his protest crying discourage you if you know he might fall from too high a jungle gym.

Now is the time to let him learn to fall asleep at night by himself, to return to sleep at night by himself, and to learn that being alone at night in slumber is not scary, dangerous, or something to avoid. Keep everything calm and not too complicated as you go through a bedtime ritual. Fathers should be involved because babies now know that they cannot be nursed by them, and any protest crying is likely to be less intense or shorter.

Once down, down is down, no matter how long she cries. Please do not return, until your baby falls asleep. Little peeks or replacing pacifiers may be harmless at age 4 months, but they will eventually sabotage your efforts because partial reinforcement has enormous teaching power.

1. When the duration of protest crying is open-ended, not limited, learning to fall asleep unassisted takes place.
2. When you put a time limit on how much protest crying you can tolerate or accept, before going to the baby, you teach the baby to cry to that time limit.

Overnight

In this age range, many babies accept naps without protest and fall asleep at night without difficulty. These easy babies still might awaken once in the middle of the night. I consider this behavior normal, natural, and not changeworthy—if it's brief and not prolonged playtime.

Choose the one time when you'll go to feed your baby and change diapers, and don't go at any other time. Please review the earlier discussion on arousals (Chapter 2) if you are puzzled why babies sometimes get up frequently throughout the night.

Most mothers will partially synchronize feedings to sleep patterns so that the child is fed around the time he gets up in the morning, around the time (before or after) the two naps, around bedtime, and one other time. In other words, bottles or breastfeedings now occur four to five times per 24 hours. Frequent sips, snacks, or little feedings throughout the day are not necessary. Gradually your child will begin to learn to associate certain behaviors on your part with certain times of the day, his crib, and his sensation of tiredness with the process of falling asleep. This learning process, when started at about 3 to 4 months of age, usually takes only about three days.

Stranger wariness or stranger anxiety may be present in some babies by about 6 months of age, and with this new behavior, some mothers even note some separation anxiety. The child shows distress when mother leaves her. I do not think this type of separation anxiety in the child directly causes more difficulty for the baby to fall asleep unassisted. I have observed that these babies learn to sleep well as rapidly as any other babies when their mothers leave them alone at sleep times. The problem is that some mothers also suffer from the thought of separation and will not leave their children alone enough at sleep times to allow healthy sleep habits to develop. This will be discussed further in Chapter 12.

When I speak of routines or schedules, please remember

that the exact number or duration of naps and the exact hour of the naptimes and bedtimes is less important than your child's behavior. A major problem in implementing this sleep schedule is that it is *inconvenient*. Many mothers resent the fact that their babies are now less portable. It is inconvenient to change your lifestyle to be at home twice a day so that your baby can nap. When parents initially suffer through but accept this inconvenience and build up a large sleep reserve by keeping their child well rested, irregularities and special occasions that disrupt sleep usually produce minor and transient disturbed sleep. The recovery time is brief and the child responds to a prompt reestablishment of the routine.

Bluntly put, when parents are unwilling to alter their lifestyle so that regular naps are never well maintained, then the child always pays a price. The child's mood and learning suffer, and recovery times following outings or illnesses take much longer. These parents often try many "helpful hints" to help their child sleep better. I'm not sure any or all of these hints can ever substitute for maintaining regular sleep schedules. Parents in my practice who have utilized regular sleep schedules have rarely, if ever, found these hints to be useful.

BUREAU OF "HELPFUL" HINTS OF DUBIOUS VALUE TO SOOTHE BABY TO SLEEP

Lamb's wool skins
Heartbeat sounds
Womb sounds
Continuous background noises
Elevating head of crib
Maintaining motion sleep in swings
Changing formulas or eliminating iron supplement
Changing diet of nursing mother
Feeding solids only at bedtime

PRACTICAL POINT

You are harming your child when you allow unhealthy sleep patterns to evolve or persist—sleep deprivation is as unhealthy as feeding an iron-deficient diet.

Babies seem to respond quickly at this age to a somewhat scheduled, structured approach to sleep. If you can learn to detach yourself from your baby's protests and not respond reflexively by rushing in to her at her slightest whimper, she will learn to fall asleep by herself. As one mother said, she now goes down like warm butter on toast!

Months 9 to 12

Strong-willed, willful, independent-minded, stubborn, headstrong, uncooperative. Sound familiar? These are the words parents often use to describe their toddlers. You may observe that your child is simply less cooperative. A psychologist might use the term "noncompliant" to describe this lack of cooperation, but the psychologist would also point out that these behaviors go hand in hand with the normal, healthy evolution of the child's autonomy or sense of independence. Usually, the experts tell us, the times when you should expect the most difficulties or so-called "oppositional behaviors" are at dressing, mealtimes, in public places, and at bedtimes. Since this is the beginning of the "stage" of autonomy (noncompliance), some experts claim that it is natural for this independence/stubbornness to cause resistance in going to sleep or to cause the appearance of night wakings. I will explain later why I think this "stage" theory is an incorrect interpretation.

Children in this age range also often develop behaviors described as social hesitation, shyness, or fear of strangers. A child also might cry or appear in distress when his mother leaves him alone in one room as she goes to another room or when she leaves the child with a babysitter. Psychologists call this behavior "stranger wariness" or "stranger anxiety" or "separation anxiety." So if a child developed increased re-sistance in going to sleep at night at this "stage," some experts might say that the "separation anxiety" or fear of being apart or away from mother was the cause. I also think that this is an incorrect interpretation.

Nap Deprivation

When parents have invested their effort to build up a reservoir of good quality sleep, occasional disruptions due to illnesses, trips, parties, or holiday visits cause only minor disruptions of sleep. These kids require only brief recovery periods before getting back on track. But when parents allow poor quality sleep patterns to emerge and persist, then there is a gradual accumulation of significant sleep deficits. Now even minor disturbances create long-lasting havoc.

Nap deprivation seems to be the major culprit, in this age range, in ruining healthy sleep patterns. Look, it's only natural that you want to get out more and do more things with your child. And, oh, what a kid he is! Full of new social charms, so cheerful, and walking now . . . why not hang out together and enjoy the good weather at the park or beach? It's your first summer together. Who wants to stay indoors anyway on such a gorgeous day?

But as naps slip and slide, a trend of increasing fatigue develops. First, the child develops a little more crabbiness, irritability, fussiness, maybe only in the late afternoon or early evening. You might think it's normal for children this age to be easily frustrated or sometimes bored. Then she starts to get up at night for the first time ever, "for no reason." Later, maybe following a cold or daylong visit with grandparents, she starts fighting going to sleep at night and you wonder why night sleep is a new problem in your house.

When you reestablish healthy, regular nap routines, the night sleep problem corrects itself. I have seen this over and over again. Although noncompliant behaviors still exist and although separation anxiety is unchanged, the night sleep problem corrects itself when nap routines are restored. That's why I think nap deprivation (which causes fatigue, which causes increased alertness/wakefulness/arousal) is the culprit behind disturbed night sleep, not a particular "stage."

PRACTICAL POINT

Boredom may be masked tiredness. If your child's motor is idling and she's not going anywhere, maybe she's tired.

Normal Naps

You may think that your baby now only needs one nap, but most babies really do need two naps in this age range. One clue that some mothers have noticed is that their babysitter can "get two good naps," but "I can get only one or none." The child is obviously more rested after the sitter leaves and the mother wonders how the sitter "does it." Well, children are very discriminating at this age. They know that the sitter, following parents' instructions, has a no-nonsense approach and will put them to sleep on a fairly regular schedule. But, with Mom, maybe if I protest long or loud enough, she'll come and we'll go out to play. After all, sometimes it works.

As long as your child retains the expectation that you will come to her and take her out of her boring, quiet room, she will fight naps.

Comforting Habits

Routines that comfort your baby include rocking, soft lullabies, stroking, patting, or cuddling. Maintain these routines so that your child learns to associate certain behaviors occurring at certain times in a familiar place with the behavior called "falling asleep."

HELPFUL HINTS FOR COMFORTING
Soft, silky, furry textured blankets, dolls, or stuffed animals in crib
A small soft blanket over forehead

Dim night light
Nursing to sleep

Nurse to Sleep?

There is nothing wrong with nursing your baby to sleep, when there is no sleep problem. Most nursing mothers in my practice do this all the time. If you have difficulty in letting your child ever learn to fall asleep unassisted so that your child always falls asleep at the breast, and your child has disturbed sleep, then nursing to sleep might be a part of the sleep problem. It may reflect the kinds of separation problems discussed in Chapter 12.

But most mothers nurse their babies for soothing and comfort, and their babies either fall asleep at the breast or they don't. In either case they are put in their cribs when they *need* to sleep, and sleep comes. I think that this intimacy between mother and infant is beautiful, and in itself, nursing to sleep does not cause sleep problems.

Q: Do I roll my child over to his favorite sleeping position when he wakes up during the night? Do I help him get down when he stands up and shakes the crib railings?

A: No. I doubt that you like playing these games with your child at night. Think, too, about what you teach him when you go to him at night to roll him over or help him down.

Q: Won't he hurt himself if he falls down in his crib? He can't get down by himself.

A: No.

Try to be reasonably regular by watching the intervals of wakefulness, not necessarily by watching clock time. For example, try not to get locked into a fixed or traditional bedtime hour but vary the bedtime hour depending on duration of naps, when the second nap ended and indoor versus outdoor activities. Often the 9- to 12-month-old needs to go to bed earlier because of increased physical activity in the afternoon.

When you are somewhat organized, planned, or programmed regarding sleep schedules, sleep is accepted and expected. But don't feel you have to be this way for feeding or other infant care practices! When mothers are creative, free-spirited, and permissive regarding solid—but wholesome—foods, feeding goes well. So try to cultivate opposite attitudes: restrictive for sleep, permissive for feeding solids.

Solving Sleep Problems: Months 4 to 12

It cannot be emphasized enough: The major sleep problems from 4 to 12 months develop and persist because of the inability of parents to remove themselves as reinforcers of bad sleep habits. Some parents don't see themselves as interfering with an important learning process in their child; namely, learning how to soothe themselves to sleep unassisted. The failure of our children to develop their own resources to fall asleep, and stay asleep, by themselves is the direct result of some parents' failure to give their child the opportunity to learn self-soothing skills. In other words, some parents can't leave their kids alone long enough for them to fall asleep by themselves. Don't underestimate children's competence and ability to learn at these early months!

Locus of Control

When your baby was younger, she slept when she needed to. She controlled your relationship with her, in the sense that you met her needs whether you wanted to or not. You didn't let her go hungry simply because you didn't want to feed her. You didn't let her stay wet because you didn't want to change her. Her needs controlled your behavior.

But from now on, a shift should occur so that *you* are in charge. For example, when your child is older, you may decide not to provide food simply because she wants it. You will not risk her physical safety by letting her climb too high on a tree simply because she wants to. And you will not let her stay up to play when she needs to sleep. What then are we to do when our child does not cooperate, and cries because she does not *want* to go to sleep when she *needs* to sleep?

"Let Cry": A Division of Popular Opinions

There is disagreement among those who write for popular magazines such as *American Baby, Working Mother, Parents,* or *McCall's* about what happens when children who are left alone at night to sleep cry:

Letting a baby 'cry it out' will not teach him the basic trust or confidence he needs to feel secure in his new world.

> *McCall's*
> September 1984

It may give him the feeling that there's nobody out there who cares. The child may become a passive, ineffective person or he may become angry or hostile . . .

> *Parents*
> November 1983

. . . there is no such thing as too little sleep for your baby . . . he will get as much sleep as his body requires.

> *American Baby*
> September 1984

Other articles in these and similar publications say:

. . . the key to solving a crying problem is teaching children to fall asleep on their own.

> *The New York Times*
> July 21, 1986

Get an early start . . . be calm and loving, but down is down.

> *Parents*
> August 1984

As the editor-in-chief of *Parents* wrote, after her third child, in the October 1985 issue:

The trick was that after eight years of parenthood, my husband and I have discovered . . . [that] the first sound does not mean that a baby needs to be picked up immediately.

Please don't wait eight years to learn what experts have long ago discovered!

"Let Cry": An Agreement of Expert Opinions

While the popular press may give all types of conflicting advice from a variety of sources, expert opinion is solidly together. In fact, all evidence accumulated by a wide array of child health specialists concludes that "protest" crying at bedtime will not cause permanent emotional or psychological problems. In plain fact, the contrary is true. For example, Dr. D. W. Winnicott, a British pediatrician and child psychiatrist, emphasizes that the *capacity to be alone* is one of the most important signs of maturity in emotional development. In his view, parents can facilitate the development of the child's ability to soothe herself when left alone. Please don't confuse this with abandonment or, on the other hand, use this notion as an excuse for negligence.

Margaret S. Mahler, a prominent child psychoanalyst, has identified the beginning of the separation–individuation process whereby the infant begins to differentiate from the mother at 4 to 5 months of age. This is the age when children naturally begin to develop some independence.

Drs. Alexander Thomas and Stella Chess, two American child psychiatrists, followed over 100 infants through young adulthood. One item they examined was regularity or irregularity of sleep and how parents responded. They wrote:

Removal of symptoms by a successful parent guidance procedure has had positive consequences for the child's functioning and has not resulted in the appearance of overt anxiety or new substitute symptoms. . . . The basic emphasis (of the) treatment technique is a change in the parents' behavior. . . .

Please don't fear that when your child cries in protest at night, because he is being allowed to "practice" falling asleep, this crying will later cause emotional or psychological problems. By itself, it will not.

Let me be very clear about this. I am talking only about children over the age of 4 months and only during normal day and night sleep times. During these periods, emotional problems do *not* develop if parents ignore protest crying. How can I be so sure?

Drs. Thomas and Chess were sensitive to irregular sleep patterns in the infants in their study. Many of those infants also had frequent and prolonged bouts of loud crying. When I asked Dr. Thomas what advice he had given to the parents of those crying babies who did not sleep at night, he responded, "Close the door and walk away." Did this create or produce any problems? He said, "No. None at all."

Always going to your crying child at night interferes with this natural learning and growth. Always going to your child produces sleep fragmentation, destroys sleep continuity, and creates insomnia in your child.

Mothers who, in general, do not feel loving or empathetic toward their child, who are insensitive or emotionally unavailable to their children, who have a lack of warmth or affection toward their child, later come to the attention of professionals. Consequently, some psychologists or psychiatrists take the attitude that parents should be encouraged *never* to let their child cry for fear of encouraging a cold parent–child relationship. As a general practice pediatrician, however, I don't share this view, because I see all kinds of parents seeking pediatric care, not just those with problems. The vast majority of parents are loving and sensitive to their child's needs. These parents should not fear letting their child cry at night to learn to sleep.

Q: How long do I let my baby cry?

A: To establish regular naps, healthy sleep schedules, and consolidated sleep overnight, there is no time limit.

If we place an arbitrary limit on the duration of crying, we train our child to cry to that predetermined time. When it is open-ended, the child learns to stop protesting and to fall asleep.

Q: Why is it good for my child to cry for hours; why not wait until he is older and more reasonable?

A: Crying is not the real issue; we are leaving the child alone to learn to sleep. We are leaving him alone to forget the expectation to be picked up. We allow him to cry, but we are not making him cry in the sense that we are hurting him. When he is older and still not sleeping, it will be harder for him to learn how to sleep well. The sleep which is lost while he is growing up is physically unhealthy, just as is too little iron or too few vitamins in his diet.

Q: But I still think the crying has to be harmful.

A: Not necessarily. In fact recent studies have proven that *crying produces accelerated forgetting of a learned response.* So when a child cries, he may more quickly unlearn to expect to be picked up. Therefore, when trying to stop an unhealthy habit, crying may have some benefit, because crying acts as an amnesic agent.

Let's look at several of the most common unhealthy sleep habits at this age, and the proven effective strategy to deal with each one.

Abnormal Sleep Schedule

When the bedtime hour and sleep periods are not in synchrony with other biological rhythms, we don't get the full restorative benefit of sleep. Please refer to Figures 5 and 6 (see pages 27–28) for age-appropriate times when children fall asleep or awaken.

At any age, abnormal sleep schedules often lead to night wakings and night terrors in older children. The schedule often gets shifted to a too-late bedtime hour because (a) Mom or Dad, returning late from work, wants to play with the baby, or (b) parents deliberately keep their baby up late to encourage a later awakening in the morning.

The strategy for bringing sleep schedules back to normal is based on developing an age-appropriate wake-up at 6 or 7 A.M.; a midmorning nap; an early afternoon nap starting before 3 P.M.; and a bedtime at 7 to 9 P.M.

PRACTICAL POINT

You are enforcing an age-appropriate nap*time* and bed*time* schedule. Your child may not cooperate initially by falling asleep immediately. Don't give up.

When your child does not promptly go to sleep at his nap times, you should leave him alone until you think that he has had about an hour of uninterrupted sleep. When you start implementing this schedule, the afternoon nap may be skipped for the first few days if the duration of morning crying and morning sleeping puts you into the mid- or late afternoon. At bedtime, put him down after his bedtime ritual, and don't attend to him until about 5, 6, or 7 A.M.

No matter how long or how loud he cries.

Studies have shown that when sleep disturbances are associated with abnormal sleep schedules, the control of the wake-up time may be sufficient to establish a healthy 24-hour sleep rhythm. In other words, you set the clock in the morning!

Here's an account of one mother who left my office determined to set the clock that night and not wait until the morning!

Wakes Up Smiling

Our son did not like to sleep. In fact, if it can be said that babies are born with an aversion to any particular thing, for Ryan, sleep was it.

From the day we brought Ryan home from the hospital, he had shown himself to be a night owl. Through *Letterman* and 2 A.M. reruns of *Mary Tyler Moore*, we would pace and nurse until sleep would overcome us sometime around *Morning Sunrise Semester*. By the time he was 4½ months old, he was down to one nap a day. He didn't sleep through the night (and in my book, that's eight hours straight or better) until he was 10 months old, and that lasted for only one night.

Not knowing any better since Ryan was our first child, I thought that this kind of behavior was perfectly normal for a majority of babies. When other moms would talk about their children sleeping through the night at 3 months of age and napping twice a day for two hours or better at a crack, I figured that it was either so much idle boasting or their children had some sort of neurological disorder. But when our pediatrician told me at Ryan's 8-month checkup that it was not normal for a child his age to go to bed at 1 A.M. and sleep until 10 A.M., I started to realize that we had a problem. The thought of my husband and I looking like *Dawn of the Dead* rejects from years without sleep was not a pretty one.

We put Ryan to bed at 9:00 that evening and, as expected, he started to cry. We shut his door and went into the den, closing two more doors between the baby's room and the den in an attempt to muffle what were now becoming very loud screams. After a half hour had passed, the crying was more muffled but continued, so I headed for Ryan's room to "reassure him." "Don't go in there now," Tom suggested. "He'll just get worked up again if he sees you. Do something else for awhile." I could see the logic and agreed to hold off. A half hour later, I cracked the door open and again heard the crying. But now I could hear something else mixed in. Ryan was talking to himself. In a very hurt tone he was babbling and complaining between the sobs. My heart was breaking. "My God," I said to Tom. "Now he's going to grow up hating us. I have to go to him." For the second time that night, Tom talked me into leaving the baby alone.

The next 15 minutes seemed like 15 hours, but the next time I opened the door, there it was . . . SILENCE. I could finally look in on Ryan without undoing all that we had just accomplished. So as not to awaken him with its squeaking, I opened the door with great caution, tiptoed into the room and clicked the light on at its dimmest setting. In this low light and from across the room, I saw what appeared to be Ryan's blanket hanging over the side of his crib. As I moved closer to remove it, however, I discovered that it wasn't the quilt draped over the side—it was Ryan. Our son had fallen asleep standing up!

The next night we again put him in bed at 9:00 and again he fell asleep standing up. But this time he only cried for one hour. The third night, he cried for 25 minutes and fell asleep lying down.

These days, with few exceptions, he cries for only a few minutes before falling asleep. He also usually wakes up smiling, thus dispelling any fears I once might have had that he would grow up to hate us for letting him "cry it out."

Nap Deprivation

This is a common occurrence between 9 and 12 months of age. Children at this age are fearless, full of grace and self-confidence, very explorative. Doing things with parents and siblings is simply a lot of fun. Unsure of when a child naturally needs only one nap, some parents try to get by with one nap before their child is ready. Afternoons full of activities help smooth over rocky moments of heightened emotionality or grumpiness. Anyway, Mom or Dad returns from work about then, so there is a loving play period early in the evening.

The fatigue from nap deprivation leads to increased levels of arousal/alertness, and this causes difficulties in falling asleep, or staying asleep, or both.

I took care of two children, 5 and 6 months of age, who had nap deprivation causing severe bobbing, turning, and jerking of the head and wincing or grimacing of the face. Both children were hospitalized and evaluated for seizures or epilepsy.

All the studies were normal and both children recovered completely when they were better rested. Subsequently, the movements transiently returned to each child during a temporary period of overtiredness.

Here is one parent's account of how shortening the interval of wakefulness helped her child sleep better.

I Was Certain That She Would Grow Out of This Bad Habit . . . Our Other Two Did

On November 19, 1984, our third daughter, Rebecca, was born. Our other girls, Lauren, 9 years old, and Karen, 4 years old, were set and busy in school activities, Hebrew lessons, and ballet. At that time I prided myself in how well I "schlepped" our new baby everywhere and how wonderfully she slept in and out of the car seat all day.

Our days were filled with errands and car pools, Rebecca nursing and napping on and off all day. What a cooperative baby . . . I used to think. Our nights were spent with her nursing on one side of me or the other. I was so exhausted by evening that I found my way to survive was to sleep with the baby, waking up every hour or so to "change her side." I knew then that having her in bed with me wasn't such a terrific idea, but it was the only way for me to get any rest.

We fell into this pattern and finally by the time Rebecca turned 5 months, I placed her in her crib and once and for all went to sleep without her at my breast.

As I expected, every few hours she began to cry, expecting me to be at her side. I quickly would run in her room, rock and nurse her back to sleep . . . until the next time she woke up.

And so our next pattern would begin! She would wake up every few hours and I would faithfully run in and get her back to sleep. I was certain that she would grow out of this bad habit . . . our other two did.

A few months passed. By now, Rebecca was weaned to a bottle and I was sure things would change for the better. That didn't happen. In fact, things got worse. There were many nights when Rebecca would get up every hour on the hour. I tried letting her cry—fifteen minutes at a time—but it was so much easier to just go in and give her a bottle.

When Rebecca was a year old, this pattern of frequent waking continued. It was so difficult leaving her with a babysitter. I knew that within an hour or so after our leaving she would be up crying for me. I actually felt sick leaving her.

When Rebecca was almost 13 months old we went to see Dr. Weissbluth. I had made the appointment when she was about 9 months old and never thought that by the time our appointment came we'd still have a problem. I was so sure that Rebecca's bad sleeping patterns would "just change." But they didn't. So we went.

Rebecca was charming for Dr. Weissbluth. Could this child really be causing all this trouble?

Our appointment went well. After our story was poured out, Dr. Weissbluth explained what our steps would be to change Rebecca's sleeping patterns. He cited studies, gave us graphs . . . this really was going to work! When we left his office I felt prepared for battle—armed with all the mental ammunition I needed to change Rebecca's nightly wakings. We started "the program" the next day.

Day #1

9:05 A.M. — Morning nap begins . . . I thought. Rebecca cried for two hours! Whose idea was this anyway? If only I could go in and rock her . . . she's got to sleep . . . but no . . . I've made this commitment.

11:00 A.M. — Two hours is enough crying—let's get her out.

1:00 P.M. — Down for afternoon nap—hold your breath. Cried for 20 minutes.

1:25 P.M. — Asleep. Slept 1 hour 10 minutes.

7:30 P.M. — Down for the night—I told her to "please go to sleep and stay asleep because I wasn't going to come in at all tonight. It's time for bed . . . I love you . . . goodnight. . ." I was glad that I could rock her to sleep. I had thought that maybe I would have to "just throw her in bed.'' Dr. Weissbluth really encouraged ''a lot of loving for the child'' before bedtime.

2:45 A.M. — Crying . . . screaming . . . more crying. I stayed in bed. Pacing wouldn't help. I'm glad that my husband was so supportive. It would have been horrible had he not reinforced me during this.

4:50 A.M. — Finally . . . asleep . . . all of us.

Day #2

7:15 A.M. — Up . . . and all smiles! I couldn't believe that after all that crying last night she could be so happy. As Dr. Weissbluth suggested, I praised her for sleeping ''like a big girl'' . . . I pulled open the shade as I explained to her that it was morning and time to get up.

9:30 A.M. — Starting to show signs of being tired. Rubbing her eyes, holding her blanket. Down for a nap . . . awake but not crying—yet . . . asleep . . .

11:00 A.M. — Awake and happy. Maybe this is going to work?

1:45 P.M. — Down for nap. Playing in bed quietly . . .

2:20 P.M. — Crying—no sleep yet.

3:00 P.M. — Still crying. This is like torture. Why did I start this whole thing? My poor baby. Maybe I should just forget this and hope that she'll grow out of it. I'm a nervous wreck from listening to all this crying.

3:30 P.M. — I've got to get her out of bed . . . she's still crying. As I walked in her room her crying became worse! Her face was red, swollen, and wet with tears. Every stuffed animal had been thrown out of bed and her sheets had even been pulled off her mattress. Oh . . . this was terrible . . . I can't go on doing this to her . . . I'll call Dr. Weissbluth—before I give up.

4:45 P.M. — I'm glad that I called Dr. Weissbluth before I threw in the towel. He gave exact directions as to how to deal with Rebecca's not sleeping this afternoon. The reinforcement that he gave me was a much needed boost to get through this. Because Rebecca hadn't napped this afternoon I was to give her an early dinner, bathe her, and rock and love her as usual and have her in bed by 6 P.M. (At first I thought Dr. Weissbluth was nuts—6 P.M.? She'll be up at 9 P.M.! But I'll trust him and try it.)

6:00 P.M. — Mission accomplished. Rebecca seemed very tired. In bed—NO CRYING.

7:15 P.M. — Wimperlike crying—for *two* minutes—stopped.

9:50 P.M. — A few cries.

Day #3

6:30 A.M. — Ma Ma Ma! Up with smiles . . . Hurrah! Last night was the first time in over a year that I slept longer than three hours!

8:30 A.M. — Dr. Weissbluth called for a report. Glad to give him the great news.

9:30 A.M. — Seems tired . . . down for nap. Singing . . .

9:50 A.M. — Sound asleep.

11:10 A.M. — Awake—happy.

2:10 P.M. — Naptime.

2:45 P.M. — Crying.

3:30 P.M. — Still crying.

3:45 P.M. — Still crying—took out of bed. She again looked like she had been in battle. Red, swollen face . . . drenched with tears.

6:10 P.M. — Well—it worked yesterday . . . let's try it again today. To bed—no crying—asleep.

9:20 P.M. — A few cries . . . but just for a few seconds each time. Coughing spells don't elicit crying either!

Day #4

7:20 A.M. — Still sleeping! Can't believe it.

7:30 A.M. — Awake—happy. Rebecca slept for 13 hours 15 minutes last night!

9:40 A.M. — Seems really tired—somewhat cranky. I'm trying to learn how to recognize the clues that

Rebecca gives me when she is tired. I need to get her to bed *before* she gets overtired.

9:45 A.M. — Rocked her—gave her a bottle—put to bed—singing.

9:50 A.M. — Asleep.

11:00 A.M. — Awake—all smiles.

2:15 P.M. — Appears tired—rocked with bottle—put to bed.

2:40 P.M. — Not asleep yet—quietly singing.

3:00 P.M. — Not asleep.

3:15 P.M. — Crying . . . crying . . . crying . . .

3:45 P.M. — Still crying. Took her out of bed—she's really upset. I'll get her to bed early tonight and tomorrow give Dr. Weissbluth a call. I don't feel comfortable with all the crying every afternoon.

6:15 P.M. — Rocked—bottle, kisses, and asleep!

7:40 P.M. — Up crying weakly.

7:43 P.M. — Asleep now—yeh!

8:45 P.M. — Crying . . .

8:49 P.M. — Stopped . . . phew!

11:10 P.M. — Crying—on and off for 10 minutes.

Day #5

7:00 A.M. — Up—smiles and hugs.

9:15 A.M. — Seems very tired—gave her bottle, blanket, rocking, and kisses.

9:20 A.M. — Quiet—humming.

9:25 A.M. — Asleep.

10:30 A.M. — Up happy! I talked with Dr. Weissbluth this morning. After I told him about our afternoons, he came up with a plan. I have to shorten the interval between Rebecca's morning nap waking time and her afternoon nap to two hours. Perhaps I have been allowing Rebecca to become overtired. Let's try it! If she still does not sleep and is up after about 3:30, get her out of bed and follow the "early to bed" routine (6 P.M.). We don't want her

exhausting herself and falling asleep at 4 P.M.
. . . she'd mess up our perfect night sleeping!
How did I ever do this with my older girls?
Every child sure presents different problems.

12:40 P.M. — Oops! Ten minutes late. Bedtime routine—
seems tired.

1:15 P.M. — Still awake—humming.

1:30 P.M. — Asleep! VICTORY!

2:00 P.M. — STILL ASLEEP—I can't believe that Dr.
Weissbluth was right again!

3:00 P.M. — Up—happy. WOW!

7:15 P.M. — Night routine—quiet—asleep! This is heaven!

7:30 P.M. — This is so strange . . . putting Rebecca to bed
for the night knowing that I won't see her until
the morning. I smile to myself just thinking
how far we've come in just a few days. I'm
really sorry that I didn't *do* something about
Rebecca's sleep problem months ago. I always
thought that it would get better by itself or that
Rebecca would grow out of it. I made so many
excuses for her, trying to make it easier for me
to deal with her night wakings. Now she's a
little person that sleeps as much as she needs.
What a difference. Right now, adhering to this
very strict schedule is a little difficult. All my
errands, car pools, and appointments must wait
. . . I've got a baby who is learning how to
sleep like one.

9:40 P.M. — She's coughing a little, a little crying too. I
hope that she'll get herself back to sleep. My
first instincts are still to run up there and give
her a bottle. I still have to hold myself back. I
guess that after a year of that behavior it is
hard for me to change, too.

9:41 P.M. — Back to sleep!

Day #6

7:15 A.M. — Rebecca is singing in bed. What a great way
to start the day.

9:20 A.M. — Seems tired—naptime. My fingers are crossed.

11:00 A.M. — Up—playing in bed.

1:10 P.M. — Nap—same routine. Not sleeping yet . . . Talking.

2:15 P.M. — Asleep.

3:00 P.M. — Up.

7:05 P.M. — Nighttime routine—no crying.

Day #7

7:15 A.M. — Up and happy.

9:15 A.M. — Came over to me, placed her head on my lap, and started humming! Naptime!

10:00 A.M. — Fell asleep.

11:15 A.M. — Up talking.

1:15 P.M. — Tired—nap routine.

1:30 P.M. — Asleep.

3:30 P.M. — Up—happy, playing in bed.

7:20 P.M. — Routine . . . in bed.

8:10 P.M. — Humming.

8:15 P.M. — Asleep.

11:00 P.M. — A few cries—a few coughs.

11:01 P.M. — Asleep.

Day #8

7:15 A.M. — Up—cheerful!

9:15 A.M. — Seems tired—nap routine—sang at first—then crying for about 45 minutes.

10:50 A.M. — Finally fell asleep. I peeked in and could smell that she had made a B.M.—maybe she had wanted me to change her.

11:30 A.M. — Woke up happy and *very smelly!*

1:30 P.M. — Naptime—same routine—humming, happy with herself . . . able to put herself to sleep.

In a week's time, the change in Rebecca has been phenomenal! She was always a happy baby, but now she's more relaxed, more affectionate, and more fun to be with.

The change in her sleeping pattern has had an effect on everyone in the family. I don't yell and lose my patience with my older children quite as much for I am better rested. Ironically, for the first few nights of our "training program" I continued to get up every two hours . . . waiting for her to cry. I now also have learned how to sleep through the night once again, and I physically and emotionally feel *so* much better.

The tone in our household is happier—we're all so better rested. What a difference our team work has made in our daily routine.

Throughout some of Rebecca's crying periods, especially in the beginning, there were moments when I was sorry that we started this whole thing. I wanted just to soothe my "poor, crying baby"! Both my husband and I kept reminding ourselves that we were trying to teach Rebecca how to sleep and that this crying was purposeful—and that we *had* to stay with it without sabotaging the plan. (Maybe knowing that we would be checking in with Dr. Weissbluth every few days helped us to stick with it.)

This has been one of the most rewarding and positive experiences that we have shared as parents. We are so proud of Rebecca and also pat ourselves on the backs for a job well done.

Shhh!!! Rebecca's sleeping!

The treatment strategy involves (a) shortening the interval of wakefulness before the first nap and reestablishing the early afternoon nap by focusing on the midday interval and making sure this wakeful period is not too long, (b) making sure the afternoon nap does not start too late in the afternoon in order to protect a reasonable evening bedtime, and (c) consistency in the naptime ritual.

PRACTICAL POINT

As long as your child retains the expectation that she can get around you and play during naptime, she won't nap well. If she thinks she can outlast you, she won't give up her protesting.

If the afternoon nap is needed but your child fights sleep the most then, consider shortening the midday interval of wakefulness. Start the afternoon nap earlier. Perhaps you were allowing him to stay up too long and he became overtired and overaroused.

It's not uncommon for a child to sleep well at night but not nap well, especially in the afternoon. At night, it is dark, everyone is more tired, parents want to be regular with bedtimes because they, themselves, want to go to sleep. During the day, it is light, everyone is more alert, and parents are more irregular because they want to run errands or enjoy recreational activities.

So during a retraining period, it's easiest to establish good night sleep and easier to establish regular morning naps than afternoon naps. Don't expect improvement to occur equally at all times.

An additional element regarding nap quality is whether the mother likes to nap or not. Naps are valuable for our children, and the most important factor in maintaining or reestablishing naps is being regular. This does not mean being regular in the afternoon according to clock time, but regular in terms of maintaining fairly regular intervals of midday wakefulness which might vary somewhat based on the length of the morning nap. Otherwise, as one mother said, "Sometimes my baby gets overtired and can't get off to sleep."

Some families have found it difficult to establish naps because they had only one bedroom which was too light or full of noise during the day. One family I know was fortunate enough to have a large walk-in closet, which was used only for naps.

Brief Sleep Durations

If your child is on an apparently normal sleep schedule and napping well, you might presume she is getting enough sleep. Overall, she doesn't look tired. But around 10, 11, or 12 months she starts new night waking. What is happening? Many times, physical and perhaps mental activity increases around 9 months. The child now is moving around more, exploring more, becoming more active and independent.

If the customary bedtime hour had been around 8 or 9 P.M. before the onset of night waking, I have observed that night waking will often disappear when the bedtime hour is now shifted earlier by a half or one hour. Usually this change is easy for the baby; sometimes it is hard to accept for the parent who returns home late from work. Small changes in sleep patterns sometimes make big differences in sleep quality when the result corrects a chronic sleep deficit.

Early Awakenings

Most children 4 to 12 months of age go to bed between 7 and 9 P.M. and awake at 5 to 7 A.M. Some also get up once around the midnight hour for a brief feeding. This pattern is very common, but many parents don't like the idea of getting up so early! In this age range, though, it seems that the wake-up part of our brain is like a neurological alarm clock.

For well-rested children, this neurological alarm clock is fairly regular, and I don't think we can ignore crying at 5 or 6 A.M. simply because we don't want to get up so early. Because they are well-rested, having slept overnight, it seems unreasonable to expect children to go back to sleep without any kind of response. Instead I would suggest a prompt, brief, soothing response so that perhaps both child and parent can return to sleep. Sometimes over-tired children start to wake up in a new pattern at 4 A.M. or to wake up at the usual 6 A.M. and *not* respond by returning to sleep after a prompt, soothing parental response. These kids are *really* up and want to play, yet they are often not well rested. When the parents put these children to bed earlier, they get more sleep at the front end and they sleep in later in the morning because they are more rested and are thus able to sleep better.

This means that when your child has disturbed sleep and (a) an abnormally late wake-up time, you might decide to control his schedule by waking him up earlier so that the naps and bedtime hour all occur earlier, or (b) an abnormally early wake-up time, shorten the intervals of wakefulness before naps and bedtimes so that the bedtime hour is earlier without worrying about an earlier wake-up time. When your child is well rested and has no disturbed sleep, an early wake-up hour may be inconvenient but not necessarily changeable.

METHODS THAT USUALLY FAIL TO PREVENT EARLY AWAKENINGS
Keeping your child up later at bedtime.
Waking him for a feeding when you go to sleep.
Giving solid foods late at night.

If your child is near her first birthday, you might consider some of the items discussed in the next section for older children.

Different Sleep Patterns: No Problem

Sleep patterns are as varied as children themselves, family sizes, and parental lifestyles. One 5 month-old child briefly awoke at 6 A.M. and promptly returned to sleep until 10 A.M. A long midday nap occurred from noon to 3 P.M. and a brief nap from 5 to 5:45 P.M. Between 7:30 and 8:00 P.M. the child went to sleep for the night, until about 6 the following morning. This child was well rested, and the midday nap coincided with his older brother's single nap. For the time being, this pattern met both children's sleep needs. By 6 or 7 months, this child developed a more common midmorning and early afternoon nap.

PRACTICAL POINT

A temporary disturbance or mild variation in sleep schedules, nap patterns, amount of sleep, or early awakenings may not be changeworthy. But if chronic or severe problems cause your child to become tired, then do try to help your baby become more rested. Watch your child's behavior, not some inflexible schedule.

Night Wakings

In this age range, night wakings typically are normally occurring complete arousals from sleep associated with (1) post-colic disturbed sleep, (2) partial airway obstruction during sleep, (3) general disorganization of sleep with chronic fatigue, or (4) parent reinforcement only at night. (See Chapters 2, 4, and 10 for discussions of points 1, 2, and 3.)

Let's consider the child who naps well, has a reasonably normal sleep schedule, and does not appear overly tired, but simply gets up too often and/or stays up too long in the middle of the night. We want to help this child learn how to soothe herself to sleep unassisted when she wakes up. This skill also will help her fall asleep at bedtime, so the two strategies outlined here can also be used when the problem is *"prolonged latency to sleep,"* commonly known as *fighting going to bed*. The first technique, called *fading*, is a more gradual approach, while the second, called *extinction*, is an abrupt, cold-turkey solution. Let's look at how each works, and their pluses and minuses.

PRACTICAL POINT

Do not attempt to correct unhealthy sleep habits unless you see a clear period ahead when you will be in control. Don't trust most relatives or babysitters to do as good a job as you can to correct unhealthy sleep habits. Also, if your child's sleep improves during a retraining period but suddenly he becomes worse, appears ill or in pain, let your pediatrician examine him for the possibility of an ear or throat infection.

Fading

A gradual approach to reduce the number of night wakings until the baby can return to sleep independently is called a "fade" procedure. Over a period of time, you gradually reduce your efforts at night, so that your child takes over for himself and falls asleep or returns to sleep by himself. This is like teaching your older child how to ride a bike. You first provide balance and support and gradually withdraw your efforts as the child gains confidence and skill. Here is an example of a fade-sequence to eliminate night wakings:

> Respond promptly, spend as much time as needed.
> Father gives bottle or mother doesn't nurse.
> Change from milk to juice.
> Dilute juice to only water.
> No bottle.
> No pick-up.
> No singing, talking, verbal communication.
> Minimal contact, petting, hand holding.
> No eye contact, sober, unresponsive face.
> No physical contact, sit next to child.
> Move chair away from crib toward door.
> Reduce time with child.
> Delay response.

The apparent advantage of gradually weaning the child from prolonged, complex contact is its seeming gentleness. A disadvantage is that it does span several days or weeks, during which many brief crying spells may occur. The major reasons why this approach usually only partially succeeds, or fails completely, are: (a) unpredictable, real-life events interfere with parents' best plans and schedules; (b) parents do not appreciate the enormous power of intermittent positive reinforcement that maintains the behavior ("I'll just nurse him this one time!"); and (c) parents' resolve weakens from their own fatigue and sometimes impatience. Here is an account of one mother's attempt to use a gradual approach.

Exhaustion Wins Out Over Patience
Lauren was 8 months old when I finally sought help from the doctor; her sleep schedule could only be described as unbearable.

When we brought her home from the hospital after birth, she would have a very long, wakeful period in the evenings from about 8 P.M. to 1 A.M. We can't say that she was colicky, as she was really quite pleasant most of the time. Only about once a week did she have an extended crying spell during which she would be inconsolable. Most other evenings, she would nurse often and sometimes fall asleep for a few minutes at a time, but would awaken as soon as put down. The great thing was that once she fell asleep at 1 A.M. she would sleep until 6 or 7 A.M. We thought she was terrific for a newborn. (During the day she would stay up for about a half to two hours between naps of varying length.)

The problems started when we tried to move bedtime up (after about 3 months of age). We started being able to get Lauren to sleep around 11:30 P.M., but she would always wake once in the middle of the night, sometimes twice. Usually after nursing, she would fall back to sleep, but often she would end up spending the rest of the night in our bed. If I tried to put her back into her crib, she would wake up instantly and have to be nursed again. Interestingly enough, if we let her stay up until 1 A.M., she could still make it through the rest of the night. For fleeting moments, we actually considered moving to the Orient where her body clock might coincide better with the time zone.

At around 7 months or so, we decided to try nursing Lauren and putting her back in her own bed consistently. That's when the trouble really began! Lauren would wake up every few hours, and it would take one and a half to two hours to get her back to sleep. By now she had learned how to stand up, and I think that made it even more difficult for her to settle down.

The other thing Lauren did was to fall asleep easily at about 9 P.M. and wake up a half hour later, inconsolable. Eventually (after nursing, rocking, etc.), she would perk up and become very pleasant and often stay up and play happily for anywhere from two to four hours. Any attempt at putting her to bed was met with great resistance. Even letting her stay up until 1 A.M. no longer guaranteed us the rest of the night's sleep. She would awaken at least twice during the night no matter what! It was no longer necessary to move to Japan—now we were considering the land of the midnight sun!

At the same time, naps were totally irregular and unpredictable. She would sometimes sleep 20 minutes—sometimes two hours—usually 20 minutes.

When I saw the doctor, Lauren was about 8½ months old and sleeping no longer than two to three hours at a stretch at night. When I explained that I was one of those people who didn't think I could let my baby cry herself to sleep, the doctor recommended a plan of action that involved a gradual withdrawal process that would stretch out over 7 to 10 days. The response to Lauren's waking was supposed to be consistently prompt, but there was to be less handling of the baby at each step of the plan. One stage of the plan was to respond to her middle-of-the-night crying by entering her room, but trying to leave her in her bed. Singing, talking, and stroking her were fine.

On the night that we reached that point of the plan, I could soon see that there would be no way Lauren would lie down and calm down enough to fall back to sleep. She just stood in her crib and got angrier and angrier that I wasn't picking her up. Of course, I eventually picked her up and nursed her, and she fell back to sleep in my arms; and, of course, as soon as I placed her back in her crib, she woke up. At this point, I realized that I'd been with her for one and a half hours (3:30 A.M. to 5 A.M.). On top of all this, my older daughter had awakened at 1 A.M. that night; and I had, so far, only managed to get one hour of sleep. Finally, exhaustion won out over patience.

I put Lauren in her crib, kissed her goodnight, walked out, and closed the door. She screamed for *45 minutes* and finally went to sleep. They were the longest 45 minutes of my life—longer than labor! But it worked!

The next few nights Lauren slept all night—once we got her to sleep. And that was the next thing we needed to deal with. It was still pretty easy to get her to sleep around 9 P.M.—only to have her awaken in a half hour. A few nights after our first success, we decided to leave her alone when she woke up at 9:30. Well, that crying session, when we did it, lasted for about 35 minutes. The next night Lauren went to bed about 9 P.M. and got up at 7:30 A.M.!

Since then, that has been pretty much her nighttime sleeping schedule. Occasionally, Lauren awakens in the middle of the night, but only cries for about two or three minutes and goes back to sleep.

Naps were still not too consistent at this time, but Lauren has recently worked herself into a two-nap-a-day routine. She manages to get another two to four hours of sleep a day. She's always been a pretty pleasant baby—now she's almost all smiles all the time, because she's well rested.

I can't tell you why it was so difficult for me to follow the doctor's advice right away about letting Lauren cry, except that I empathize with the baby completely and entirely. I kept thinking to myself that it must be horribly frightening for a baby, who is unable to communicate except through crying, to be left alone in a room to cry. What helped to convince me, however (in addition to utter, complete and entire exhaustion), was the realization that as long as I stayed in Lauren's room she screamed anyway. Walking, rocking, singing, etc.— none of these quieted her anymore, the only thing that calmed her was endless, nonstop nursing! I finally came to the conclusion that as long as Lauren was going to be miserable crying anyway, she might as well be learning something positive from it—learning to go to sleep. Even now, if I stay in her room after I put her in bed, she stands up and cries; but as soon as I kiss her goodnight, walk out, and close the door, she lies down and goes to sleep!

Extinction (Or Going "Cold Turkey")

When parents—however well intentioned—stop reinforcing a child's night waking, the habit can be eliminated quickly. In fact, psychologists have shown that the more continuous or regular you had been in reinforcing the night waking during the first few months, the more likely it will be reduced rapidly simply by stopping it. The advantages of ending the habit of going to your baby at night are that the instructions are simple and easily remembered, and the whole process takes only a few days. But the seeming disadvantage is that a few nights of very prolonged crying are unbearable for many parents. This procedure strikes many people as harsh, too abrupt, or cruel. Those are personal value judgments, but bear in mind—this procedure is *effective*. It works.

Here is an account of one mother who decided to stop cold turkey in order to eliminate her child's night wakings. Stimulus control was also used, so that the child could nap well. In other words, certain behaviors in certain places at naptime *and* bedtime (the stimuli) became associated with "falling asleep."

One of the Hardest Things I've Ever Had to Do

At 6 months of age, Stephen was strong, happy, and healthy in every respect but one—he didn't sleep well. He did all his daytime napping in the car, the stroller, or our arms. If we put him in his crib, he awoke immediately and cried until we picked him up. His nighttime pattern was different, but equally exhausting. He went to sleep in his crib promptly at 8 P.M., but usually awoke within the first hour for a brief comforting and two or three times between 11 P.M. and 5 A.M. for a feeding.

This routine was taking its toll. I was almost as tired as when Stephen was a newborn and had no emotional reserve for handling everyday problems. I was sharp with the rest of the family and got angry if my husband was even 10 minutes late getting home from work. We needed to make a change.

We discussed the problem with our pediatrician, and he suggested leaving the baby alone to cry both at naps and at night, but I just wasn't ready to do it. I hoped Stephen would outgrow his sleeping problems. Two weeks later, I decided to try a limited program of letting him cry at naptime. Because I was still going to him at night, however, I think he was confused. After a week, he still cried for up to an hour before each nap. I felt depressed and even more discouraged than when he wasn't napping at all. But, at the same time, I knew we couldn't go back to the way things had been.

We made another appointment with the doctor and for an hour talked over all my anxieties about going "cold turkey" and letting Stephen cry at night. I wanted to know about all the "what-ifs"—what if he's afraid, hungry, too cold, too warm, uncomfortable from a dirty diaper, awakened by a noise outside? I wanted to raise every concern I had, no matter how insignificant it might seem.

During that appointment, the doctor also explained to us the importance of regular day- and nighttime sleeping for babies, and how they need to learn to use their own resources for falling asleep. He said we were perpetuating Stephen's night waking habit by going to him whenever he awoke, and told us that sleeping problems tend to persist and even get worse. I began to see that I was doing Stephen a disservice, as well as myself, by continuing the pattern we were in. He needed the sleep as much as I did.

The doctor gave us explicit instructions for instituting morning and afternoon naps and unbroken nighttime sleeping. At the end of the appointment, I was full of resolve. Stephen was free of any illness, and we had the weekend ahead of us, when my husband would be around for support, so we decided to start that night.

We put the baby to bed at 8 P.M. and he awoke the first time around 9:30. He cried for *20 minutes* and went back to sleep. He awoke again around 2 and 4 A.M. and cried about 20 minutes each time. When he cried at 6 A.M., I rushed into his room, anxious to hold him and be sure he was the same healthy, happy baby I had put down the night before.

Over the next few days it was amazing to see how quickly he fell into the schedule we had set up for him. He cried 10 to 15 minutes several times, but never again for an hour. Now he naps regularly and sleeps all night, occasionally crying for one or two minutes during the night as he puts himself back to sleep.

For the first two weeks after we began the program I felt tense every time I put Stephen in his crib, wondering if he would cry a long time before falling asleep. Finally, I began to relax and unwind from the weeks of indecision and tension we had been through surrounding this problem.

Letting my baby cry was one of the hardest things I've ever had to do. Now that the experience is behind us, however, I have no doubt at all that it was right. Both he and I are better rested, and he can enjoy outings in the car or stroller without falling asleep and missing the activity. During his naps, I have time to do household tasks or simply catch my breath. I feel refreshed and delighted to be with him when he wakes up. At night, I look forward to several hours of uninterrupted rest, rather than falling asleep feeling tense and wondering when the first waking will occur.

In a broader sense, too, this experience had value. It gave me more confidence in my abilities to handle tough issues as a parent and respect for my child's ability to learn and adapt to the guidelines I establish for him.

PRACTICAL POINT

Small, soothing efforts such as kissing the forehead, rearranging blankets, comforting, and patting appear trivial to parents, but they interfere enormously with learning to fall asleep *unassisted*.

HELPFUL HINT FOR AVOIDING MIDNIGHT DIAPER CHANGES

Use thick layers of zinc oxide *paste* in the diaper region so that no rash will develop when you do not go to your baby at night to change diapers. Ordinary mineral oil will make removal of the paste easier in the morning. Or consider using the extra-absorbent disposable diapers specially designed for nighttime use in this weight range.

Here are some other typical questions and answers for this age group:

Q: I've heard that if I nurse my baby to sleep, I'll create a night waking problem.

A: The issue is not whether nursing to sleep is good or not but rather is nursing too frequently or nighttime nursing part of a night waking problem. Please include nursing, if you wish, in naptime or bedtime rituals. But after you spend the time you want to spend nursing, whether the child's asleep or awake, put her down, kiss her cheek, say good-night, walk away, turn lights off, and close the door.

Q: Once I let my child cry a long time and she vomited. Won't I be trading one problem for another?

A: If the vomiting always occurs, I think you will want to always go in to clean her promptly and then leave her again. If the vomiting is irregular and occasional, you should try waiting until after you think she is deeply asleep before checking, and then quickly clean her if needed.

Q: Won't my baby simply outgrow this habit? My doctor says to try these procedures later, if needed then, when she's a few years old. She'll understand more then.

A: Believe it or not, college freshmen, at age 18, who don't sleep well, had difficulties sleeping as infants, according to their mothers, as reported in one study. It seems that if the child doesn't have the early opportunity to practice falling asleep by herself, she'll never learn to fall asleep easily by herself.

Q: Even if she won't outgrow this habit, what's really wrong with my still going to her at night?

A: Consider your feelings. Good studies at Yale University show that *all* mothers eventually become anxious, develop angry feelings toward their child, and feel guilt about maintaining poor sleep habits. These feelings may persist for years. True, you will also feel guilty letting your baby protest cry, but this will last only several days. Here's one mother's account.

I Felt Cruel, Insensitive, and Guilty

The moment my daughter, Amanda, arrived home from the hospital, she exploded with a very bad case of colic. I took her to the pediatrician's office several times, only to be told there was "not a thing wrong, relax," and received several suggestions about nursing and a pat on the back. All of these suggestions irritated me, and I felt as though I were being perceived as an anxious, first-time mother.

After 12 weeks of crying at best and screaming at worst, Amanda was evaluated by two child development specialists. I decided we should work with one until my daughter's crying and screaming settled down. We also saw a psychiatrist, who recommended medication and also suggested that we continue to be followed by the development specialists. In the meantime, our lives had become a nightmare. Amanda cried most of the day and always screamed in the evening. To our horror, this behavior had worked itself into the entire night hours also.

By 5 months, we were referred to Dr. Weissbluth for what was hoped to be a sleep disorder. I say hoped, because we were at the point of seeing a pediatric neurologist and having an EEG done. I was very frightened for my daughter, and my husband and I were exhausted. We had read Dr. Weissbluth's *Crybabies*, and I was eager for the consultation. My daughter had definitely been cursed with colic. Could this now be wired exhaustion from a sleep disorder caused by the treatment for colic—rocking, swinging, motion all the time? It was.

Amanda was old enough now to try "crying it out." It was the most difficult thing I've had to do as a new mother.

The first night Amanda screamed, choked, and sobbed for *32 minutes*. I remember I felt sick to my stomach and kept following my husband around reading parts of *Crybabies* out loud. It wasn't that he needed to hear any of it, but rather, I needed to hear the statistics and conclusions of Dr. Weissbluth as an encouragement.

The first two days weren't too terrible. However, the third and fourth were almost intolerable. Amanda would cry through her entire naptime. Then I would get her up to keep Dr. Weissbluth's time frame going. Her temperament after these episodes is only known to mothers who have been through the same ordeal! When she would scream for *over an hour* during a naptime and in the evening, I felt cruel, insensitive, and guilty.

Three things kept me going: my husband's support; Dr. Weissbluth's concern, encouragement, and compassion; and the fact that I knew it had to be done—Amanda had to learn to sleep.

It took Amanda about a week to catch on to the idea. The bags under her eyes faded, her sporadic screaming attacks stopped, and her personality was that of a predictable baby— a sweetheart when rested and a bear when she's past a nap or bedtime.

I would offer these suggestions to other mothers and fathers who have to take this measure in order to teach their baby to sleep:

You, as parents, have to understand and believe intellectually it is the right thing to do. Otherwise, your feelings of guilt will overpower you, and you will give in. You must have the support of your spouse, as it will be too much of a strain on you.

You are doing what is best for your baby. It seems cruel and unacceptable as a loving new mother to let your baby cry. But it is a fact of parenting—many, many things will bring tears and protests in the years to come.

Enlist the support of a sympathetic friend as much as you feel the need to. I found close telephone contact a tremendous help. Some parents may not need this close interaction, but many of us do.

In your role as parents, perhaps teaching your child to sleep may be the very first difficult task you have to undertake. Those parents who do should feel a special sense of accomplishment, for it is a very difficult task! Those of us who have been through a baby with a sleep disorder know what misery is. But so does the baby, who is crabby and exhausted all the time. Once patterns and the practice of sleep are established, everyone benefits and finally life can be somewhat predictable again will get better!

A few more typical questions and answers:

Q: Look, I grew up in the sixties; I don't believe in this kind of unnatural programming.

A: Just consider the "unnatural" effects of chronic sleep fragmentation on your child.

Q: I just don't think I can do nothing when my baby cries for me at night.

A: Letting your baby cry is *not doing nothing*. You are actively encouraging the development of independence, providing opportunities for her to learn how to sleep alone, showing respect for her capability to change her behavior.

Q: Maybe you're right, but why do I feel that I just can't do it?

A: If you want to do it but can't do it, consider the following possibilities:

WHY CAN'T I LET MY BABY CRY?

1. *Unpleasant childhood memories* surface and remind you of loneliness, of feeling unwanted.
2. *Working mother's guilt*—from being away from the child so much.
3. *We already tried it and it didn't work*—maybe the child was then too young; maybe you time-limited your inattention; maybe you unknowingly provided partial reinforcement.
4. *I enjoy my baby's company too much at night*, because I'm not a good sleeper myself.
5. *If I don't nurse my baby at night* she might lose weight. Not true.
6. *We're under a lot of stress.* In *My Child Won't Sleep*, Jo Douglas and Naomi Richman write: "If you are feeling stressed, your child may respond by not sleeping so well. If the stress is related to difficulties between you as parents, you may think that your young child will not notice, but the chances are that he will. His way of waking at night and coming into your bed can be a way of preventing you from talking to each other and sorting out your problems, and his presence can act as a useful contraceptive." Although this quote applies to older children, it's possible that maintaining baby's night waking or having the baby sleep with you when

the baby is younger also serves the purpose of avoiding marital problems.

PRACTICAL POINT

When your overly tired child first starts to sleep better during a retraining period, he may appear, in the beginning, to be more tired than before! You are unmasking the underlying fatigue that previously had been present but that was hidden by the turned-on, hyperalert state.

CHAPTER 7

Months 12 to 36

When your child starts to walk, babble, and show more character, you will naturally begin to treat him less as an infant and more like a little person. Please try to avoid the trap of endlessly explaining, negotiating, or threatening when it comes to sleep times. Save your breath; let your behavior do the talking.

Months 12 to 23

During months 15 to 21, you can probably expect your child's schedule to be reduced from two naps a day to only one. This transition, however, may not be smooth. You might have a few rough months when one nap is not enough, but two are impossible. Here are some ideas for making the transition easier:

Many children naturally shorten one nap on their own (either morning or afternoon or alternately either nap). Most of these children do not appear to become very tired. Other children appear to actively resist the second nap, and because it was short anyway, many parents forget it. The result is a tired child late in the afternoon or early evening. If two naps are clearly impossible but one nap is insufficient, then put your child to bed earlier. Do this even if this means that a working parent coming home late does not see the child then. You can get up extra early to have longer morning play time with your child before you go off to work. Another solution is to declare some days as two-nap days and other days as one-nap days depending on when the baby awakens, how long the morning nap lasts, scheduled group activities, or the time you want your baby to go to sleep at night. Flow with your baby and arrange naps and bedtimes to coincide with baby's need to sleep as best you can.

Obviously, any combination of parents' scheduling for their convenience and baby's need to sleep can determine nap patterns. If you are a napper yourself, you may protect your child's nap schedule differently than another parent who does not customarily take naps.

Q: How long should my child nap?

A: Does your child appear well rested? You be the judge.

All of us have good days and bad days, but if you notice a progression toward more fussiness, bratiness, tantrums . . . ask yourself, is my child tired?

Months 23 to 36

Fears

Nightmares, monsters, fear of separation, fear of darkness, fear of death, fear of abandonment . . . don't fears at this age cause disturbed sleep? By age 2, 3, or 4, many experts tell us that night fears are common. Thunderstorms, barking dogs, lightning flashes, and many other events over which we have no control might frighten our children. If your child has been a good sleeper up to now, you should expect any disturbed sleep triggered by these events to be short-lived.

Reassurance, frequent curtain calls, open doors, night lights, or a longer bedtime routine will help your child get over these fears. Some child care experts believe severe sleep disturbances are caused by night fears. Usually, though, children with these problems did not sleep well at younger ages and their current sleep problem is simply misinterpreted as caused by an age-appropriate concern or "stage." Don't worry.

If your child has been a good sleeper up to now, the disturbances related to fearful events will be brief and infrequent.

Routines and Schedules

At about 2 years of age, most children go to sleep between 7 and 9 P.M. and awaken between 6:30 and 8 A.M. A single nap between one and three hours occurs in over 70% of children. Try to be *reasonably* regular according to clock times with naptime and bedtime routines and consistent in your behaviors for bedtime rituals. There are no absolute, rigid, or firm rules, because every day is somewhat different. *Reasonable* regularity and consistency implies *reasonable* flexibility. Be aware of how your lifestyle helps or hinders your child's sleep patterns. As natural as seasons change or tides rise and fall, there will be changes due to growth and rearrangements in relationships within your family.

Regular Bed

One rearrangement is moving your child to a "big kid's" bed. There is no special age when you should make this change. As long as the crib is large enough, you should not feel that your child must be placed in a regular bed by a certain age. Many parents will do this around the second or third birthday.

If the move to a regular bed is needed because of a new baby brother or sister, consider making the move when the newborn is about 4 months old. Then the newborn has regular sleep habits and the older child has become adjusted to the new family arrangements. The baby goes to the crib and the older child graduates with pride to the big bed for big kids. He does not feel displaced. Moving too early, before the birth of the new baby, often invites a problem: The commotion and excitement of the arrival of a new baby creates confusion or insecurity in the older child who starts to get up every night to visit his parents.

If the move to a regular bed is associated with frequent nocturnal visits, curtain calls, calls to help go to the bathroom, or calls for a drink of water . . . think before you act. A habit may slowly develop so that your child learns to expect you to spend more time with her putting her to sleep or returning her to sleep.

Imagine what would occur if a babysitter gave your 2-year-old candy every day instead of a real lunch? Once you discovered this, you would immediately stop the candy for meals. Your child might protest and cry but would you give in and give the expected candy? No. If you are spending too much time at night with your child when she should be sleeping, consider what you are doing to be "social candy"—not needed and not healthy for your child. Be firm in your resolve to ignore the expected protest from your child when you change your behavior.

PRACTICAL POINT

Don't confuse these issues:
Needs versus wants
A sad cry versus a protest cry
Being abandoned versus being alone

Solving Sleep Problems: Months 12 to 36

Your child's developing personality and awareness of himself as an individual means that his second and third year will be a time of testing, noncooperation, resistance, and striving for independence. Sleep problems in 12 to 36 month-olds are related to this normally evolving stubbornness or willfulness in our children who now want to do their own thing, for example: (a) to get out of their bed or crib at night; (b) not to take naps; (c) to get up too early to play and, of course; (d) to resist falling asleep and to wake up at night. This last problem might have started during the first year and may now continue during the second year as an ingrained habit. Let's look at each of these major problems in turn.

Getting Out of the Crib or Bed (Or, the "Jack-in-the-Box" Syndrome)

It's quite natural for 2- or 3- year-olds to climb out of the crib or bed to check out the interesting things that they think their parents are up to. Or maybe they just want to watch the late late movie or have a bite to eat. Of course, what they like to do most is to come visit with us and/or get into our bed. This not only disrupts our sleep, but it also harms the child. Here's how.

When the child has a naturally occurring partial arousal during sleep, instead of soothing himself back to sleep, he learns to force himself completely awake to get out of his bed or crib. The result is sleep fragmentation—for him, and us, too. Here's a five-step treatment plan to put your Jack back into his "box" at night:

Step 1: Keep a chart, log, or diary to record key sleep events: time asleep, time awake, number of times out of bed, and duration of protest calling, fussing, or crying. This will make you a better observer of both your child's and your own behavior. The chart enables you to determine whether the strategy is working, and helps remind you to be regular according to clock times and to be consistent in your responses.

Step 2: Ask yourself, does my child behave as if he is tired in the late afternoon or early evening? If the answer is yes, then consider the possibility that naps are insufficient or that the bedtime hour is too late. Deal with these problems at the same time you are working on his getting out of the crib or bed. If needed, keep data in your sleep chart regarding naps, such as time he falls asleep, how long he slept during the day, how long he cried in protest before napping, and the interval between the end of his nap and when he went to sleep for the night.

Also, consider whether your child is snoring or mouth breathing more and more at night. Please review the section on snoring in Chapter 10 if this is now a problem.

Step 3: Announce to your child that there is a new rule in the house which is: Down is down—no getting out of bed until morning. Tell him that you love him very much, that you need your sleep, and he needs to put himself back to sleep by himself; getting out of bed is not allowed. Tell him that when he gets out of bed, you are going to put him back to bed and you are not going to talk to him or look at his face.

Depending on whether he has just turned 3 or about 3, he may or may not understand what you are saying. But he senses or understands that tonight, something different is going to occur.

PRACTICAL POINT

Be silent, unemotional, appear disinterested or mechanical. No more night entertainment!

Step 4: Place yourself somewhere where you can easily hear him get out of his crib or bed. Place a bell-rope on his door or your door to signal you when he leaves his room or enters your room, or use an intercom if you must be out of earshot.

Every time you determine that he is out of his crib or bed or discover him in your bed—gently place him back in his bed. *Maintain silence.* Plan not to sleep the first night as he may try many, many times to get back to his old style. Parents might want to alternate nights so that at least someone gets some sleep. Do not take turns on the same night because the child might think one parent will behave differently. Children learn quickly that there's no benefit in getting out of bed, so they stay in bed and sleep through the night.

Step 5: Every morning, shower the child with praise or affection for cooperating with the new rule. Perhaps offer a favorite food that was previously withheld or go on a special outing. Try small rewards for partial cooperation and larger rewards for more complete cooperation.

In addition to praising or rewarding your child when he cooperates, you might consider changing some of the routines when he does not cooperate. For example, past 15 to

18 months, you might close the door in a progressive fashion every time he gets out of bed. You can put three or four white tape marks on the floor and for the first 3 or 4 times he gets out of bed, the door is more and more closed until it is barely open or completely closed. If he stays in bed, the door is left open to the first tape mark. A similar progressive strategy could be used with brighter or dimmer night lights.

Expect this plan to dramatically reduce or eliminate the getting-out-of-bed routine within a few days, usually three or four. All you had to do was remove the previous nighttime social interaction (whether pleasant or unpleasant) as a reinforcer to the habit of getting out of the crib.

Here are some typical questions and answers about this strategy:

Q: Won't my child hurt himself when he climbs or falls out of his crib?

A: This is a common worry and often used as an excuse to go to your child or buy a "big kids" bed. But the truth is that serious injuries rarely occur when the child bumps on the floor as he lets himself down.

Q: Can the plan fail?

A: Yes, when both parents aren't committed, so that one partner passively or actively sabotages the program. One father in my practice loved to sneak a bottle of formula to his baby once or twice a night. This caused the baby to suffer excessive wetness and a severe, persistent, and painful monilial diaper rash. Only in the course of trying to eradicate the rash did his behavior come to light. Failures also sometimes occur when the child is still chronically fatigued from too late a bedtime hour or nap deprivation.

Q: What if he stays in his crib but cries?

A: Letting your child cry when he protests going to sleep or staying in his crib is not the same as making your child cry as if you were hurting him. Leave him alone.

PRACTICAL POINT

Do not underestimate the enormous power of partial reinforcement to ruin your efforts to overcome baby's habit of getting out of the crib. If you are not silent and you discuss getting out of bed when it is occurring, your social behavior reinforces getting out of the crib.

One family instituted this five-step program when their daughter was 26 months old—after 26 months of poor sleeping. She always had difficulty in falling asleep and difficulty in staying asleep. Nicole always wanted to, and did, get out of her bed and go into her parents' bed. After the birth of Daniel, her brother, her parents decided that this had to stop.

Their records showed the following results:

NIGHT 1: Between 8:13 and 9:45 P.M.—*69* return trips to bed. Slept until 8:30 A.M. with one brief awakening at 2:15 A.M.

NIGHT 2: Between 8:20 and 10:30 P.M.—*145* return trips to bed. Slept until 7:20 A.M. with one brief awakening at 2:15 A.M.

NIGHT 3: After 9:14 P.M. (bedtime)—*0* return trips to bed! Slept until 7:40 A.M., awakening at 3:20 A.M.

That's it!

From then on, the curtain calls at bedtime ceased. Furthermore, at naps the mother would now leave after 15 or 20 minutes of reading, whereas before she had stayed in the room until Nicole fell asleep. The parents described Nicole as easier in many ways: less resistant in dressing, less argumentative, more charming, and better able to be by herself.

Another family made a poster for their 2-year-old which they put on the wall:

BEDTIME RULES
At bedtime we . . .
1. Stay in bed.
2. Close our eyes.
3. Stay very quiet.
4. Go to sleep.

Next to the poster was a calendar called a Bedtime Star Chart. The rules were read by the parents at bedtime. If the child followed the rules, she put a star on the chart in the morning, which meant that she could choose a treat later on that day. No star, no treat. She caught on very quickly to the relationship between following the rules and getting treats.

PRACTICAL POINT

Problems may get worse before they get better during a retraining phase.

Refusal to Take Naps

Playtime in the park or gym or shopping together is so much fun; who wants to take a nap? Ask yourself, is "not napping" my *child's* problem or *my* problem: "I have so many things I want to do". Some parents simply find it too inconvenient to hang around the house so that their child can get their needed day sleep. But reflect on how "inconvenient" it is to drag a tired child around while shopping. Please review the first chapter of this book, if you feel that naps are not that important.

Let's consider two common problems regarding naps: (a) resistance for one nap and (b) no naps.

Resistance for one nap: This often occurs after a special event, such as a holiday, party, or vacation. There was so much excitement the day before, the children don't want to miss anything again! Sometimes this becomes apparent because of unappreciated chronic fatigue due to an abnormal sleep schedule, brief night sleep duration, or sleep fragmentation. If these problems are present, work on them as you work on day sleep.

The trick to solving the problem of resisting a nap is judging when your child is tired, but not overly tired. This is usually after being up about three to four hours. If the interval is too short, the child may not be tired enough. If the interval is too long, she may be overpooped and not able to fall easily asleep.

Keep a sleep chart, log, or diary; pick a time interval that you think is right, and then put your child down in the crib at that time. *You* are controlling the naptime. Spend the time you want, 10, 20, 30 minutes hugging, kissing, rocking, nursing to soothe your child. Then down is down . . . no matter how long he cries, don't go in until you think he has slept for about an hour without interruptions.

If your child has been quite well rested up to now, the crying may only be an hour or two. But if your child has had a background of chronic fatigue, prepare yourself for several hours of crying. Here's one mother's account of how her 14-month-old daughter responded.

She Woke in the Morning Smiling . . . We Were Reassured That She Loved Us

My daughter was 14 months old, ate poorly, resisted naps, woke two to three times in the night, needed to be rocked to sleep, and was tired all the time. My husband and I were exhausted, angry, resentful, and blaming each other for the situation we were in.

We were ambivalent, scared, concerned, and skeptical about letting our daughter cry [as the treatment plan recommended]. We thought she would feel unloved and worthless, if no one responded to her.

After only one episode of crying, she learned how to lie

down and fall asleep on her own! It was very difficult listening to her crying, but when she woke in the morning smiling and kissing us good morning, we were reassured that she loved us. Now she naps regularly, sleeps through the night, eats better, plays better, and is able to play in her crib before going off to sleep on her own.

The more well rested the child is, the quicker you'll see improvement. A very tired child might require several days of training before he learns to nap.

Your goal is to establish a routine, so that the child learns to associate being left alone in a certain place and a familiar soothing routine with feelings of being tired—with taking a nap. No more playtime. No more games. Just sleep. Parents who would rather hold their child in a rocking chair, let them snooze in a sofa with one hand on the back, or catch catnaps in the stroller are robbing their children of healthy sleep. This lighter, briefer, less regular sleep is less restorative—it's not as effective in returning your child's energy and attentiveness to its best levels.

No Naps: If your child is a young 2-year-old, you might find that simply establishing a pattern as described under "Resistance to One Nap" and sticking with it works best, especially if the duration of not napping was not too long. But if you have an older 2-year-old or a 2-year-old who hasn't napped for a long time or is very tired because of unhealthy sleep habits in general, try the methods described in the next section on how to reestablish naps in the older child.

Q: My problem is not refusal to nap or resistance to naps, but *irregular* naps. What's wrong?

A: If your child is well rested, it may be that you are in fact very sensitive to his need to sleep and place him in an environment conducive to sleep when he needs it. Differences in daily activities produce differences in wakeful intervals and differences in the durations and timing of naps.

Perhaps you have an unrealistic expectation regarding regularity of naps according to clock times. If your child is very tired, he might be crashing at irregular times when he is totally exhausted.

Now, let's look at another major problem in this toddler age group.

Getting Up Too Early

The first question to ask is, how early is too early? If your child gets up at 5 or 6 A.M. and is well rested, maybe this pattern is not changeable. Perhaps getting everyone together in a family bed at that hour will allow everyone to get some more snooze time. Often families have established the habit of giving the baby a bottle at this early hour, after which the baby returns to sleep for a variable period of time.

Bottles given early in the morning may help the child return to sleep, but if the baby is allowed to fall asleep with the bottle in her mouth, the result is decayed teeth. This will not occur if the bottle contains only water. Unfortunately, many parents go to their child at 4 or 5 A.M. with a bottle of milk, and then let the baby feed herself.

Treatment for the well-rested child who has the early morning awakening-bottle habit is to first switch to juice, and then gradually over about a week dilute the juice to only water. Now that the child is drinking only water, place two water bottles at either end of the crib and point them out to the child at bedtime. If your child is not well rested, work hard to establish a healthy sleep pattern. In the morning, don't go to him until the wake-up hour.

Controlling the wake-up hour involves *stimulus control*. Place a digital clock in her room and set the alarm for 6 or 7 A.M., *after* the expected spontaneous wake-up time. You do not respond to her cries before this wake-up time. Then at the wake-up time *you* have decided, you bounce into her room, shower her with affection, open the curtains, turn on the lights, bring her into your bed, or give a bath. Be dramatic, wide-eyed, and happy to see her. Point out the numbers on the digital clock and exclaim, "Oh, see, it's time to start the day!" The child learns that the day's activities start at this time. The pattern on the digital clock acts as a cue, just as a green traffic light tells you to start moving. Before the wake-up time, the child has her water bottles but no parental attention.

The last major sleep problem centers on the bedtime hour and on waking at night.

Resistance to Falling Asleep/Night Waking

Cues can also be used to control the bedtime hour. Use a digital clock and say "Oh, look, it's 7:00 (say, "seven, zero, zero"), time for bath." After bath, hugs, stories, kisses, say, "It's now seven, three, zero (7:30), time to go to sleep." Lights out. Door closed. No returning or peeking. The child learns that after a certain hour, no one will come play with him, so he falls asleep and stays asleep until the morning. He learns to amuse himself with crib toys or other toys in his room until the wake-up time.

If your child has had a long history of resistance to falling asleep or night waking, then read the earlier chapters in this section and work on establishing a healthy sleep pattern in general. Prepare yourself for some long or frequent bouts of crying as your extinguish this habit. A fade procedure probably won't work if your child is chronically tired and has longstanding disturbed sleep; he'll outlast you. The following published account of a "cold turkey" strategy in a 21-month-old boy shows that it is effective, that the improvement occurs over several days, and that the treatment has *no ill effects*. This account was published in a professional journal for psychologists, so please forgive the dry style of writing.

Case Report
The Elimination of Tantrum Behavior
by Carl D. Williams

This paper reports the successful treatment of tyrant-like tantrum behavior in a male child by the removal of reinforcement. The subject child was approximately 21 months old. He had been seriously ill much of the first 18 months of his life. His health then improved considerably, and he gained weight and vigor. The child now demanded the special care and attention that had been given him over the many critical months. He enforced some of his wishes, especially at bedtime, by unleashing tantrum behavior to control the actions of his parents.

The parents and an aunt took turns in putting him to bed both at night and for the child's afternoon nap. If the parent left the bedroom after putting the child in his bed, the child would scream and fuss until the parent returned to the room. As a result, the parent was unable to leave the bedroom until after the child went to sleep. If the parent began to read while in the bedroom, the child would cry until the reading material was put down. The parents felt that the child enjoyed his control over them and that he fought off going to sleep as long as he could. In any event, a parent was spending from one-half to two hours each bedtime just waiting in the bedroom until the child went to sleep.

Following medical reassurance regarding the child's physical condition, it was decided to remove the reinforcement of this tyrant-like tantrum behavior. Consistent with the learning principle that in general, behavior that is not reinforced will be extinguished, a parent or the aunt put the child to bed in a leisurely and relaxed fashion. After bedtime pleasantries, the parent left the bedroom and closed the door. The child screamed and raged, but the parent did not re-enter the room. The duration of screaming and crying was measured from the time the door was closed.

The results are shown in the figure. It can be seen that the child continued screaming for 45 minutes the first time he was

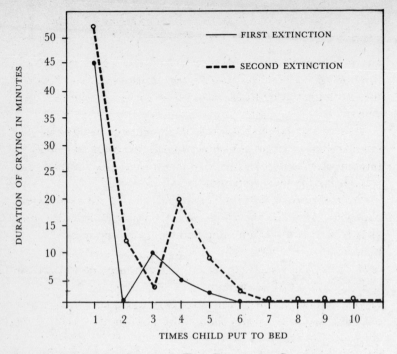

FIGURE: LENGTH OF CRYING IN TWO EXTINCTION SERIES AS A
FUNCTION OF SUCCESSIVE OCCASIONS OF BEING PUT TO BED.

put to bed in the first extinction series. The child did not cry
at all the second time he was put to bed. This is perhaps
attributable to his fatigue from crying.

By the tenth occasion, the child no longer whimpered,
fussed, or cried when the parent left the room. Rather, he
smiled as they left. The parents felt that he made happy sounds
until he dropped off to sleep.

About a week later, the child screamed and fussed after the
aunt put him to bed, probably reflecting spontaneous recovery
of the tantrum behavior by returning to the child's bedroom
and remaining there until he went to sleep. It was necessary
to extinguish this behavior a second time.

The figure shows that the second extinction is similar to
the first. Both curves are generally similar to extinction

curves obtained with sub-human subjects. The second extinction series reached zero by the ninth occasion. No further tantrums at bedtime were reported during the next two years.

It should be emphasized that the treatment in this case did not involve aversive punishment. All that was done was to remove the reinforcement. Extinction of the tyrant-like tantrum behavior then occurred.

No unfortunate side- or after-effects of this treatment were observed. At three and three-quarters years of age, the child appeared to be a friendly, expressive, outgoing child.

Here are some final questions for this age group:

Q: Does this mean that after my baby falls asleep I can never peek, never go in to soothe him or comfort him?

A: No. Only during the period when you are establishing a new sleep pattern is it important to avoid reinforcement. After your child is sleeping better and becomes well rested, there is nothing wrong with going in to check on him at night.

Q: I took his older brothers out of their bedroom so his crying wouldn't disturb them. When can they go back into their old bedroom?

A: Allow several days or a couple of weeks to pass before making changes. The more rested the baby becomes, the more flexible and adaptable he will be. Changes then will be less disruptive.

Q: My 2½-year-old son understands what I'm saying; why can't I discuss these problems with him?

A: You want to avoid discussions or lectures at the time when the problem is taking place because your reasoning calls attention to the problem and thus reinforces it. Instead, choose some low-keyed playtime to voice your concerns regarding his lack of cooperation. But when there is some cooperation, make sure to praise the specific behavior: "Thank you for staying in bed" or "Thank you for trying to sleep." Praising the child ("Thank you for being a good boy") does not tell him exactly what it is that you want him to do again.

SEPARATION ANXIETY

Q: My 15-month-old child shows separation anxiety during the day, and at night she wants me to hold her and sit with her on the sofa until she falls asleep. How can I leave her alone at bedtime, when she is most anxious?

A: Separation anxiety, stubbornness, or simply exhibiting a preference for parents' company over a dark, boring room might separately or in combination cause your child to behave this way. Please understand that it is normal for children to feel some anxiety, and learning to deal with anxiety and not be overwhelmed by it is a healthy learning process.

Let's not use separation anxiety in our child as an excuse for our own problems in dealing with a child's natural disinclination to cooperate at bedtime.

If there has been longstanding ambivalence or inconsistency regarding putting your child to bed at night, then the naturally occurring separation anxiety will only aggravate or magnify the problem. The same could be said of the naturally occurring fears of darkness, death, or monsters that older children around age 4 often express. For separation anxiety or for fears at night to be dealt with, we must understand that all children experience them, and that they can learn not to be overwhelmed by them at the bedtime hour with the help of the consistent, calm resolve of their parents at bedtimes. The routine of a set pattern in a bedtime ritual reassures the child that there is an orderly sequence: Sleep will come, night will end, the sun will shine again, and parents will still be there smiling.

PRACTICAL POINT

Don't hide behind excuses; there is always one handy!
Some families use colic (0 to 6 months), teething (6 to 12
months), separation anxiety (12 to 24 months), terrible-
twos (24 to 36 months) and fears (36 to 48 months) to
''explain'' why their child wakes up at night and has
trouble returning to sleep by himself.

Young Children:
Years 3 to 6

Between 3 and 6 years of age, most children still go to sleep between 7 and 9 P.M. and awaken between 6:30 and 8 A.M. Naps gradually decrease in duration; few children are still napping after 5 years. Sleep problems and disturbed sleep usually do not develop in those children who previously had been good sleepers.

The major problem occurs when parents push their children too soon into preschool, nursery school, or other scheduled activities. The children are overprogrammed, and naps get scheduled out before the child is ready.

PRACTICAL POINT

A missed nap is sleep lost forever.

Some parents provide partial compensation for their children's increased mental and physical stimulation by shifting bedtime to an earlier hour. Working parents may not accept this solution, because it shortchanges their playtime with their children. When you sign up your child for courses, classes, or activities, another solution to prevent sleep deficits is to simply enforce a policy of declared holidays: Once or twice a week the child stays home and naps, or he engages in more unstructured, low-intensity, quieter activities.

Solving Sleep Problems in Young Children

Three-year-olds may no longer have tantrum behaviors, but they may call parents back many times and clearly express their feelings of love for their parents or fears of the dark. Let's look at the problems that may occur with night- and daytime sleep habits and some of the strategies we can use to deal with them.

Night Sleep

Here's one mother's account of how hard it was to ignore her 3-year-old child at night.

Mom, I Need a Hug and Kiss Goodnight

Here'a a quiz! What does every parent want to be, but most parents aren't? The answer is *CONSISTENT*. How many times has "one more time" turned into two or three more times? If we don't fulfill our promises to our children, then the inconsistency in our behavior sparks inconsistency in their behavior.

My daughter Chelsea is almost 3 years old. Putting her to bed has always been an ordeal. At 18 months of age, she started to climb out of her crib anywhere from 75 to 100 times a night. The problem seemed to be solved with the advent of a "big bed." She now sleeps through the night. However, having her stay in bed and fall asleep is still an ordeal.

I have yelled and screamed. I have used gates and locks on Chelsea's door to physically keep her in her room. I have used treats as an incentive for positive reinforcement of desired behavior. Unfortunately, the only consistent behavior has been my inconsistency.

You may ask, why? What is so hard about being consistent? I have thought about this and analyzed and agonized over it for quite some time. I have concluded that consistency is difficult, because we look at it as a punishment rather than as a means to develop positive behavior in our children.

If Chelsea knows that I will put a gate on her bedroom door if she leaves her room, even once, then she will gradually conform and stay in her room. But there is a catch! She eventually will start to challenge my consistent behavior. One night she will appear in the living room and say, "Mom, I need a hug and kiss goodnight." As a parent, do you deny your child such a loving request and lock her in her room? So, you give her a hug and kiss and send her off to bed, again. Then, the next night she wants water and before too long, she's out of bed three or four times a night for hugs and kisses, water, band-aids, scary noises, you name it! Within a week, saying goodnight and falling asleep takes one hour or more. Now, we have to start over.

Webster's dictionary defines the word "consistent" as "free from self-contradiction; in harmony with." I long for the night when I'm in harmony with Chelsea.

As this mother said, "Unfortunately, the only consistent behavior has been my inconsistency." In other words, when a behavioral approach fails with older children, it almost always is not a failure of the methods, but rather a failure of the resolve of the parents to implement it.

In one English study of children about 3 years old, psychiatrists examined: (a) difficulty in going to bed (defined as requiring parents' presence until going to sleep in bedroom or falling asleep downstairs before going to bed); (b) night waking at least three times a night or for more than an hour, or waking and continuing sleeping in parents' bed; or (c) both. Treatment consisted of keeping a sleep diary for a week and establishing goals with the parents for the child that included:

> Sleeping in his own bed.
> Remaining in his bed throughout the night.
> Not disturbing his parents during the night.

The treatment consisted of identifying the factors that reinforced the child's sleep problem, and then gradually withdrawing them or temporarily substituting less potent rewards. It was a "fade" strategy, not a "cold-turkey" approach.

Here's an example of how subjects gradually reduced reinforcement: (1) father reads story to child in bed for 15 minutes; (2) father reads newspaper in child's bedroom until child falls asleep; (3) child is placed back in bed with minimal interaction; and (4) gradual withdrawal of father from bedroom before the child is asleep.

Another example: (1) parents alternate, but respond to the child; (2) give no drinks but provide holding and comforting until crying stops; (3) parent only sits by the bedside until child is asleep; and (4) less physical contact at bedtime.

PRACTICAL POINT

At every stage of reduction of parental attention, expect the problem to get worse before improvement begins. That's because the child will put forth extra effort to cling to the old style.

In the Oxford study, 84% of the children improved. Not surprisingly, the two factors that most likely predicted success were both parental: the absence of marital discord and the attendance of both parents at the consultation sessions. Also, when one problem such as resistance in going to sleep was reduced or resolved, other problems such as night waking rapidly disappeared. And lastly, although half of the mothers in this study had current psychiatric problems requiring treatment, this did *not* make failure more likely.

I think this study points out the importance of working with professionals who can provide parent-guidance advice directed toward changing the child's behavior without dwelling on current psychological/emotional problems within the mother or father. The exception, of course, is when *these problems directly are related to marital discord or parents' ability to maintain a behavioral management program.*

Another study from England included children who took at least an hour to go to bed, awakened at least three times a night or for more than 20 minutes, or who went into their parents' bed. Treatment started with the parents recording the present sleep pattern in a sleep diary. A therapist worked with the parents to develop a program of treatment based on gradually reducing or removing parental attention, adding positive reinforcement for the desired behavior, making bedtime earlier, and developing a bedtime ritual. Target behaviors were identified, and an individual treatment program was developed for each child. Also, mothers were evaluated for psychiatric symptoms. Mothers rated as showing psychiatric symptoms were more likely to terminate treatment, again pointing out how stressful treatment can be. But for those families who completed about four or five treatment sessions, 90% of the families showed improvement. The authors concluded that:

The evidence that children's night-time behavior could thus change so radically often within a surprisingly short time, suggests that parental responses were extremely important in maintaining waking behavior . . . A rapid achievement of improved sleep pattern with reduced parental attention would be unlikely if anxiety in the child or *lack* of parental attention were causing the sleep difficulty . . . Parents needed help in analyzing goal behavior into graded steps so that they could achieve successes. Once some success was obtained, the morale and confidence of the parents rose and they were reinforced in their determination to persist by the more peaceful nights.

I have seen this over and over again; when you see even partial improvement, you gain confidence and you no longer feel guilty or rejecting when you are firm with your child.

Often it appears that the child is listening to the treatment plan in the office, because they often sleep better that very night . . . as if they knew something was going to be different.

I think they are responding to the calm resolve and firm, but gentle, manner in their parents, which tells them that things are going to be different.

Q: Do I ever lock my child in her room?

A: Let's say that you've already tried patient reasoning, threats, criticisms, perhaps you've even tried spanking— which of course never works by itself—and all methods have failed. Also, let's assume that you are not working with a therapist to gradually reduce reinforcing behaviors. What's left to be done? Maybe a stiff door hook which, when locked, holds the door in a slightly open position but prevents opening or completely closing is the answer. The door is held locked in a slightly open position to protect the child's fingers from a crush injury. Completely closing and locking the door may be an overwhelming degree of separation for either you or your child. What have you accomplished? You have established an unambiguous routine; leaving the room after a certain time is unacceptable. The child learns that you mean business. The usual result is that after a night or two the child negotiates to stay in bed, and does, even if you do not lock the door. Also, you avoid the repeated prolonged stresses of your trying physically to separate from a child who is clinging to you or your trying to pull the door closed while your child is in the room trying to pull the door open.

Rewards are often used to encourage the child to cooperate. They must be items the child really wants. One mother placed a piece of candy, at night, after some cooperation, in a wicker basket which was under a special doll. Part of the motivation was the excitement of discovery in the morning when the child looked for her treat. Paper stars on a chart may be used but they might be ineffective. One strategy that often works is withholding a favorite wholesome food and giving it only as a reward for cooperation. Other rewards might be small toys, surprise trips, or wholesome snack foods. By using a timer, you can give rewards as measured amounts of extra time for games, stories, TV, or free play. The expectation of a specific reward is usually forgotten as the new behavior becomes a habit. The child's heightened self-esteem seems to substitute for the pleasure of the reward.

PRACTICAL POINT

Always reward even partial cooperation. Small rewards for small efforts, bigger rewards for more cooperation. Rewards are best given in the morning after awakening or immediately following a nap.

Day Sleep

You may conclude that life is impossible without your child taking a nap, but it is impossible to get him to nap. You've worked at sleep schedules, night wakings, resistance to sleep and things *are* better, but he also really needs a nap. Not necessarily a long one, but no nap at all is no good.

Some mothers have successfully reestablished naps as a routine even when the naps have been absent or sporadic for several months. The method involves taking a nap with your child (at least initially): Take her into your own bed, dress yourself for sleep, and nap together. The idea is to make this a very comforting, soothing event. Try to be fairly regular according to clock time. Use a digital clock as a cue, and be consistent with the routine of a glass of warm milk and cookies or reading from a favorite book. Try to fall asleep yourself. Tell your child what is expected of her if she sleeps with you, then A occurs, if she rests quietly next to you but doesn't fall asleep, then B occurs. You decide what kind of reward A and B will be.

If she doesn't cooperate at all and jumps on the bed or runs around the room, then you might restrict or withdraw some pleasurable activity or privilege. If you are able to get her to nap with you, then eventually you'll want to try to shift her napping to her own room. This should be done in a graded or staged fashion. You might decide the next step is for your child to be in her bed and you're in her room resting as long as needed. Rewards are now given *only* for this new behavior. This process of reinforcing successive approximations to the desired target behavior is called "shaping."

Preschool children who slept well when they were younger might develop problems because too many activities interfere with napping or, as discussed in Chapter 10, because allergies occur interfering with sleep at night. Reorganizing daytime activities or managing allergies may provide a rapid solution. On the other hand, preschool children who have not previously slept well may have ingrained habits or expectations which are not easily changed. Parents should seriously consider working with a professional if they think their child is so tired that he might not do well in school.

CHAPTER 9

Older Children: Years 7 to 12 and Adolescence

The list of new concerns for our older children is long: school assignments, organized after-school activities, individual lessons, parties, more homework, dating, driving cars, drugs, and alcohol. Health habits may appear to be less important to parents than the development of our children's academic, social, athletic, or artistic skills. But as you will see, the contribution of healthy sleep habits to our child's wellbeing does not diminish with age.

Years 7 to 12

School-aged children are sleeping less and less as the bedtime hour gradually is shifted to later hours. Most 12-year-old children go to sleep around 9 P.M.; the range is from about 7:30 to 10 P.M. The range for total sleep duration for most 12-year-old children is about 9 to 12 hours. This data, from a large survey of middle-class families I performed a few years ago, and the data from an ongoing study at Stanford University are in close agreement. Researchers there have shown that the prepubertal teenager needs 9½ to 10 hours of sleep to maintain optimal alertness during the day.

PRACTICAL POINT

As your preteen grows older, he will need more sleep, not less, to maintain optimal alertness.

If healthy sleep habits are not maintained, the result is increasingly severe daytime sleepiness.

Recurrent Complaints

Many children in this age range complain of aches and pains for which no medical cause can be found: abdominal pains, limb pains, recurrent headaches, and chest pains. Children who suffer from these pains often have significant sleep disturbances. Stressful emotional situations thought to cause these complaints include real or imagined separation of or from parents; fear of expressing anger which might elicit punishment or rejection; school, social, or academic pressures; or fear of failure to live up to parents' expectations.

These are real pains in our children, just as our tension headaches are real pain. When we work too hard or sleep too little we might have ordinary tension headaches. All laboratory tests or studies during these episodes of tension headache will be normal. So will all the tests be normal in our children who have similar somatic complaints. Performing laboratory tests should be discouraged, unless there is a strong clinical sign pointing toward organic disease. The reasons that tests, to "rule out" obscure diseases, should be avoided is because of the pain of drawing blood, irradiation, expense, and most importantly the possible result of creating in the child's mind the notion that he is really sick. Also, a slightly abnormal test result might lead to more and more tests, all of which in the end turn out to show basically normal results.

Adolescence

Surveys of sleep habits of teenagers show that the gradual decline in total hours of sleep flattens around age 13 or 14. Many 14- to 16-year-old children now actually require more sleep!

PRACTICAL POINT

Many teenagers over age 15 require more sleep than in previous years to maintain optimal daytime alertness.

Excessive tiredness, daytime sleepiness, or decreased daytime alertness develops in many adolescents—there simply are not enough hours in the day to do everything. The time demands for academics, athletics, and social activities are enormous. Even without worrying about sex, drugs, alcohol, and loud music, parents worry that their teenagers may become burned out from lack of sleep.

PRACTICAL POINT

Social pressures, not changing needs, cause reduced sleep times and chronic sleep deficits.

Chronic sleep deficits were observed in 13% of teenagers in a Stanford study which included over 600 high school students. These poor sleepers attributed their sleep problems to worry, tension, and personal, family, and social problems. The students appeared to be mildly depressed. Of course, we don't know which came first: disturbed sleep or the mood changes. Perhaps both the mood and sleep disturbance changes develop from the same endocrine change naturally occurring during adolescence. But healthy lifestyle habits, including sensible sleep patterns, might prevent or lighten the emotional depression seen in so many adolescents.

Here's how the Stanford sleep researchers defined chronic and severe sleep disturbances in adolescents:

1. 45 or more minutes required to fall asleep on three or more nights a week.

   or

2. One or more awakenings a night followed by 30 or more minutes of wakefulness occurring in three or more nights a week.

   or

3. Three or more awakenings a night on three or more nights a week.

So if your teenager has this kind of sleep pattern, don't consider it a "normal" part of growing up. There are other abnormal sleep patterns and problems that begin in adolescence which you should note.

Delayed Sleep Phase Syndrome

You notice that your teenager is going to bed later and later. Eventually, she might consider herself to be a "night" person. You may have heard of "owls" or "larks" and if you are an owl, you might consider this tendency for your teenage daughter to delay going to sleep as "normal." After all, she has so much to do and thankfully, she's a good kid who studies hard and stays away from hard drugs. What may result is the development of an inability to fall asleep at a socially and biologically appropriate time. The child has no difficulty in falling asleep or staying asleep but only when the sleep onset is delayed, maybe to 1, 2, or 3 A.M. When she tries to go to sleep earlier, she can't. On weekends and vacations, she'll sleep in later so that her total sleep time is about normal. But school days, it's always a struggle to get her up for those early classes.

As a consequence, school work suffers, and the child's mood swings widely, because the long-term result is brief sleep during school times and chronically abnormal sleep schedules.

Kleine-Levin Syndrome

This is a rare condition but it may be mistaken for other psychiatric or neurological illnesses. The major features include excessive sleepiness, excessive overeating, and loss of sexual inhibitions. The exact cause of this problem is not known, but if you notice dramatic abnormalities in sleeping, eating, or other behaviors, do not simply assume this is a teenage "phase." Other uncommon disorders involving abnormal sleeping might be associated with changes in temperature sensitivity, thirst, or mood.

Chronic Mononucleosis

Infectious mononucleosis is caused by a virus infection. Children as young as 14 years have been identified as having a chronic condition, following the acute infection, characterized as disabling daytime sleepiness. Because of the daytime sleepiness, the children's school performance deteriorates. Not surprisingly, misdiagnoses of depression are sometimes made among these children. The correct diagnosis is made only after blood tests confirm the viral infection.

Solving Sleep Problems in Older Children and Adolescents

Let's look at two major areas of concern for children in this age group, namely falling asleep and maintaining a healthy sleep schedule.

Falling Asleep

Working with a therapist, older children can learn to sleep better with relaxation training techniques similar to those used for adults. Here are a few:

1. *Progressive relaxation* is a method whereby you tense individual skeletal muscle groups, release the tension, and focus on the resulting feeling of relaxation.
2. *Biofeedback* involves focusing on a visual or auditory stimulus which changes in proportion to the tension within skeletal muscles. Both progressive relaxation and biofeedback techniques can help reduce muscle tension and thus make it easier to fall asleep.
3. *Self-suggestion* to produce relaxation involves repeating suggestions of heaviness and warmth to your arms and legs.
4. *Paradoxical Intention.* Trying hard to spontaneously fall asleep might create a vicious cycle that might be broken by focusing on "staying awake."
5. *Meditative relaxation* procedures vary, but simple instructions

to focus on the physical sensation of breathing seem to help some people fall asleep.

6. *Stimulus-control* treatment tries to make the bedroom environment function as a cue for sleep. This means that spending lots of time in bed watching television, reading, or eating directly competes with sleeping and, therefore, is discontinued in the bedroom.

7. *Temporal control* means establishing a regular and healthy sleep schedule. The elements of stimulus control and temporal control are incorporated in the following instructions developed by Richard R. Bootzin at Northwestern University:

STIMULUS-CONTROL INSTRUCTIONS

1. Lie down intending to go to sleep *only* when you are sleepy.
2. Do not use your bed for anything except sleep; that is, do not read, watch television, eat, or worry in bed.
3. If you find yourself unable to fall asleep, get up and go into another room. Stay up as long as you wish and then return to the bedroom to sleep. Although we do not want you to watch the clock, we want you to get out of bed if you do not fall asleep immediately. Remember, the goal is to associate your bed with falling asleep *quickly*! If you are in bed more than about 10 minutes without falling asleep and have not gotten up, you are not following this instruction.
4. If you still cannot fall asleep, repeat step 3. Do this as often as necessary throughout the night.
5. Set your alarm and get up at the same time every morning, irrespective of how much sleep you got during the night. This will help your body acquire a consistent sleep rhythm.
6. Do not nap during the day.

If these instructions or programs do not provide help, consider pushing your child into sports programs to increase the amount of physical exercise. If this fails and your child can't sleep well and appears exhausted, too tired, and not interested in outside activities, ask yourself whether the problem might not be depression.

Children do get depressed and some crazy, risk-taking "accidents" in overtired teenagers are really deliberate suicide attempts. If this is a concern of yours, seek outside help immediately. Start with school social workers, your physician, or local suicide prevention centers.

Maintaining a Healthy Sleep Schedule

As already discussed, some teenagers suffer from what we call delayed sleep phase syndrome. This occurs when teenagers usually are unable to fall asleep at a desired conventional clock time, but have no difficulty falling asleep well after midnight. On vacation, they sleep a normal duration, do not wake up at night, and feel refreshed in the late morning or midday when they awaken. The problem lies in the disrupted sleep schedule often developing during the school year, when "sleeping-in" is not possible.

Treatment is called "chronotherapy," or resetting the sleep clock. Let's say your child can easily fall asleep at 2 A.M. The therapy consists of forcing him to stay up until 5 A.M., and then letting a natural sleep period follow. Obviously, we don't do this during the school year! The next time sleep is allowed to start is at 8 A.M. the following day and at 11 A.M. the next day. In other words, you are allowing sleep to occur about three hours later every cycle. Over the next few days, sleep begins at 2 P.M., 5 P.M., 8 P.M., and finally 11 P.M. Now, keeping careful watch over clock time, you *always* try to have the child go to sleep at 11 P.M. You have shifted the sleep clock around to a more conventional time, and usually this can be maintained by sustaining a regular nighttime sleep schedule.

Drugs and Diet to Help Us Sleep

Drugs don't solve sleep problems. Diphenhydramine, which is sold as Benylin and Benadryl or other antihistamines, is often used to induce sleep in children. The common situation is for these drugs, or others, to be thought of as a temporary, short-term measure, "just to give everyone a break." It sounds great—get your strength back to muster up enough courage to try to correct problems caused by your own mismanagement. I have observed many times that those parents who most demand drugs are those who are least likely to change their behaviors, so the basic sleep problems continue. No study has shown that sleep-inducing drugs are really useful and safe for our children. Diphenhydramine has been shown *not* to be an effective hypnotic in adults. A hypnotic drug like phenobarbital can actually cause sleep disturbances, daytime fussiness, and irritability.

Other drugs that can interfere with good sleeping include nonprescription decongestants, such as phenylpropanolamine, and caffeine. So let's sleep better by not taking any drugs. An important exception might be drugs used by an allergist or pediatrician to help the child breathe easier at night, if he is suffering from allergies.

PRACTICAL POINT

Don't depend on drugs to solve your child's sleep problems.

Dietary changes that are known to make some people sleepy include high carbohydrate meals and the amino acid, tryptophan. It is possible that the content of a nursing mother's diet affects the carbohydrate content of her breast milk, and this may indirectly influence the levels of tryptophan in the baby. In one study of infants, tryptophan caused the babies to begin quiet sleep 20 minutes earlier and active sleep 14 minutes earlier. But the total amount of sleep time was not affected. So giving tryptophan to infants or other children will probably not make them sleep longer. The effects of high carbohydrate or high protein meals in adults show differences between sexes and differences based on age. There is no scientific nutrition data on children that could be translated into a sleep-promoting diet. Eliminating refined sugar, because of the commonly held belief that this makes children hyperactive, also does not appear to have any effect on sleep patterns.

Another recent report suggested that cow's milk allergy could cause insomnia. But the results of the study could have been caused by a placebo effect because the parents knew when they were giving a cow's milk challenge and when they were eliminating cow's milk from the diet.

Dietary challenges and eliminations are best performed when the parents and the researchers, at the time of the challenge, are ignorant of whether the child is or is not receiving the substance in question. Only then can bias or wishful thinking be reduced.

Many school-aged children have difficulty falling asleep because they worry about their grades, test scores, appearance, or sports skills. Anxiety about not doing well academically or athletically might lead to impaired performance. The same is true about worrying or nagging too much about not getting enough sleep. Worrying too much about not sleeping well creates anxiety or stress interfering with the relaxation needed to successfully perform the task which is to fall asleep. If your child, at any age, appears to need more sleep and he wants to sleep but he cannot easily fall asleep, please consider working with a professional to help your child learn to relax and avoid performance anxiety.

PART III

Other Sleep Disturbances and Concerns

CHAPTER 10

Special Sleep Problems

Specific sleep problems may occur at different ages and it would be useful to read the earlier sections to determine whether your child's sleep pattern is appropriate for his age. Some specific sleep problems such as sleep walking, sleep talking, or night terrors appear to occur more frequently when children have abnormal sleep schedules. Most of these common problems are bothersome to the family but they are not harmful to your child. However, severe and chronic snoring may be hazardous to your child's health. Please read the section on poor quality breathing even if your child has no specific sleep problems or you think he does not snore. Snoring is sometimes not appreciated as a problem because the child has always snored or because allergies developed when the child was older, in his own bedroom, and the parents were unaware of how much snoring was occurring every night.

Sleepwalking

Between the ages of 6 and 16, sleepwalking occurs about 3 to 12 times each year among 5% of children. An additional 5% to 10% of children walk in their sleep once or twice a year. When it starts under age 10 and ends by age 15, sleepwalking is not associated with any emotional stress, negative personality types, or behavioral problems.

Sleepwalking episodes usually occur within the first two to three hours after falling asleep. The sleepwalk itself may last up to 30 minutes. Usually, the sleepwalker appears to be little concerned about his environment. His gait is not fluid and his movement not purposeful. In addition to walking, other behaviors such as eating, dressing, or opening doors often occur.

Treatment consists only of safety measures to prevent sleepwalkers from falling down stairs or out of open windows. Try to remove toys or furniture from your child's path, but don't expect to be able to awaken him. Trying to awaken him won't hurt, but usually the child spontaneously awakens without any memory of the walk.

Sleeptalking

Sleeptalkers do not make good conversationalists! They seem to talk to themselves and respond to questions with single syllable answers. Adults appear annoyed or preoccupied. Infants often repeat simple phrases like "get down" or "no more," as if they were remembering important stressful events that had occurred that day.

Between the ages of 3 and 10 years, about half of all children will talk in their sleep once a year. Older studies had suggested that sleepwalking and sleeptalking tended to occur together and were more common in boys; however, newer studies do not support this association.

Night Terrors

Your child has a piercing scream or cry and you rush to see him. He appears wild-eyed, anxious, frightened. The pupils are dilated, sweat is covering his forehead, and as you pick him up to hug him you notice his heart is pounding and his chest heaving. He is inconsolable. Your heart is full of dread, and you fear this evil spirit which has gripped your child. After 5 to 15 minutes, the agitation/confused state finally subsides. This is a night terror.

Night terrors, sleepwalking, and sleeptalking all occur *during* sleep. They do not occur when we dream; they are not "bad" dreams. In fact, children have no recall or memory of them.

Night terrors usually start between 4 and 12 years of age.

When they start before puberty they are not associated with any emotional or personality problems. Night terrors appear more often with fever or when sleep patterns are disrupted naturally, such as on long trips, during school vacations, during holidays, or when relatives come to visit. Recurrent night terrors also are often associated with chronically abnormal sleep schedules. Overtired children who have frequent night terrors are best treated by enabling them to get more sleep. I have observed night terrors disappear when the parents moved the bedtime hour earlier by only 30 minutes.

Drug therapy is not warranted for most children with night terrors, sleepwalking, or sleeptalking problems. Most children should be allowed to outgrow these problems without complex tests, such as CAT scans, drug treatments, or psychotherapy.

Nightmares

In Old English mythology, a nightmare was "a female spirit or monster supposed to beset people and animals by night, settling upon them when they are asleep and producing a feeling of suffocation by its weight."

I have nightmares of suffocation, strangulation, breathlessness, choking, being crushed or trapped, drowning, entrapment, asphyxiation, and of being buried alive only when I sleep on my back. When my wife wakes me, she says I sound like a diesel truck with a bad motor that can't get started. She pokes me to get me up, the nightmare ends, and I breathe normally again. You see, my nightmares occur when my upper airway is partially blocked. This obstruction only occurs when I sleep on my back or drink alcohol before bedtime. Occasionally, my dreams are not so dramatic, but consist only of breathlessness such as running, flying (by myself, without a plane, of course), or being chased. If my wife does not awaken me, I wake up to breathe, but I have no dream recall. Maybe some children have similar nightmares when they have bad colds or throat infections that partially obstruct their upper airway.

The child with a nightmare can be awakened and consoled

in contrast to the child with a night terror, which spontaneously subsides. About 30% of high school students have one nightmare a month. Adults who have more frequent nightmares (more than two per week) often have other sleep problems: frequent night awakenings, increased time required to fall asleep, and decreased sleep duration. They appear more anxious and distrustful, and experience fatigue in the morning.

But nightmares in most young children do not seem to be associated with any specific emotional or personality problems. Analysis, really guesswork, of dream content in disturbed children who have been referred to psychologists or psychiatrists should not be generalized to normal populations of children with the assumption that normal anxieties or fears represent a mental or emotional problem. We really do not know the exact value or limitations of dream interpretation. If you think your child is having a nightmare, shower him with hugs and kisses and try to awaken him.

Head Banging and Body Rocking

My third son banged his head against the crib every night when we moved into a new house. Actually, he struck his shoulder blades more than his head against the headboard of his crib. My solution was to use clothesline rope and sofa cushions to pad both ends and both sides completely. Now, when he banged away, there was no racket, no pain, and no parental attention. After a few days he stopped. Thank goodness, because my wife's back was killing her because we could not lower the side railing! Other parents are not so lucky.

About 5% to 10% of children will bang or roll their heads before falling asleep during their first few years. This usually starts at about 8 months of age. No behavioral or emotional problems are seen in these children as they develop, and they certainly have no neurological problems. Body rocking before falling asleep also occurs in normal children.

All this rhythmic behavior usually stops before the fourth

year, if there are no underlying neurological diseases. Your pediatrician can diagnose these uncommon conditions if they are present.

Bruxism

Teeth grinding during sleep occurs commonly in children. At the Laboratory School at the University of Chicago, about 15% of the students were reported by their parents as having a history of bruxism. In the age range of 3 to 7 years, the percentage of bruxists was about 11%; between 8 to 12 years it was 6%; and between 13 to 17 years the percentage dropped to about 2%.

The teeth grinding does not occur during dreams or nightmares. Furthermore, there is no association between emotional or personality disturbances and teeth grinding. No treatment is needed for bruxism in children.

Narcolepsy

The major characteristic of narcolepsy is excessive or abnormal sleepiness. It appears as if the child has a sudden sleep attack while engaged in ordinary activities such as reading or watching television. The child with a mild form of narcolepsy may drift into a state of excessive drowsiness; the child with a more severe form might fall stone asleep in the middle of a conversation.

Narcolepsy is less common under the age of 10. When it begins in older children it may be mistaken for "lack of concentration" or inattentiveness.

Other features of narcolepsy seen in older children are (a) cataplexy, a muscular weakness triggered by emotional stress; (b) sleep paralysis, a passing sensation of inability to move during drifting off to sleep; and (c) hypnagogic hallucinations, visual or auditory experiences occurring as sleep begins.

Poor Quality Breathing (Snoring and Allergies)

If you've ever suffered through a head cold, I'm sure you'll agree that when you can't breathe easily during sleep, you can't sleep easily, either. In turn, this makes you sleepy during the day, which can affect your mood and performance. When the cold finally disappears, you feel like your "old self" again, and your mood improves as does your performance. Some children experience the same type of disrupted sleep *every night* due to snoring or allergies. Let's look at them both.

Snoring

Two of the world's leading sleep researchers, Drs. Christian Guilleminault and William C. Dement, published a landmark paper in 1976. This was the first careful study of how impaired breathing during sleep destroys good quality sleep. At Stanford University School of Medicine, they studied eight children (seven boys and one girl, aged 5 to 14 years), all of whom snored. Here's how their symptoms were described:

All eight children snored loudly every night, and snoring had been present for several years. Snoring started in one child at age 6 months, and while the snoring in most children was originally intermittent, the snoring eventually became continuous.

Daytime Drowsiness: Five of the eight children experienced excessive daytime sleepiness. The report noted that: "The children, particularly at school, felt embarrassed by their drowsy behavior and sleep spells and tried desperately to fight them off, usually with success. To avoid falling asleep, the children tended to move about and gave the appearance of *hyperactivity*."

Bed Wetting: All the children had been completely toilet trained, but seven started to wet their beds again.

Decreased School Performance: Only five of the eight children had learning difficulties, but all the teachers reported lack of attention, hyperactivity, and a general decrease in intellectual performance, particularly in the older children.

Morning Headaches: Five of the eight children had headaches only when they awoke in the morning; the headaches lessened or disappeared completely by late morning.

Mood and Personality Changes: Half the children had received professional counseling or family psychotherapy for "emotional" problems. The report noted that "three children were particularly disturbed at bedtime: they consistently *avoided going to bed, fighting desperately against sleepiness*. They *refused to be left alone* in their rooms while falling asleep and, if allowed, would go to sleep on the floor in the living room."

Weight Problems: Five of the children were underweight, and two overweight.

Overall, we have a picture here of impaired mood and school performance which deteriorated as the children grew older or as the snoring became more continuous or severe. Sleep is definitely not bliss for these children!

But was this a new discovery? Not really. As I will discuss further, most snoring children have enlarged adenoids, which medical texts such as one written by Dr. Ballenger in 1914 acknowledge can disrupt sleep and cause behavior problems:

Restlessness during the night is a prominent symptom; the patient often throws the covers off during the unconscious rolling and tossing which is so characteristic . . . Daytime restlessness is also a characteristic sign. The child is fretful and peevish, or is inclined to turn from one amusement to another . . . The mental faculties are often much impaired . . . difficult attention is very often present. The child is listless and has difficulty in applying himself continuously to his play, studies, or other tasks, of which he soon tires. He has fits of abstraction.

The increased motor activity or physical restlessness during sleep, the distractability, and the "difficult" attention described in this 1914 report are characteristic features of children who have been diagnosed in more modern times as "hyperactive."

A 1925 study from the Department of Preschool and Elementary Education at Kansas State Agricultural College included enlarged adenoids and tonsils as a physical cause of poor sleep. So educators also were aware of this problem a long time ago. Even a major pediatric professional journal as far back as 1951 cited "difficulty in breathing, such as seen with extreme enlargement of the adenoids" as a common cause of "infantile insomnia." In truly severe cases of enlarged adenoids and tonsils, affected children appear to be mentally retarded and have retarded physical growth or short stature, even enlargement of the right side of the heart.

In one study of children who had documented difficulty breathing during sleep, the following problems were observed in addition to snoring:

"Breath holding," "stopping breathing" during sleep
Frequent nighttime awakening
Breathing through an open mouth
Sleeping sitting up
Excessive daytime sleepiness
Difficulty concentrating
Bedwetting
Decreased energy, poor eating, weight loss
Morning headaches
Hyperactivity

Some parents also have described to me their child's apparent "forgetting to breathe" during sleep. Their child's chest is heaving, but during those moments of complete airway obstruction, airflow is stopped. These periods are called apnea. With only partial airway obstruction, though, excessively loud snoring throughout the night is the result. In either case, it's the poor *quality* sleeping that's the culprit, causing daytime sleepiness, difficulties in concentration, school and behavioral problems, decreased energy, and hyperactivity . . . even though the *total* sleep time may be normal!

Why, then, has kid's snoring practically been ignored? Are there more snorers around today? Perhaps yes, because surgical removal of tonsils and adenoids up until recently has been a very popular procedure for recurrent throat infections and this also "cured" snoring children. And, perhaps yes, because the air we breathe is increasingly polluted and our processed foods increasingly allergenic, causing reactive enlargement of adenoids or tonsils in more of our children. This brings us to allergies, a second major cause of poor quality breathing.

Allergies

Allergies frequently are suggested as a cause of typical signs and symptoms characterizing snorers. Here's a list of symptoms from one study of children with difficulty breathing during sleep, conducted at the Children's Memorial Hospital in Chicago.

Snoring
Difficulty breathing during sleep
Stopping breathing during sleep
Restless sleep
Chronic runny nose
Breathing through mouth when awake
Frequent common colds
Frequent nausea/vomiting
Difficulty swallowing
Sweating when asleep
Hearing problem
Excessive daytime sleepiness
Poor appetite
Recurrent middle-ear disease

Perhaps the "chronic runny nose" and "frequent common colds" are due to allergies.

Allergists have long associated sensitivity to environmental allergies or food sensitivites to behavioral problems, such as poor ability to concentrate, hyperactivity, tension, or irritability. Terms such as "tension-fatigue" syndrome or "allergic-irritability" syndrome are used by allergists to describe children who exhibit nasal or respiratory allergies, food allergies, and behavioral problems. It is possible that allergy causes behavioral problems in many children by producing swollen respiratory membranes, large adenoids, or large tonsils which partially obstruct breathing during sleep. The difficulty these children experience in breathing during sleep causes them to lose sleep and thus directly causes fatigue, irritability, and tension.

Also perhaps due to allergies, large adenoids or tonsils can partially or completely obstruct breathing during sleep as well as cause hearing problems or recurrent ear infections. So, either because of the actual enlargement of the tonsils or because of the underlying allergies that cause swelling of the membranes in the nose and throat, these children suffer from frequent "colds"—runny nose, sneezing, coughing, and ear problems.

Snoring Revisited

We've seen so far that children who snore aren't getting the best quality sleep. Now we'll see that generally they aren't getting as much, either. One Children's Memorial Hospital study of snorers also showed that children with documented obstruction to breathing generally slept less than normal children. At about age 4 years, the night sleep durations were only 8½ hours in affected children, and 10¼ hours in normal children.

In another study which I performed, also at Children's Memorial, the affected snoring children were somewhat older, about 6 years of age, and their total sleep duration was only about one-half hour less. They also had longer duration of night wakings, went to bed later, and took longer to fall asleep after going to bed. These affected children exhibited snoring or difficult or labored breathing when asleep, or mouth breathing when asleep. Parents described problems in their snoring children as overactivity, hyperactivity, short attention span, inability to sit still, learning disability, or a nonspecified academic problem. And as we've seen, just a chronic sleep deficit of only one-half hour per night might cause impaired intellectual development.

Even in infants, snoring might be a problem. I studied a group of 141 normal infants between 4 to 8 months of age. In these infants, 12% exhibited snoring and 10% exhibited mouth breathing when asleep. These snoring infants slept 1½ hours less and awoke twice as often as infants who did not snore.

In another study of infants about 4 months of age, cow's milk allergy was thought to be the cause of brief night sleep durations and frequent awakenings. Other studies have suggested that cow's milk protein allergy can cause respiratory congestion.

PRACTICAL POINT

Although snoring reflects difficulty breathing during sleep, it is not related to Sudden Infant Death Syndrome or "crib" death.

The night waking in these snoring infants and the restless, light sleep in older children probably represent protective arousals from sleep. As we learned earlier, these arousals mean that the child awakens or sleeps lightly in order to breathe better. When awake, the child breathes well, but the brain's control over breathing is blunted during deep sleep stages. So, to prevent asphyxiation and perhaps even death, the child awakens frequently, cries out at night, and has trouble maintaining prolonged, consolidated, deep sleep states. Here, the crying and waking at night and resistance to falling asleep are caused by a valid medical problem—not a behavioral problem, not nightmares, not a parenting problem.

PRACTICAL POINT

All children sometimes snore a little, and frequent colds or a bad hay fever season might cause more snoring, which usually does no harm. But consider snoring a problem when it progressively gets worse, is chronic or continuous, disrupts your child's sleep, and affects daytime mood or performance. About 10% to 20% of children snore frequently.

Not all children who snore a lot have all of the problems listed above. Differences among snorers can probably be explained by differences in the severity and duration of the underlying problems. Also, I have encountered many monster snorers with minimal problems because they habitually take very long naps or have been able to go to bed much earlier than their peers. In other words, there are snorers and there are snorers! Some, like myself, have never been studied, and except for occasional nightmares—like the ones of asphyxiation, drowning, or strangulation I have when sleeping on my back—do not suffer adversely from snoring. Other snorers are not so fortunate because their snoring is more severe due to enlarged adenoids or tonsils.

The reason that attention recently has been focused on this problem of enlarged adenoids and tonsils is because sleep researchers only lately have proven that breathing actually is disordered during sleep. This is an important point, because when the child opens his mouth, the tonsils do not necessarily look enlarged. In fact, the adenoids and tonsils may cause partial airway obstruction in some children during sleep only because the neck muscles naturally relax and the airway thus narrows. In other words, the basic problem in some children might not be enlarged adenoids or tonsils, but rather too much relaxation in the neck region during sleep. If snoring appears to be disrupting your child's sleep, consult with your physician. Your child's doctor may have to do some tests to determine how serious the problem really is.

Locating the Problem

Try to suck through a wet soda straw . . . you can't, because it collapses. When we breathe in, the air flows into our lungs and active, neuromuscular forces keep our neck from collapsing like a wet straw. Sometimes things don't work well during sleep, and our neck muscles lose their tone. Sometimes the major problem involves the tongue; the tongue does not stay in its proper position during sleep and flops backwards, causing upper airway obstruction.

Think of this as a neurological problem involving the brain's control over our muscles while we sleep. The result is that the airway is not kept open during sleep. If it's a neurological problem, then consider the possibility that there are other associated problems involving the brain: difficulty in concentrating, poor school performance, excessive daytime sleepiness, or hyperactivity. If the major problem involves the tongue or neck muscles, removing the tonsils or adenoids might not help. So, determining the cause of the problem is obviously important before considering surgery.

Children who snore and have many of those problems associated with poor breathing during sleep often have abnormal X rays of the neck when viewed from the side. Obviously, the most common abnormality is enlargement of adenoids or tonsils. A simple X ray might tell the entire story. But some children who snore might have normal X rays, and will require other studies designed to document airway obstruction; this is important to pursue before clinical problems develop.

Studies used to document obstructive breathing problems during sleep include actual measurements of respiratory flow through the nose, skin oxygen levels, and the carbon dioxide concentrations in the expired air during sleep. Another type of sleep study, using fluoroscopy, may visualize the level of obstruction. Computerized axial tomography or CAT scans during sleep also have been used to measure the cross-sectional area at different levels of the airway to determine the anatomic location of the airway narrowing.

Electrocardiograms are useful because in severe instances,

the right side of the heart shows signs of strain. This right-heart strain can lead to pulmonary hypertension in longstanding cases.

Pulmonary hypertension also occurs with massive obesity in the "Pickwickian Syndrome." In *The Pickwick Papers*, an extremely fat boy is pictured as standing motionless, barely awake and feebly snoring. Massive obesity itself apparently causes difficulty in breathing.

Finding the Answers

If the tonsils or adenoids are causing significant airway obstruction, they should be removed. Sometimes a surgical procedure to correct an abnormal nasal septum solves the airway problem. Tracheostomy or creating a breathing hole in the neck occasionally is needed when the obstruction is due to airway closure or narrowing not caused by enlarged adenoids or tonsils. During the day, the hole is closed and covered by a collar. Oral devices are now becoming available which keep the tongue from flopping backwards, when that's the major problem.

Weight reduction to correct obesity and management of allergies may be crucial nonsurgical treatments in some children. The management of allergies might include a trial of a diet without cow's milk, making the bedroom dust-free by using large air purifiers, reducing molds by using dehumidifiers, or getting rid of pets. Nightly administration of decongestants or antihistamines sometimes are needed to reduce the allergy symptoms. Often, intranasal steroid sprays are used to keep the nasal airway open; this treatment avoids the side effects of oral decongestants. A "snore ball," which is a small glass marble or half of a rubber toy ball sewn or attached with a Velcro strap in the midback region, will prevent a back snorer from sleeping on his back.

Enjoying the Cure

When treatment restores normal breathing during sleep, the loud snoring, daytime sleepiness, morning headaches, and all other problems either disappear or are reduced. Sleep

OBSTRUCTIVE SLEEP APNEA

SNORING, DIFFICULT BREATHING, OR
MOUTH BREATHING WHEN ASLEEP

↓

DISTURBED SLEEP

ABNORMAL SLEEP SCHEDULE
BRIEF SLEEP DURATIONS
SLEEP FRAGMENTATION (PROTECTIVE AROUSALS)
NAP DEPRIVATION
PROLONGED LATENCY TO SLEEP

↓

BEHAVIORAL, DEVELOPMENTAL & ACADEMIC PROBLEMS

REVERSIBLE

FIGURE 9: POOR QUALITY BREATHING CAUSES PROBLEMS

patterns and electrocardiogram abnormalities return to normal. These changes are rapid and dramatic. For example, in one report, a 13-month-old boy had a standardized development score of 11 months before surgery, but during the five months after surgery, his score had jumped to the 20-month level!

Remember, sleep deficits may directly cause behavioral, developmental or academic problems. These problems are *reversible*, when the sleep deficits are corrected (see Figure 9).

One word of caution: Once children are cured of their snoring or their allergies are under control, if the problem has been longstanding, then bad social or academic habits or chronic stresses in the family or school will still require the continuous attention of professionals, such as psychologists, tutors, or family therapists. The treated child is now a more rested child, however, and he is now in a better position to respond to this extra effort.

Hyperactive Behavior

Educators and parents have used different terms to describe children with hyperactive behavior, but the current popular diagnoses are "attention deficit disorder" or the commonly used term "hyperactivity." Hyperactive children are not usually thought to be related to snorers or children with severe allergies, although they have similar academic problems and characteristically poor sleep patterns.

Yet restless sleep, or increased amounts of movement during sleep, have been documented in hyperactive children. Could these turned-on school-aged children be cranked-up from chronic, poor sleep habits starting in infancy?

I studied a group of boys from ages 4 to 8 months. Only boys were included, because most hyperactive school-aged children are boys. The infant boys in my study also had active sleep patterns—they moved throughout the night in a restless fashion with many small movements of the hands, feet, or eyes. They also had difficult-to-manage temperaments: They were irregular, withdrawing, had high intensity, were slowly adaptable, and were moody. This temperamental cluster also is thought to be common among hyperactive children. The results of my study showed that infant boys at age 5 months with more difficult temperaments and active sleep patterns also had briefer attention spans. Perhaps their motors were racing so fast, day and night, that they couldn't sleep quietly at night or quietly concentrate for prolonged periods when awake during the day.

Another study I did was performed on preschool children, at age 3 years. It also showed that children who had increased motor activity when awake had a physically active sleep pattern. A child with active sleep patterns was more likely to be described in the following terms from the Conners' Questionnaire used to help diagnose hyperactivity:

1. Restless or overactive
2. Excitable, impulsive

CONGENITAL: ↑RHYTHMICITY/↑PERSISTENCE
(↑MOOD, ↑ADAPTABILITY)

↓

IMPAIRED LEARNING   HOW TO FALL
ASLEEP UNASSISTED

↓

CUMULATIVE SLEEP LOSS

↓

CHRONIC FATIGUE

↓

↑NEUROTRANSMITTERS

↓

ACQUIRED: ↑ACTIVITY/↑INTENSITY (↑MOOD, ↑ADAPTABILITY)

FIGURE 10: TRANSFORMATION OF TEMPERAMENT CHARACTERISTICS
ASSOCIATED WITH BRIEF SLEEP DURATIONS

3. Disturbs other children
4. Fails to finish things he starts—short attention span
5. Constantly fidgeting
6. Inattentive, easily distracted
7. Demands must be met immediately—easily frustrated
8. Cries often and easily
9. Mood changes quickly and drastically
10. Temper outbursts, explosive and unpredictable behavior

Figure 10 summarizes my research suggesting how a
transformation could take place from a colicky/difficult temperamental boy with brief sleep durations to a hyperactive
school-aged child. The upgoing arrows mean that high ratings for rhythmicity signify irregularity and high ratings for
persistence signify short attention spans. These infant traits
are replaced by hyperactivity and increased intensity as the

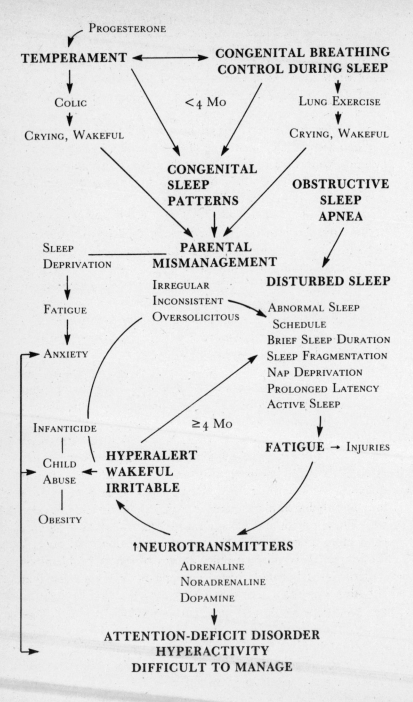

FIGURE 11: Disturbed Sleep

child becomes more fatigued. As an infant, the child would have been negative in mood and slowly adaptable due to brief sleep durations, and would have remained so at age 3 years.

Such children never learned how to fall asleep unassisted and had accumulated a chronic sleep loss which caused chronic fatigue. As previously discussed in Chapter 3, this long-lasting fatigue turned such children on, made them more active night and day, and interfered with learning.

Learning may suffer, then, in kids who do not sleep well, because they breathe poorly during sleep or sleep too little and in turn suffer from chronic fatigue which causes hyperactivity.

Figure 11 summarizes this entire cycle. It shows how crying and sleeping problems present at birth can trigger parental mismanagement. Parental mismanagement or breathing problems during sleep can in turn cause disturbed sleep, elevated neurotransmitters, and a more aroused, alert, wakeful, irritable child. This turned-on state directly causes even more disturbed sleep, because of heightened arousal levels. It also may indirectly cause parents to misperceive their child as not needing much sleep: "Johnny just won't quit—he certainly doesn't seem to be running out of gas."

All of these factors in combination—the fatigued child who is too alert to sleep well, plus irregular, inconsistent, fatigued/anxious parents—conspire to produce a child who may find it difficult to concentrate, who may seem hyperactive, or who may have behavioral problems that make him difficult to manage. These school and behavioral problems make the parents even more anxious, and the cycle continues on, and on . . . Of course, there may be other causes of school problems or hyperactivity, but disturbed sleep appears to be *one* cause that is both preventable and treatable.

CHAPTER 11

Special Events and Concerns

As if growing up were not hard enough, there are inevitable events that might significantly disrupt your child's healthy sleep habits. Other special concerns, such as frequent injuries, may well be the *result* of unhealthy sleep habits. Here are some examples.

Moving

The only thing worse than moving is moving with children. You pack, they unpack. You clean up, they make a mess. Here is one account of how moving upset the child's routine.

Nicholas Knew This Was the Time to Really Stick It to Me

Nicholas had an established sleep pattern before we moved, but after . . . !

Bill and I started packing up the apartment about two months before we moved; Nicholas's response to this preparing to move was to change his sleep pattern. But we weren't too worried, since we assumed it would change back once we were moved and settled. It didn't. We moved when he was about 8 months old. Well, by the time Nicholas was 9 months, I needed another chat with Dr. Weissbluth to discuss Nicholas's frequent night wakings.

My husband was with my father for the opening of trout season that weekend, and Nicholas knew this was the time to really stick it to me.

Nicholas had had a cold for weeks. Thursday night he cried from 7 until 11. I went in several times to try to calm him. I knew that what I should be doing was turning off, or down to a whisper, the intercom and letting him work it out, but I thought the cold had something to do with it. Dr. Weissbluth said the cold *did* have something to do with it—plain and simple, Nicholas needed more sleep to shake it, but just as important was the routine Nicholas had to learn (again!). The doctor made me promise not to go in the room at all until between 5 and 7 A.M. "Load him up with Desitin and hugs and kisses and close the door." The first night the crying stopped after an hour and a half, but by Saturday Nicholas only cried for five minutes. Now he will perhaps play for at least a few minutes, then before I know it, his head is down and we have a quiet happy baby 12 hours later!

Your general goal is to maintain as regular and consistent a pattern as reasonably possible when preparing for and following a move. If your child is young, say less than a year old, quickly reestablish the bedtime rituals and sleep patterns that worked best before the move. Be firm and after a day or two for adjustment to the new surroundings, ignore any protest crying that may have evolved from the irregularity and inconsistency during the move. If your child is older, say a few years, go slower. Fears of newness, excitement over novelty, uncertainty regarding further changes may create resistance with naps, difficulty falling asleep at night, or night waking as new problems. Be gentle, firm, and decisive. Reassurance, extra time at night, night lights, and open doors may have a calming or soothing effect. Be somewhat consistent in controlling this extra comfort so that the child does not learn that it is completely open-ended. For the older child, consider using a kitchen timer to control the amount of "extra" time you are going to spend with him. The timer helps the child to learn to expect that mom or dad will leave for the night after a predictable time period. Anxiety or fear in your child regarding a move is natural, normal, and not something which should unduly alarm you. After several days, start a deliberate social weaning process to encourage a return to your old, healthy sleep habits. Gradually reduce the duration on the timer. This should usually take no longer than several days in most instances.

Vacations

Think of a vacation with your child as sort of a semi-holiday. After all, you may spend a lot of time babysitting among the palms and on sun-drenched beaches. I have spent many hours building simple sand castles, trying to keep one eye on the castle architecture and the other eye on a nonswimmer jumping over small waves. This intense concentration is not very relaxing!

Try to flow with your child; be flexible if you want to, forget schedules, try to have as much fun as possible, and don't worry much if your kids become tired. Irregularity and spontaneity are part of what makes vacations fun.

But when you return home, you know—back to the basics; it's boot camp again with all the regular routines. Within a few days, if you are firm, consistent, and regular, your child will learn quickly that the vacation is over. If your child had been well rested prior to this vacation, expect only one rough, crazy recovery day of protest crying. Trying to gradually soothe your child back to her previous good sleep routine over several days often fails because the child fights sleep for the pleasure of your soothing efforts.

You may avoid having a "reentry" problem by careful planning, as did Claire's parents.

Claire's First Vacation

Having spent our previous vacations as young marrieds jaunting lightheartedly to Hawaii, the Canadian Rockies, England, Europe, and New England without an itinerary or reservations, it was with some trepidation that my husband, Tom, and I launched off on our first vacation as new parents with our 8-month-old daughter in tow. As a working couple, we were unable to face the prospect of missing the pleasure of our daughter's company while on vacation—and yet, how to arrange it so that we could enjoy both her and our holiday!

The answer for us proved to be limiting our wanderings to a resort where we could ensconce ourselves for an entire week—quite a change, considering that on our previous trips the longest we had perched in one locale had been only two or three nights! We chose a family-oriented beach resort (only one time zone away), which was conveniently located near a major city of historic interest that we had never visited. We decided to spend our money on above-average accommodations, knowing that with an 8-month-old, we would be spending more time there and might as well make ourselves comfortable. We selected a two-bedroom/two-bath condo with a kitchen and large living/dining area, which ensured that Claire's naps and bedtimes wouldn't interfere with our activities—and vice versa.

Our daily schedule certainly was not as hectic as when we were just a couple, but we did manage to relax more and have a great deal of fun. We tried to preserve Claire's two-nap-a-day schedule and approximate bedtime hour, but be flexible, too. A typical day for us would begin with breakfast at the condo followed by a walk on the magnificent beach looking for shells and sand dollars. Because the sand is firmly packed there, we could push Claire's stroller right along on the beach, which allowed us to venture further than if she'd been in the backpack. About midmorning, we'd return to the condo for Claire's nap. One of us would lounge on the sundeck while Claire was sleeping, while the other would be free to go swimming, shopping, cycling or whatever.

After lunch—either a picnic at the park/playground near our condo or at the snack bar by the pool, we'd pack up the car and head to a nearby attraction. Claire would promptly fall asleep in her car seat for her afternoon nap, a habit we never practiced back home, and be ready to go again after we reached our various destinations about an hour or so later. In this way, we visited the local historic district, a famous antebellum plantation, and a World War II aircraft carrier and other vessels at a floating naval museum. By late afternoon, we'd head home, perhaps picking up some shrimp or the catch-of-the-day at the seafood shop en route.

We ventured out to dinner with Claire on several occasions, picking one of the resort's family-oriented restaurants and arriving early (both before the larger crowds and to be closer to her typical suppertime). After another walk on the beach, we'd follow Claire's bedtime routine, and put her to sleep at about her normal hour in the rented full-size crib in her own room. We then had time to enjoy some wine, read, catch up on our conversation, or plan the next day's activities.

Yes, it was quite a different style of holiday for us! But, the new scenery was fascinating and with some advance planning (like arranging for the crib rental and packing a special box with Claire's "walker," backpack, and favorite toys), we all were able to enjoy our first vacation as a family.

Frequent Illnesses

Night wakings routinely follow frequent illnesses. First, let's have a clear understanding of what is happening. Videotapes of healthy young children in their homes at night show that many awakenings occur throughout the night, but the children usually return to sleep without any help. Fever can alter sleep patterns and can cause light sleep or more frequent awakenings. So it is not surprising that a painful illness with fever, such as an ear infection, causes an increased number of night wakings. These more frequent and prolonged arousals often require your intervention to soothe or calm the child back to sleep. Your child might now begin to associate your hugging, kissing, or holding at night with returning to sleep. This learning process might then produce an alteration in the child's behavior or expectations that continue long after the infection passes. Now we have a problem; usually it's called "night waking."

Actually, awakening at night is *not* the problem. As we have seen, spontaneous awakenings are normal, as are increased awakenings with fever. Naturally, parents should go to their sick children at night. The real problem now is the child's learned inability or difficulty in returning to sleep unassisted, once the child is healthy and not bothered by pain or fever. You should view this development as an unhealthy habit. As you now know, prolonged and uninterrupted sleep is as health-promoting a habit as are other health habits, such as teeth brushing or hand washing. How can you now reteach your child to develop her own resources to return to sleep after awakening? Remember, parents are teachers and we teach health habits, even if the child might not initially cooperate or appreciate our efforts. Here are three options.

Option One: You might decide that since the child is frequently ill and you can't let him down when he needs you, you will always respond and wait for the child to "outgrow" this habit. The problem with this option is that the awakenings initially tend to become more frequent, because your child learns to enjoy your company at night. After all, who wants to be alone in a boring, dark, quiet room in the middle of the night? Eventually, months or years later, the child sleeps through the night and the parents can congratulate themselves for always having attended to their child's crying at night. You have, however, paid a price. Parents following this course of action often become sleep deprived or chronically fatigued, and occasionally feel resentful toward the child for not appreciating their dedicated efforts. Additionally, the sleep fragmentation and sleep deprivation in the child often produce a more irritable, aroused, agitated, hyperexcitable behavior in the child, *because the child is always fighting chronic fatigue and drowsiness*.

Option Two: You might try on your own to go to your child at night only when the child is really sick and to leave the child alone at night when the child is healthy. This is a hazardous strategy that often fails, because you often are uncertain whether frequent illness represents painful, serious problems or minor concerns. After all, at 7 P.M. you might decide that your child has only a minor common cold and that you are going to ignore his crying, but by 2 A.M. you begin to worry about the possibility of an ear infection. Is it still reasonable to ignore the crying? What usually occurs is intermittent reinforcement: You sometimes go to your child and sometimes do not go to your child. This behavior generally teaches your child to cry longer and louder when he awakens at night, because the child learns that only loud and persistent crying will bring his parents. Quiet or brief crying often fails to get the parents' attention.

Option Three: Work closely with your pediatrician to devise a reasonable strategy whereby frequent visits or phone calls permit a clearer distinction between nonserious common colds and more distressing or disturbing illnesses. Generally speaking, the child's playfulness, sociability, activity, and appetite during the day are good clues; common colds do not cause much change in your child's behavior when awake. Then, in a planned and deliberate fashion, your child is left alone more and more at night, so that he learns to return to sleep without your help. When an acute illness develops that is associated with high fever or severe pain, of course, do that which most comforts the child, both night and day. But when the acute phase of this illness is over, start again to give the child less and less attention at night. Remember, most children sleep through most common colds; with your pediatrician's help, you can learn to distinguish between habit crying occurring with a common cold and more painful crying associated with a serious and painful, acute infection.

Mother's Return to Work

Some adults develop a sensitivity to children's needs and appreciate the benefits of regularity, consistency, and structure in child care activities. Some do not. The quality of the caretaker is what is important, not whether the person is or is not the biologic parent.

Do not assume that when mother returns to work outside the home your child will automatically suffer in the quality of her sleep habits. Keep data, track the schedule of naps when she is cared for by someone else, watch for signs of tiredness in the early evening that might suggest nap deprivation, and become aware of your own feelings.

Please don't let your guilt about being away so much during the day cause you to keep the child up too late, to reinforce night wakings for sweet nocturnal private time with your baby, to cause nap deprivation on weekends when you cram in too many activities. Please don't let household errands, chores, or nonessential social events rob you and your child of unstructured, low-intensity playtime.

PRACTICAL POINT

To help your child sleep better during natural room changes such as vacations, moves, or bringing her to your workplace, try to build an environment of familiarity by using certain cues *only* for sleeping:

> The same bumper pads
> The same music box
> The same stuffed animal or blanket
> A lamb's wool blanket
> A spray of perfume

The child will then learn to associate these sensations with falling asleep, and this will help reduce the disruptive effect of the novelty of any new surroundings. None of these items will work in the absence of regularity and consistency of parent care.

Injuries

Injuries occur to children of all ages. Some can—or should—be prevented, some cannot. Examples of preventable injuries include leaving a 4-month-old infant alone on a changing table from which she falls, poisonings occurring when safety seals are not used or medicines are left lying around, or electrical shocks from uncovered wall sockets. A nonpreventable injury is truly an accident, for example, those resulting from an earthquake or a lightning bolt.

The truth is, though—and I realize this sounds harsh to

many parents' ears—that most so-called childhood "accidents" are really preventable injuries that occur because of parental neglect or the lack of parental forethought. These injuries can be one consequence of home routines that create tired children—and tired *families*.

But wait, what about the child's responsibility? Is there such a thing as an "accident-prone" child? To determine if traits within the child cause him to suffer frequent injuries, various studies have examined babies before the injuries start to occur. (After a child has had several injuries, a "halo" effect develops and adults are more likely to perceive traits in the child—clumsiness, lack of self-control, etc.—that "explain" why he has had so many injuries.)

One study included 200 babies who were evaluated between 4 and 8 months of age. Some of the infants were difficult to manage. As we saw earlier, these infants were called "difficult" because they were irregular, low in adaptability, initially withdrawing, and negative in mood. During the next two years, difficult babies were much more likely to have cuts requiring sutures than were babies with the opposite or easy-to-manage temperaments. This study showed that during the first two years of life, about one-third of the difficult children had cuts deep or severe enough to require stitches, while only 5% of easy babies had similar cuts.

Remember also my data—at 4 to 8 months of age, the difficult babies slept about three hours less than easy babies, and at age 3 years, the difference was about one and one-half hours. By age 3, the briefer the sleep, the more active, excitable, impulsive, inattentive, and easily distracted the child appeared—the perfect description of an "accident-prone" child. Little wonder, then, that these tired children fell more often, sustaining deep cuts.

Obviously, for both the "difficult" kids and all other children, chronic fatigue can lead to more injuries, such as cuts and falls. More sleep is the remedy.

Another study which supports this fatigue–injury connection included over 7,000 children who were 1 to 2 years old. Researchers compared those children who frequently woke up at night with those who slept through the night. They defined night waking as waking five or more nights a week plus one or more of the following traits: (a) waking three or more times a night, (b) waking for more than 20 minutes during the night, or (c) going into the parents' room. Among the night wakers, 40% had injuries requiring medical attention compared to only 17% of the good sleepers. The parents of the children who were night wakers reported that they immediately went to their child when they heard a cry to prevent further crying. There was a tendency for the mothers of the night wakers to feel more irritable in general and "out of control." One sign of family tension was that these mothers felt unable to confide in their husbands; the association of marital difficulties with disturbed sleep has been mentioned in many studies.

Maybe the parents who don't supervise sleep patterns to meet sleep needs are the same ones who don't supervise children at play to protect physical safety. The message is clear: If your child is often injured, it's not necessarily because he is careless or clumsy—he may be exhausted instead.

I have cared for many children who were so overtired that they fell down only a stair or two or fell from a very low height. But because they hit their head and were later noted to be sleepy or wobbly, the parents worried about a head injury or concussion. They needed more sleep, not a CAT scan!

Overweight

Difficult-to-manage children fuss and cry a lot. One way to respond to their demands is to put food in their mouths. This certainly quiets them. Coincidentally, their fussiness also might ensure their survival in times when food is scarce. As mentioned previously, this was shown to be the case among Masai people of East Africa during drought conditions in 1974. But in a study conducted in a white, middle-class Pennsylvania pediatric practice, the more difficult babies tended to be fatter babies. Perhaps this connection between fussiness and being fed sets the stage for obesity in later years.

In my own pediatric practice, fat babies are almost always

tired babies. That's because their mothers have incorrectly attributed their babies' crying to hunger instead of crying from fatigue. The mothers are always feeding their babies, then telling me that their babies can't sleep because they're always hungry! The major point here? Overfeeding the crying child to keep him quiet could cause unhealthy obesity.

This overfeeding habit may actually begin innocently enough in some children at 3 to 4 months of age, when nutritional feedings in the middle of the night give way to recreational feedings. Later, the bottle or breast is used as a pacifier and the frequent sipping and snacking causes excessive weight gain. Please try to become sensitive to the difference between nutritive and nonnutritive feeding. Overdoing milk or juice bottles is a common way babies learn to not "like" eating solids. After all, they are getting calories, so they have no appetite to motivate them to eat solid foods when they are older.

Q: If I give my child a bottle at naps or at bedtime, will I make him fat? When should I not include a bottle in the bedtime ritual?

A: Most babies and even older children are comforted by sucking or sipping a bottle before falling asleep. There is no harm in doing this and there is no particular age when you should stop as long as (a) you prop the baby, not the bottle, so he drinks in your arms, (b) the rate of weight gain is not too fast, and (c) frequent or prolonged feedings are not part of a sleep problem.

Child Abuse

Let's get one ugly fact out in the open so we can see what our true feelings are. No more pretending. When we are very, very tired of hearing our baby cry at night to fight sleeping, we would like to shut him up. We don't act on our feelings, we don't harm our babies. But at nighttime, the thought might have occurred to us: "What if I weren't so much in control, might I . . . ?"

The tired, difficult-to-manage infant, whose howling at night will not stop, becomes a target or "elicitor" for abuse or infanticide. Crying is the behavior that seems to trigger child abuse in some parents, and crying at night instead of sleeping is the historical setting for infanticide.

So when your baby gets all cranked up late at night with her desperate, angry, or relentless screaming, when she should be asleep, and you feel like a tightly wound spring, don't be surprised if you feel that you want to "get even" or "shut her up for good." If you and your child don't get the sleep you need, you may have experienced these intense feelings of anger, resentment, or ill will toward your child.

Contact the following organizations, social workers at local hospitals, or your pediatrician if you feel the need for help.

Parents Anonymous
(800) 421-0353

National Committee for the Prevention of Child Abuse
(312) 663-3520

Parents Without Partners
(800) 638-8078

CHAPTER 12

A Sleep Disorder: My Child?

by Patricia Della-Selva, Ph.D.

What do we mean by a sleep disorder? To be honest, this is usually defined by the parent. When the child's sleep, or lack thereof, becomes troublesome to the parent, it gets identified as a problem. Because you are reading this book, you probably already have decided a problem may exist and are looking for help.

At some point in time, almost all children have trouble either going to sleep or waking at night. Perhaps they can't settle down after a particularly exciting day or have trouble saying goodnight following a separation from Mommy. Disruptions in a young child's life are bound to affect his eating and sleeping habits for a while, and we expect this. We comfort the child and it soon passes.

We had a recent example of this in our own home. My 2½-year-old daughter became fearful of being alone at night when we moved to a new house. She would call me back several times after being put to bed, wanting "just one more song" or another "night-night story." I realized her need for extra assurance and provided it. After several weeks, she had settled into the house but had gotten into the habit of calling me and resisting sleep. She would cry and say she was scared, but as soon as I'd arrive, she'd laugh. It became clear that she had learned how to get me to respond to her protests. I told her that she no longer seemed frightened, but just wanted to stay up late. I told her it was bedtime and that I'd see her in the morning. She was angry at being found out and put up quite a protest, but I remained firm and didn't return to her room. This isn't as easy as it may sound. She screamed on and off for 40 minutes and really tested our resolve, but we held out. It worked! The very next evening our regular routine was restored. If I hadn't been able to determine when she was really frightened and when she was play-acting, this could have dragged on endlessly.

The move to our new house was the obvious cause in this example, but many parents complain of chronic sleep problems in their children with no idea whatsoever regarding its cause. Since all children have trouble with sleep at some time in their early lives, we as parents need to find ways to handle it before it becomes a chronic problem. In preceding chapters, Dr. Weissbluth has outlined clear, well-researched guidelines to help you and your family enjoy more silent nights. Some parents can't seem to make them work. What gets in their way?

Whose Problem Is This, Anyway?

Let's begin by talking about the feelings that surface in you as your baby develops. Often, our own very early memories return when we become parents. Thoughts and feelings that may have been buried for years arise when we have our own babies. Sometimes, without even thinking, we find ourselves saying things we never dreamed we'd utter. We vowed not to be like our parents, but when asked "Why?" for the tenth time by our curious 2-year-old, we find ourselves saying, "Because I said so." Sometimes old feelings about our own childhood get in the way of our being effective parents.

You may find what I'm saying painful, but bear with me. If you can understand what you're feeling and why, you'll be well on your way to resolving your baby's sleep problem.

While it seems to the casual observer that the problem of going to sleep is clearly the baby's, I have frequently found that the mother—as baby's primary caregiver—subtly and unconsciously either encourages wakefulness or prevents the development of independent self-soothing in her child. Here is just one example.

A professional who returned to work after a three-month maternity leave felt very guilty about the limited amount of time she had to spend with her new baby. She kept him up late and always responded to his calls at night. At the age of 18 months, her son still failed to sleep through the night. Upon reflection, she admitted that she cherished these times alone with her baby and wouldn't want to see them end. Her need to have contact with her baby and her guilt over leaving him during the day prevented her from allowing her baby to learn to sleep on his own. As our talk continued, she said her husband was now refusing to have any more children and she realized her son would be her only child. Now she clung to him and this period of "babyhood" even more tenaciously, because she knew she would never again have the chance to experience this special closeness. She required some professional help to separate her needs from those of her baby and to learn to behave in his best interest, while dealing with her own feelings and problems in an appropriate way.

Marital Problems

Another type of problem that can wind up contributing to baby's sleepless nights is within the marriage itself. In fact, marital problems are frequently present in the families of the children I've seen who have sleep disorders. Often, the woman feels unloved and unappreciated by her husband and seeks solace in her child. This was dramatically demonstrated by one mother who would leave her husband's bed to go sleep with her baby, who was waking in the night. This mother's view was: My baby needs me, wants me, and is happy to see me when I enter the room. This mother felt none of this warm, loving acceptance from her husband, so the lure of her baby's cry was too much for her to resist.

In this example, the mother's own needs colored her judgment. Unconsciously she was using the baby to soothe herself, but she was convinced consciously that she was being a good mother by responding to every call. Her husband couldn't very well get angry with her for being such a devoted mother, so a confrontation was avoided. This points out the other crucial area of difficulty I've noticed in these mothers—their inability to express anger directly.

Anger

A third area in which mother's problems can contribute to baby's sleep problems is the inability to express anger. Even successful professional women can feel dependent and frightened in an intimate relationship and fear that any expression of anger will disrupt or even destroy it. By being continually preoccupied with her baby, the woman expresses her anger and dissatisfaction with her husband in an indirect fashion. Not only is this destructive for the marriage itself, it also hampers the baby's development.

The Need to Be Needed and Loved

As you can see from these examples, several themes recur again and again in these women. The central issue seems to be a strong need to be needed and loved. Some women have a poorly developed sense of self and are, therefore, overly dependent on others for feelings of self-worth. If their baby is unhappy and making a fuss, they feel personally inadequate and will do whatever is necessary in order to quiet him down— and make them *both* feel better. I have found, too, that many women fear being alone and need another's presence to feel safe. Nighttime can be especially difficult, and some women may go to their children for soothing and companionship if their husband is away or emotionally unavailable.

How About Father?

Why am I addressing myself to mothers? In this country, the great majority of babies are cared for primarily by their mothers. Even though fathers are more involved than ever, very few assume the role of primary caretaker. While both parents may discuss child-rearing practices, the mother is usually the one who implements these practices on a day-to-day basis. This does not mean, however, that fathers don't influence their children or contribute to their baby's sleep problems. Here are only a few cases that illustrate how they certainly can and do.

A mother came to me recently for advice regarding her 2-year-old son, who cried for "Momma" throughout the night and demanded her presence before returning to sleep. She felt this was becoming a real problem and wanted to correct it. A plan was devised which involved her telling her son that she would no longer be coming to him at night. The parents agreed to let him cry, if that's what it would take. But the father backed out after hearing his son cry for 10 minutes. He began to yell at his wife, saying, "Are you really going to let him cry like this? If you don't go to him, I will!" Needless to say, the plan went down the drain and night waking continued.

Another father in a similar situation yelled, "I have to work in the morning. I need my sleep. Go shut him up!" As these examples illustrate, *both* parents have feelings about child rearing, and they need to agree and *stick together* if their plan is going to work. I hope that both mothers and fathers will read this and work out a strategy for solving their child's sleep difficulties together. Children gain a great deal of security from the knowledge that parents are unified, rather than split, on important issues.

The Whole Family Gets Involved

As the divorce rate has soared, remarriages have become commonplace and stepfamilies are more prevalent than ever. When a new baby enters the picture, frequently the older siblings from the previous marriages have to deal with the new arrival. As a mother in this situation, you may worry that if you allow yourself to be absorbed with your new infant, the others will feel neglected and get angry. On the other hand, you may receive all sorts of advice from your older children about how to handle the new baby. You may try to please everyone, and end up feeling like no one is happy. One woman told me she continued to go to her baby at night long after she would have if he were her only child. She had teenage stepchildren in the house, and didn't want to keep them up. She went to her baby "to keep him quiet." Things certainly do get complicated in these situations, but solutions can be found.

It would be great if everyone could sit down, talk about the situation, agree on a solution, and carry it out. But things aren't always so easily resolved. You, as parents, have to decide what's best and let the older children know about your decision. They should be told to abide by your wishes, even if they don't agree with them. They'll eventually get their turn at parenting.

Whose Advice Do I Follow?

I've had many parents ask me how to determine which route to follow in this or other areas of child care. It seems as though every "expert" has a different opinion and technique. Parents today are often alone in the demanding task of child rearing, having moved away from their family and friends, and they rely on books and professionals for help. One mother said she understood the position being taken in this book, but worried about letting her baby cry because she had read elsewhere that you should "never let your baby cry."

Penolope Leach, who wrote the popular book, *Your Baby and Child From Birth to Five*, even contradicts herself on this issue. At one point she says: "Ignore a brief protest on being left— any sensible, well-attached baby is bound to announce that he would prefer you to stay with him." Later she addresses herself to the issue of ignoring a toddler's cry at bedtime by saying it won't work. She says that the child "can't bear your going away" and that leaving him alone at sleeptimes gives the message: "It's no good you're crying because I'm not going to come back no matter how sad you are." First of all, in many cases of crying at bedtime, the cries are those of angry protest, not sadness.

Leach also raises the issue of the message that the parents communicate by their actions. If you are affectionate at bedtime and confident that it is in his best interest to have your baby learn to sleep on his own, you will convey that message rather than one of abandonment, as Leach suggests. Being alone is not the same as being abandoned, and both you and your baby can understand that.

Some experts try to simplify the complex task of childrearing by concentrating on one principle or guideline. La Leche League provides both useful information and much-needed support to nursing mothers, but the organization oversimplifies the task of development by using one parental response—that of offering the breast—as the answer to all dilemmas. La Leche addresses the baby's need for love and nurturance to the exclusion of all other needs. Babies are complicated creatures and they need to be able to be alone, to be angry, and even to be sad at times without being forced into "blissful union" with a mother who can't tolerate hearing her baby cry.

Recent research has been done on babies who are unable to fall asleep on their own and require holding in order to do so. It was discovered that the mothers of these babies wouldn't allow them to separate, to grow, and to learn how to do things on their own. This discouraged the baby's attempts to soothe himself by sucking his thumb or using a pacifier. These babies were described as "addicted to mother's presence." Some recent attention has been directed at adults who become "addicted" to their lovers. It's my suspicion that an addiction to mother, like the one described in this research, is at the root of this problem as well.

How Can Theory Help?

We no longer need to rely on old wive's tales or the latest fashion in child-rearing advice to guide our behavior with regard to child care. Great strides have been made in research concerning babies over the past 20 years, and the findings can be of great help. It's my belief that most parents will respond when given clear, accurate information along with a feeling that they are being supported in this complex and anxiety-arousing job of parenting. In this light, let me briefly review what we know about babies and the process of separation as it unfolds in the first few years of life.

The *"Hatching Process"*

According to the research conducted by Margaret Mahler, the first signs of individuation, or development as an individual, normally occur at the beginning of the baby's fourth month. Up until that time, baby and mother are as one. The infant is totally dependent on the mother for all his physical and psychological needs. Optimally, the baby's needs and the mother's ability to give are balanced. During the late stages of pregnancy and the first few months of extrauterine life, the normal mother finds that she is preoccupied with her baby. This allows her to tune into and get to know her baby in a special way. In addition to providing warmth and food, the mother provides the vital function of soothing the infant, who is being bombarded with stimulation from both internal (hunger) and external (noise) sources. By responding immediately to your baby's cry, you are providing a basis for trust essential in healthy emotional development. The result of a successful "dance" between you and your baby is that the world is felt to be manageable rather than an overwhelming or threatening place.

The First Few Months

During the first few months of life, babies sleep a lot and do so according to their own needs and rhythms. Research suggests this cannot and should not be altered. When your baby is tired and fretful, he needs your soothing ministrations to lull him to sleep. Being left alone to cry is overwhelming for an infant. The baby is absolutely dependent on you for soothing and has no internal resources on which to rely. Only by having the soothing provided externally on a reliable basis will your baby eventually be able to internalize it in order to calm himself and feel a safe, whole being even when alone.

Given the total dependence of newborn infants, one cannot speak of an infant without referring to and understanding the mother. The physical process of birth does not coincide with psychological birth. In her pioneering studies of mother–infant pairs, Mahler found that mothers' conscious and, more importantly, unconscious attitudes, had a significant impact on the course and outcome of the "hatching" process that begins in the fourth month of life. At that time, bodily dependence decreases and the baby's focus gradually changes from the inner world to the world around him. The baby shows interest in objects and pursues goals. At this time your baby will start to push away from you in order to explore your face. He'll express active pleasure in the use of his entire body. If your baby has had an optimal experience of unity with you in the first, symbiotic phase of development, he will take your presence for granted and play confidently at your feet.

Some mothers find this first step toward independence painful, and interpret the baby's pushing away as rejection. While some become angry and withdraw emotionally, others cling to their babies and try to prolong the feeling of oneness they so enjoyed. It is these mothers who seem to have the greatest difficulty putting their babies down to sleep. They continue to feel that their babies must fall asleep before being put down. While they consciously feel this is essential for the baby, it has become clear, as I've explored these issues with them, that it is their need to feel needed that motivates their hanging onto the baby.

In the first three months of her life, my youngest daughter slept a good deal. She tended to wake up at around 6 A.M., and fall right back to sleep after being nursed. She'd get up again around 8 A.M., sleep again from 10 to 12 A.M. and 2 to 4 P.M., and was in for the night at 7 P.M. It seemed she was content to just eat and sleep. Between 3 and 4 months, she became far more sociable and playful. I noticed that she began to have difficulty falling asleep. At first we were perplexed, because the child who had always slept so much was now fighting sleep. All my holding and rocking seemed in vain. I soon came to realize that she was confused. Her growing awareness of the world and desire to explore it were at odds with her need to sleep. My typical method of holding her until she dropped off wasn't working, because her closeness to me was now stimulating her curiosity and desire to interact. Her lack of sleep was taking its toll and she became very cranky. I decided that I needed to put her down in her crib when I saw signs of sleepiness. She cried for a minute or two, but the familiarity of the crib and the music from her mobile soon lulled her to sleep. It was clear she needed help regulating her sleep/wake cycles at this point in development, and she readily accepted the routine. Her waking hours were filled with active exploration of the environment, and her naps were consistent and restorative.

Was putting my baby down and letting her cry for a few minutes cruel? Would she feel abandoned and lose confidence in the world around her? This is what many mothers fear. In fact, by understanding the needs of a baby at this stage of development, you'll find that the opposite is true. You interfere with development when you fail to recognize your baby's growing ability to do for himself what you once did for him. This is where theory can help in a practical way.

About 4 to 9 Months

It used to be thought that babies were totally dependent upon mother for a year or more. Now we know from research that they are able to do more earlier than we ever thought possible. At this age, a baby needs and responds to regularity in his day. Be beginning to institute a reasonable nap schedule, you are making life predictable and reducing anxiety. Imagine how interminable a day must seem to a 4-month-old infant. By having a fairly routine day of meals, naps, play time, and bath you are providing a structure which can be internalized over time. Trying to impose a schedule on a 6-week-old infant will prove futile, but three months later the baby can respond to it. To be effective parents, we need to understand and respond to these changing capabilities in our babies. Yes, respecting your baby's need for regularity in his day may entail some sacrifice on your part. But adapting yourself to your baby's needs now will lay the foundation for healthy development later.

This sort of adaptation to your baby's needs does not come naturally and usually needs to be learned. A couple with children my own kids' ages proved a vivid example of this. Upon discovering the similarity in our family structure, we decided to get together with this couple and their children one afternoon. When naptime came, I put my baby to sleep and rejoined the company. They were amazed that I could just put her down. They said their 6-month-old rarely napped. They attributed this to luck and heredity, but it became clear as the day progressed that the differences between the babies reflected the differences in the way they were handled. I watched as the couple talked, played with, and fed their baby. When she began to cry, squirm, and rub her eyes, they interpreted this as a need for more active intervention. They took her on their lap and began to bounce her up and down. This worked for a few minutes, but the crying returned. Then they tried pushing her back and forth in the stroller. The baby was clearly tired and all these attempts at entertainment were causing her to get more keyed up and less able to get the sleep she needed. Babies at this age don't just fall asleep in the midst of commotion the way a newborn will. We need to understand their cues and respond accordingly.

What interfered with this couple's ability to recognize their daughter's crankiness as fatigue and put her to bed? I learned that both parents, professionals with demanding careers, worked full time and wanted to be with their children as much as possible on weekends. As much as they complained about their children's lack of sleep, it was obvious that they enjoyed the extra time this afforded them. They were not able to separate their need for time with the children from the children's need for rest. They tended to pack weekends full of visits and activities. They wanted to take them to zoos and parks and didn't want naps to interfere. What they failed to recognize was that the children were so fatigued that they couldn't enjoy or learn from these experiences. Their toddler would tend to pass out from exhaustion while riding in the stroller. Accommodating to his needs might have meant forgoing day trips until he got a little older.

Some may say you are being overly protective if you schedule around your children, but for the first two years or so this is essential to their health and wellbeing. Some professionals undertake the role of parenthood with the same gusto and ambition that made them successful in their chosen field, but it is misplaced here. Children need to develop at their own pace and will suffer if pushed to do too much, too soon. This is the other extreme of the overly protective mother we discussed earlier.

A *"Love Affair With the World"*

The next stage of development, referred to as the "practicing" phase, ushers in what's been called by Mahler the infant's "love affair with the world." It lasts from approximately 10 to 15 months. The baby's increased motor skills and exploration of the environment make this an active time, one in which sleep difficulties often arise. The baby is so taken with the world and his ability to affect it, that he won't willingly retreat. Many parents subscribe to the notion that the child knows best and will sleep when tired. I've seen parents use this excuse to justify allowing their infants to go all day without a nap. Research tells us that babies of this age continue to require naps and reasonable bedtimes, but they also may require more help in settling down than they did several months ago. Why is this? Your baby is increasingly able to determine cause and effect. You'll notice babies of this age playing endlessly with toys like "Poppin Pals," where they vividly experience the effects of their actions. This newfound ability will also affect your baby's relationship with you. Their desire to control the world, including you, is more powerful than their desire for sleep. So, it's up to you to help your baby turn off the world and go to sleep.

One mother, whose baby had always been a great sleeper, suddenly had a problem during this stage of development. The infant refused naps and prolonged sleeptime at night by calling mother back each time he was left in his crib. The first step in tackling the problem was to understand it. The baby was exercising his newfound powers of control by calling mother back when he wanted her. It was an ongoing peek-a-boo game! She decided it was time for her baby to learn the limits of his control. *She* decided on a reasonable sleep schedule and, following a lullaby, would say to her son, "It's naptime now. I'll see you in a couple of hours." At night she'd say, "I'll see you in the morning." While a prolonged period of screaming and protest was anticipated, it only lasted 10 minutes the first night and 5 minutes the second night. How can this be explained? Did this 9-month-old understand what mother was saying? Obviously he didn't comprehend the words, but mother had spoken his language—one of action, and her attitude—one of calm assurance—relayed the message. This sort of assurance is very important, because babies pick up on their mother's feelings. They will respond to any tension or ambivalence they perceive. Rather than being traumatized, as some parents fear (and Penelope Leach contends), this baby seemed happier than ever. Bedtimes were no longer a struggle, and both parent and child were able to enjoy this special closeness before bed without dreading a confrontation.

I have found that refusing to set limits and continuing a struggle with going to bed over a period of weeks and months has a more damaging effect to the parent–child relationship than a few night's crying in the process of establishing good sleep habits. There is an added benefit to settling this problem as soon as it arises. First of all, it's easier to get rid of a habit that's just forming than one that's well established. Most importantly, though, is the fact that a well-rested child enjoys his waking hours and can be at his best all day.

Now we'll get back to the task of development. Weaning your baby from his total dependence on you is the central issue when the baby is 10 to 15 months old. Weaning means more than the gradual elimination of the breast. It signals the start of baby's identity as a separate individual. Both sadness and anger can, and frequently do, accompany this period of transition. Mother needs to help her child in this process, which has been referred to as one of disillusionment. Up until now, mother has given her baby the illusion that the world is his oyster and that all needs will be satisfied immediately. This belief in things and people is necessary in infancy. But gradually. the child must discover that, while the world can provide satisfaction for some needs and wants, it does not do so automatically. A switch must occur from the notion of need to that of wish or desire. This signals an acceptance of external reality, including the awareness of other people and their feelings.

Anger Need Not Be Destructive

Learning to wait is not easy, and anger is not an uncommon response during this process. Mothers who fear anger and associate it with abandonment, can't tolerate anger in their children. They want to be loved at all times, even idealized. Without realizing it, they prevent their children from learning that anger is not destructive. By tolerating the anger and surviving it you provide reassuring proof that thoughts and feelings can't destroy. Your baby will eventually come to realize that you are neither a wicked witch nor a good fairy, but a human being. He will then be better able to accept himself as such. This may sound reasonable and it shouldn't be difficult to pull off. But, from my experience, many mothers have a great deal of trouble during this stage in their child's development. What makes it so rough?

I have found that these women have had a troubled relationship with their own mother that was never resolved, got replayed in marriage, and activated again when they themselves became mothers. A large number of them have come from divorced homes. As well as losing their father via divorce, they frequently suffered the loss of their mother through work and/or depression. Their mothers may have used them to satisfy their own emotional needs, never giving them the room they needed to develop as individuals. It is no wonder that a similar pattern gets activated when these children become women and have children of their own. They are so afraid of the loss of important relationships, that they cower in the face of confrontation and would rather give in, even to their own child, than face these feelings again.

Separation Without Trauma

The task of the next phase, called "raproachment," is for the baby to learn how to separate without trauma. Mothers need to be "emotionally available" during this period, while physically giving the child some breathing room. Donald Winnicott, a British pediatrician who was also a psychoanalyst, spoke of the ability to be alone as beginning to develop here, when the child is alone in the presence of his mother. What does that mean? It means being left alone to explore the world and discover one's own inner life, free from intrusions by mother and her needs. The alternative is what Winnicott calls a "false self." The "false self" is built up of reactions to mother's and others' needs and expectations for the child, rather than reflecting the unique individuality of the child.

Troubles Later On

Each new stage of development brings with it special problems and concerns as well as new-found abilities. The 2-year-old begins to experience fears. He now recognizes the limits of his power, and tends to feel small and helpless in a big and often confusing world. Fears can make going to sleep at night problematic.

Graduating from a crib to a bed can also cause new difficulties with sleep. While understanding and accommodation to your child at these junctures in development are necessary, your firm attitude regarding sleep will carry over to each new stage. If a good, solid sleep habit has been formed in the first year of life, all subsequent trouble spots, like fear of the dark, getting up to go to the potty, or needing a drink of water, will die out in a short time. If a sleep problem has existed from infancy, these new difficulties just get added to the existing problem and you will be faced with a complex and tenacious situation. At this point, unlike the case of a 9-month-old who is having new difficulties falling asleep due to a spurt in motor development, a simple solution is unlikely. This doesn't mean you should throw in the towel and forget about trying to find a cure for the sleep disorder. But it does mean looking at your contribution to the problem, as well as the child's, and instituting a program of change—as outlined in this book—based on your unique history together.

The fact that you're reading this book signifies a desire to begin the process of change. Understanding your baby's needs is paramount, and this book, along with others cited at the end of this book, can broaden that understanding. An understanding of your own reactions and difficulties also may be a necessary step. Further reading in this area can be of great value as well. If you find that you're still struggling with mixed feelings about letting your baby separate, you might consider professional counseling.

Books for Parents to Share with Children at Sleepy Times

Bang, M. *Ten, Nine, Eight.* New York: Picture Puffins, 1983, ages 6–36 months.

Brown, M. W. *Goodnight Moon.* New York: Harper & Row, 1947, ages 1–3.

Hoban, R. *Bedtime for Frances.* New York: Harper & Row, 1960, ages 2–6 years.

Larrick, N. *When the Dark Comes Dancing: A Bedtime Poetry Book.* New York: Philomel, 1983, ages 1-10 years.

CHAPTER 13

The Pros and Cons of Other Approaches to Sleep Problems

Notions, theories, and opinions on how to prevent or solve sleep problems abound. Let's look at some ideas published recently, and see how they stand up to the facts about children's sleep habits that we've just reviewed together in this book.

Checking: A Method of Helping Fall Asleep *(by Jo Douglas and Naomi Richman)*

The Theory:

Go into your child's room when he starts to cry; provide reassurance and comforting. "A firmness of approach, without undue sympathy or contact, is necessary." Then leave the room, even if he is still awake and continues to cry. Wait up to five minutes, then return and repeat the same procedure. Continue to do this, back and forth, until the child realizes he will not be picked up, "[he will] normally fall asleep quickly." This pattern of checking is repeated consistently each time the child cries: "He should learn within 3 or 4 nights his crying no longer achieves the desired end of getting up." This procedure is implemented after the age of 1 year, "because of the vagaries of the first year." The authors do not recommend totally leaving the child alone because the distress to the parents is unbearable. They state that the advantage of checking

— 246

is that "the regular visits reassure you that your child is safe and well." In other words, they think this is an *easier* approach for the *parents*, not a more *effective* approach for the *child*.

My Comment:

I think checking would work well for some families, but not for those families who start off with a very tired child, perhaps one who had had colic, or for some mothers who have trouble separating from their child. It is equally unbearable *not* to pick up and hug or nurse—just once. And as we've seen, once is all it takes to start the habit all over again.

Shaping an Infant to Sleep
(by Rita J. McGarr and Melbourne F. Hovel)

The Theory:

This is a single case report that describes awakening a child 15 to 30 minutes before her expected early awakening. For example, if the child usually got up at 4 A.M., the parents would awaken her at 3:45. Then, when awake, mother would nurse or cuddle before putting the child back to bed. Maternal attention, authors state, was thus associated with falling asleep, not waking and crying. Next, the scheduled awakenings would be shifted later by 15- to 30-minute intervals. If the baby spontaneously awakens earlier, respond immediately and on the next night awaken her 15 to 30 minutes before that unscheduled awakening the night before. The goal is to increase the child's length of sleep and eliminate night crying. The child in the study was 3 months old.

My Comment:

The data in this study looks good, but "the parents declined to conduct a formal follow-up measure . . . they acknowledged that [the baby] occasionally spontaneously awoke earlier than 5 A.M. . . . both parents reported that the procedures were difficult to employ." There is also the risk that the child learns to associate the cuddling and nursing with the immediate prior event, which was awakening.

Focal Feeding . . . Followed by Water and Love (by Joanne Cuthbertson and Susie Schevill)

The Theory:

Start on the third day of life by always feeding between 10 P.M. and midnight even if you have to awaken the baby. This is called the focal feeding.

The staged procedure is recommended to start around 6 weeks (when night sleep organization spontaneously begins!) or later if the baby has colic.

NIGHT 1

STEP 1: Have some water ready in a bottle.

STEP 2: Focal feeding; awake baby between 10 P.M. and midnight. Get him back to sleep quickly.

STEP : First spontaneous wake-up; father or assistant (not mother) change, wrap in blanket, settle back to bed. Do not now pick him up but sing, rock, offer a pacifier, or rock the crib.

STEP 4:
a) He fell asleep but now is up again, try to gain "further stretching time" by playing with him in your arms, walk around.
b) He did not fall asleep after 10 to 20 minutes, pick him up, play with him.

STEP 5: Having stretched the time with your baby as long as possible, offer the water that you prepared. Authors write, "A baby will quickly abandon nightime awakenings if water and love are the only reward."

STEP 6: Change diapers, try to settle him back to sleep . . . then or later, feed him (formula or nursing).

Repeat this procedure for three full nights, and if the child is sleeping better and awakening initially at 5 or 6 A.M., let him fuss for 10 to 20 minutes. If he is not sleeping better, try this procedure again in a few weeks.

My Comment:

In discussing this procedure with the first author, she told me that it worked 90% of the time, but that there was no data or survey to validate that claim. It would be worthwhile to know whether both the temporal control part (focal feeding) or the removal of positive reinforcement (the water instead of milk) are needed or whether only one item would work as well. Then the procedure would be simpler to execute and in my experience, the simpler the procedure, the more likely that parents will stick to it.

Proper Association With Falling Asleep
(by Richard Ferber)

The Theory:

A child associates certain conditions with falling asleep, such as being held in parents' arms, lying down on a living room sofa, or rocking in a swing. When put to sleep in a crib or bed, upon awakening, those certain conditions are missing, so the child has difficulty returning to sleep. The progressive approach is to not respond to the baby's cry at night when she awakens in her crib for a brief period of time, say five minutes. After crying for five minutes, the parents return and stay in the room two to three minutes, but do not pick up or rock the child. This is thought to reassure the parents and the child that all is well. Parents then leave, whether asleep or not, whether crying or not, and return in 10 minutes for the same brief interaction, if needed. After leaving, parents would return again after 15 minutes of crying for a brief curtain call. They would return every 15 minutes for a brief encounter until the child fell asleep during one of their 15-minute absences. If no crying or mild whimpering, then no return. If the child awoke later that night with hard crying, parents would repeat the original progressive routine of 5, 10, 15, 15, 15 . . . minutes of delay in response time. The second night would be a repeat performance except the progression would be 10, 15, 20, 20, 20 . . . The third night would be 15, 20, 25, 25, 25 . . . and so on. The child learns to associate falling asleep and returning to sleep in her bed or crib.

My Comment:

Whether we call this approach developing "proper associations" or "learning self-soothing skills," I'm sure this method can work. But the general problem is that it's very difficult to maintain any time schedule in the middle of the night for several nights in a consistent fashion—frustration, and exhaustion often override planning and patience.

Summary

The major problems with these other methods is that insufficient or no attention is given to the importance of naps and schedules. There is more to healthy sleep habits than not waking at night. Children who don't sleep well usually have developed this pattern as a result of parental mismanagement. Too much attention, or irregularity, or inconsistency in bedtime "policy" and routines interfered with the development of healthy sleep habits. Accepting this responsibility is the first step in developing a treatment plan. You may be uncertain whether you want to try a gradual, "fading" approach or an abrupt, "cold-turkey" extinguishing approach.

As a specialist doing research and providing consultative services for sleep problems, I could devote a great deal of time for coaching parents, helping them maintain their motivation, fine-tuning sleep schedules, and giving them encouragement to carry through a gradual approach. As a general practice pediatrician though, the time demands of a busy office make it more difficult to be as available. So when you try to decide between a gradual approach versus an abrupt approach in putting to rights your child's sleep habits, consider not only your own resolve but also the external supports that you know you can count on.

Many parents start with a gradual approach, see partial success, but then get worn down and recognize their evolving inconsistency. Feeling a bit more confident and competent, many parents then shift directions to a more abrupt approach. But some parents cannot even start to correct their child's sleeping problems at all, because the same personal stresses revolving around the child's emerging independence, marital discord and other problems with the parents that created the unhealthy sleep habits in the first place, are still present. To maintain or develop healthy sleep habits for your child, please have the courage to do what is best for your child. You will create a loving home with a happy, well-rested child with well-rested parents.

References

Chapter 1. Why Healthy Sleep Is So Important

Bernstein, D. Emde, R., and Campos, J. (1973). REM sleep in four-month infants under home and laboratory conditions. *Psychosomatic Medicine*, *35*, 322–329.

Coons, S. & Guilleminault, C. (1982). Development of sleep-wake patterns and non-rapid eye movement sleep stages during the first six months of life in normal infants. *Pediatrics*, *69*, 793–798.

Emde, R.N., Metcalf D.R. (1970). An electroencephalographic study of behavioral rapid eye movement states in the human newborn. *Journal of Nervous and Mental Disorders*, *150*, 376–386.

Fish, B. (1963). The maturation of arousal and attention in the first months of life: A study of variations in age development. *Journal of the American Academy of Child Psychiatry*, *2*, 253–270.

Harper, R.N., Leake, B., Miyahana, L., Mason, J., Hoppenbrouwers, T., Sterman, M.B., and Hodgman, J. (1981). Temporal sequencing in sleep and waking states during the first six months of life. *Experimental Neurology*, *72*, 294–307.

Jacklin, C.N., Snow, M.E., Cozahapt, M., and Maccoby, E.E. (1980). Sleep pattern development from 6 through 33 months. *Journal of Pediatric Psychology*, *5*, 295–302.

Klein, K.E., Hermann, R., Kuklinski, P., and Hans-M, W. (1977). Circadian performance rhythms: Experimental studies in air operations. In R. R. Mackie (Ed.), *Vigilance: Theory, operational performance and physiological correlants* (NATO

Conference Series III, Human Factors, Vol. 3). New York: Plenum Press.

Salzarulo, P., and Chevalier, A. (1983). Sleep problems in children and their relationship with early disturbances of the waking-sleep rhythms. *Sleep*, *6*, 47–51.

Schulz, H., Salzarulo, P., Fagioli, I., and Massetani, R. (1983). REM latency: Development in the first year of life. *Electroencephalography and Clinical Neurophysiology*, *56*, 316–322.

Still, G. F. (1931). *The History of Pediatrics*. London: Oxford University Press.

Sundell, C. E. (1922). Sleeplessness in infants. *Practitioner*, *109*, 89–92.

Chapter 2. Healthy Sleep

Sleep Duration

Anders, T. F., Carksadon, M. A., and Dement, W.C. (1980). Sleep and sleepiness in children and adolescents. *Pediatric Clinics of North America*, *27*, 29–43.

Anders, T. F., and Keener, M. A. (1985). Developmental course of nighttime sleep-wake patterns in full-term and premature infants during the first year of life: Part I. *Sleep*, *8*, 173–192.

Anders, T. F., Keener, M. A., and Kramer, H. (1985). Sleep-wake state organization, neonatal assessment and development in premature infants during the first year of life: Part II. *Sleep*, *8*, 193–206.

Parmelee, A. H., Schulz, H. R., and Disbrow, M. A. (1961). Sleep patterns of the newborn. *Journal of Pediatrics*, *58*, 241–250.

Parmelee, A. H., Wenner, W. H., and Schulz, H. R. (1964). Infant sleep patterns: From birth to 16 weeks of age. *Journal of Pediatrics*, *65*, 576–582.

Weissbluth, M. (1981). Sleep duration and infant temperament. *Journal of Pediatrics*, *99*, 817–819.

Weissbluth, M. (1984). Sleep duration, temperament, and

Conner's ratings on three-year-old children. *Journal of Developmental and Behavioral Pediatrics, 5,* 120–123.

Weissbluth, M., Poncher, J., Given, G., Schwab, J., Mervis, R., and Rosenburg, M. (1981). Sleep durations and television viewing. *Journal of Pediatrics, 99,* 486–488.

Naps

Coons, S., and Guilleminault, C. (1984). Development of consolidated sleep and wakeful period in relation to the day/ night cycle in infancy. *Developmental Medicine and Child Neurology, 26,* 169–176.

Daiss, S. R., Bertelson, A. D., and Benjamin, L. T. (1986). Napping versus resting: Effects on performance and mood. *Psychophysiology, 23,* 82–88.

Emde, R. N., and Walken, S. (1961). Longitudinal study of infant sleep: Results of 14 subjects studied at monthly intervals. *Psychophysiology, 13,* 456–461.

Folkard, S., Hume, K. I., Minors, D. S., Waterhouse, J. M., and Watson, F. L. Independence of the circadian rhythm in alertness from the sleep-wake cycle. *Nature, 313,* 678–679.

Minors, D. S., and Waterhouse, J. M. (1984). The sleep-wakefulness rhythm, exogenous and endogenous factors (in man). *Experientia, 40,* 410–416.

Wladimorva, G. (1983). Study of cyclic structure of daytime sleep in normal infants aged 2 to 12 months. *Acta physiologica et pharmacoligica Bulgarica, 9,* 62–69.

Sleep Consolidation

Bonnet, M. M. (1985). Effect of sleep disruption on sleep, performance, and mood. *Sleep, 8,* 11–19.

Coons, S., and Guilleminault, C. (1985). Motility and arousal in near miss sudden infant death syndrome. *Journal of Pediatrics, 107,* 728–732.

Stepanski, E., Lamphere, J., Badia, P., Zorick, F., and Roth, T. (1984). Sleep fragmentation and daytime sleepiness. *Sleep, 7,* 18–26.

Weissbluth, M., Davis, A. T., and Poncher, J. (1984). Night

waking in 4- to 8-month-old infants. *Journal of Pediatrics, 104,* 477–480.

Sleep Schedule

Abe, K., Sasaki, H., Takebayashi, K., Seki, F., and Roth, T. (1978). The development of circadian rhythms of human body temperature. *Journal of Interdisciplinary Cycle Research, 9,* 211–216.

Czeisler, C. A., Weitzman, E. D., and Moore-Ede, M. C. (1980). Human sleep: Its duration and organization depend on its circadian phase. *Science, 210,* 1264–1267.

Dreyfus-Brisac, C., and Monod, N. (1965). Sleep of premature and full term neonates—A polygraphic study. *Proceedings of the Royal Society of Medicine, 58,* 6–7.

Emde, R. N., Swedberg, J., and Suzuki, B. (1975). Human wakefulness and biological rhythms after birth. *Archives of General Psychiatry, 32,* 780–783.

Onishi, S., Miyazawa, G., Nishimura, Y., Sugiyama, S., Yamakawa, T., Inagaki, H., Katoh, T., Itoh, S., and Isobe, K. (1983). Postnatal development of circadian rhythm in serum cortisol levels in children. *Pediatrics, 72,* 399–404.

Reppert, S. M. (1985). Maternal entrainment of the developing circadian system. *Annals New York Academy of Science, 453,* 162–169.

Weissbluth, M. (1982). Modification of sleep schedule with reduction of night waking: A case report. *Sleep, 5,* 262–266.

The Question of the Family Bed

Elias, M. F., Nicolson, N. A., Bora, C., and Johnston, J. (1986). Sleep/wake patterns of breast-fed infants in the first 2 years of life. *Pediatrics, 77,* 322–329.

Klackenberg, G. (1982). Sleep behavior studied longitudinally. *Acta Paediatrica Scandinavia, 71,* 501–506.

Lozoff, B., Wolf, A. W., and Davis, N. S. (1984). Co-sleeping in urban families with young children in the United States. *Pediatrics, 74,* 171–182.

Lozoff, B. L., Wolf, A. W., and Davis, N. S. (1985). Sleep problems seen in pediatric practice. *Pediatrics*, *75*, 477–483.

Rosenfeld, A. A., Wenegrant, A. O., Haavik, D. K., Wenegrant, B. C., and Smith, C. R. (1982). Sleeping patterns in upper-middle-class families when the child awakens ill or frightened. *Archive of General Psychiatry*, *39*, 943–947.

Solid Foods and Feeding Habits

Beal, V. A. (1964). Termination of night feeding in infancy. *Journal of Pediatrics*, *75*, 690–692.

Deisher, R. W., and Goers, S. S. (1954). A study of early and later introduction of solids into the infant diet. *Journal of Pediatrics*, *45*, 191–199.

Grunwaldt, E., Bates, T., and Guthrie, D. (1960). The onset of sleeping through the night in infancy: Relation to introduction of solid food in the diet, birth weight and position in the family. *Pediatrics*, *26*, 667–668.

Jones, N. B., Brown, M. F., and MacDonald, L. (1978). The association between perinatal factors and later night waking. *Developmental Medicine and Child Neurology*, *20*, 427–434.

Lavie, P., Kripke, D. F., Hiatt, J. F., and Harrison, J. (1978). Gastric rhythms during sleep. *Behavioral Biology*, *23*, 526–630.

Parmelee, A. H., Wenner, W. H., and Schulz, W. R. (1964). Infant sleep patterns from birth to 16 weeks of age. *Journal of Pediatrics*, *65*, 576–582.

Robertson, P. M. (1974). Solids and "sleeping through." *British Medical Journal*, *1*, 200.

Salzarulo, P., Fagioli, I., Salomon, F., and Riccour, C. (1979). Alimentation continue et rhythmic veille-sommeil chez l'enfant. (Continuous feeding and the waking-sleeping rhythm in children.) *Archives Francaises de Pediatrie (Suppl)*, *36*, 26–32.

Schultz, H., Salzrulo, P., Fagiolo, I., and Massetani, R. (1983). REM latency: Development in the first year of life. *Electroencephalography and Clinical Neurophysiology*, *56*, 316–322.

Schulz, H., Massetani, R., Fagioli, I., and Aalzarulo, P. (1985). Spontaneous awakenings from sleep in infants. *Electroencephalography and Clinical Neurophysiology*, *61*, 267–271.

Wright, P., MacLeod, M. A. & Cooper, M. J. (1983). Waking at night: The effect of early feeding experience. *Child Care Health Development*, *9*, 309–319.

The Effects of Healthy Sleep: Sleep Patterns, Intelligence, Learning, and School Performance

Anders, T. F., Keener, M. A., and Kraemer, H. (1985). Sleep-wake state organization, neonatal assessment and development in premature infants during the first year of life: Part II. *Sleep*, *8*, 193–206.

Bonnet, M. H. (1985). Effect of sleep disruption in sleep, performance, and mood. *Sleep*, *8*, 11–19.

Busby, K., and Pikik, R. T. (1983). Sleep patterns in children of superior intelligence. *Journal of Child Psychology and Psychiatry*, *24*, 587–600.

Denenberg, V. H., and Thoman, E. B. (1981). Evidence for a functional role for active (REM) sleep in infancy. *Sleep*, *4*, 185–191.

Dunst, C. J., and Lingerfelt, B. (1985). Maternal ratings of temperament and operant learning in two- to three-month-old infants. *Child Development*, *56*, 555–563.

Fibiger, W., Singer, G., Miller, A. J., Armstrong, S., and Datar, M. (1984). Cortisol and catecholamine changes as functions of time-of-day and self-reported mood. *Neuroscience Biobehavioral Reviews*, *8*, 523–530.

Hayaski, Y. (1927). On the sleeping hours at school, children of 6 to 20 years. *Psychological Abstracts*, *1*, 439.

Johs, M. W., Gay, T. J. A., Masterton, J. P., and Bruce, D. W. (1971). Relationship between sleep habits, adrenocortical activity and personality. *Psychosomatic Medicine*, *33*, 499–508.

Matheny, A. D., and Dolan, A. B. (1974). Childhood sleep characteristics and reading achievement. *JSAS Catalog of Selected Documents in Psychology, 4,* 76.

Terman, L. M. (1925). *Genetic studies of genius: Vol. 1. Mental and physical traits of a thousand gifted children.* Palo Alto: Stanford University Press.

Weissbluth, M. (1981). Sleep duration and infant temperament. *Journal of Pediatrics, 99,* 817–819.

Weissbluth, M. (1984). Sleep duration, temperament, and Conners' ratings of 3-year-old children. *Journal of Developmental and Behavioral Pediatrics, 5,* 120–123.

Weissbluth, M. (1985). How sleep affects school performance. *Gifted Children Monthly, 6,* 14–15.

Chapter 3. Disturbed Sleep

Mood and Performance

Beltramini, A. U., and Hertzog, M. E. (1983). Sleep and bedtime behavior in preschool-aged children. *Pediatrics, 71,* 153–158.

Dement, W. C., and Carskadon, M. A. (1982). Current perspectives on daytime sleepiness: The issues. *Sleep, 5* (Supplement 2), S56–S66.

Dixon, K. N., Monroe, L. J., and Jakim, S. (1981). Insomniac children. *Sleep, 4,* 313–318.

Fibiger, W., Singer, G., Miller, A. J., Armstrong, S., and Datar, M. (1984). Cortisol and catecholamines changes as functions of time-of-day and self-reported mood. *Neuroscience Biobehavioral Reviews, 8,* 523–530.

Gaillard, J. M.(1985). Neurochemical regulation of the states of alertness. *Annals of Clinical Research, 17,* 175–184.

Gunner, M. R., Malone, S., Vance, G., and Fisch, R. O. (1985). Coping with aversive stimulation in the neonatal period: Quiet sleep and plasma cortisol levels during recovery from circumcision. *Child Development, 56,* 824–834.

Harrison, G. A. (1985). Stress, catecholamines, and sleep. *Aviation, Space and Environmental Medicine, 56,* 651–653.

Hauri, P., and Olmstead, E. (1980). Childhood-onset insomnia. *Sleep, 3*, 59–65.

Hicks, R. A., and Pellegrini, R. J. (1977). Anxiety levels of short and long sleepers. *Psychological Reports, 41*, 569–570.

Johs, M. W., Gay, T. J. A., Masterton, J. P., and Bruce, D. W. (1971). Relationship between sleep habits, adrenocortical activity and personality. *Psychosomatic Medicine, 33*, 499–508.

Kales, A., Bixler, E. O., Vela-Bueno, A., Cadieux, R. J., Soldatos, C. R., and Kales, J. D. (1984). Biopsychobehavioral correlates of insomnia: Part III. Polygraphic findings of sleep difficulty and their relationship to psychopathology. *International Journal of Neuroscience, 23*, 43–56.

Lucey, D. R., Hauri, P., and Snyder, M. L. (1981). The wakeful "Type A" student. *International Journal of Psychosomatic Medicine, 101*, 333–337.

Price, V. A., Coates, T. J., Thoresen, C. E., and Grinstead, O. A. (1978). Prevalence and correlates of poor sleep among adolescents. *American Journal of Diseases of Children, 132*, 583–586.

Simonds, J. F., and Parraga, H. (1982). Prevalence of sleep disorders and sleep behaviors in children and adolescents. *Journal of the American Academy of Child Psychiatry, 4*, 383–388.

Sundell, C. E. (1922). Sleeplessness in infants. *Practitioner, 109*, 89–92.

Tan, T. L., Kales, J. D., Kales, A., Soldatos, C. R., and Bixler, E. O. (1984). Biopsychobehavioral correlates of insomnia: Part IV. Diagnosis based on DSM III. *American Journal of Psychiatry, 141*, 357–362.

Night Waking

Coulter, D. L., and Allen, R. J. (1982). Benign neonatal sleep myoclonus. *Archives of Neurology, 39*, 191–192.

Earls, F. (1980). Prevalence of behavior problems in 3-year-old children. *Archives of General Psychiatry, 37*, 1153–1157.

Fukumoto, M., Muchozuki, N., Tekeishi, M., Nomura, Y.,

and Segawa, M. (1981). Studies of body movements during night sleep in infancy. *Brain and Development*, *3*, 37–43.

Karacan, I., Wolff, S. M., Williams, R. L., Hurscl, C. J., and Webb, W. B. (1968). The effects of fever on sleep and dream patterns. *Psychosomatics*, *9*, 331–339.

Oster, J., and Nelson, A. (1974). Growing pains: A clinical investigation of a school problem. *Acta Paediatrica Scandinavia*, *61*, 329–334.

Radbill, S. X. (1965). Teething in fact and fancy. *Bulletin of the History of Medicine*, *39*, 339–345.

Richman, N. (1981). A community survey of characteristics of 1- to 2-year-olds with sleep disruption. *American Academy of Child Psychiatry*, *20*, 281–291.

Tasanen, A. (1969). General and local effects of the eruption of deciduous teeth. *Annales de Paediatrac Fenniae*, *14*, Supplement 29.

Weissbluth, M. (1982). Modification of sleep schedule with reduction of night waking: A case report. *Sleep*, *5*, 262–266.

Weissbluth, M., Christoffel, K. K., and Davis A. T. (1984). Treatment of infantile colic with dicyclomine hydrochloride. *Journal of Pediatrics*, *104*, 951–955.

Weissbluth, M., Davis, A. T., and Poncher, J. (1984). Night waking in 4- to 8-month-old infants. *Journal of Pediatrics*, *104*, 477–480.

Excessive Daytime Sleepiness

Hoddes, E., Zarcone, V., Smythe, H., Phillips, R., and Dement, W. C. (1973). Quantification of sleepiness: A new approach. *Psychophysiology*, *10*, 431–436.

Stepanski, E., Lamphere, J., Badia, P., Zorick, F., and Roth, T. (1984). Sleep fragmentation and daytime sleepiness. *Sleep*, *7*, 18–26.

Chapter 4: How Crybabies Become Crabby Kids: Colic and the Postcolic Child

Introduction

Breslow, L. (1957). A clinical approach to infantile colic: A review of 90 cases. *Journal of Pediatrics, 50,* 196–206.

Illingworth, R. S. (1954). "Three months" colic. *Archives of Diseases of Children, 29,* 167–174.

Meyer, J. E., and Thaler, M. M. (1971). Colic in low birth-weight infants. *American Journal of Diseases of Children, 122,* 25–27.

Pierce, P. (1948). Delayed onset of "three months" colic in premature infants. *American Journal of Diseases of Children, 75,* 190–192.

Wessel, M. A., Cobb, J. C., Jackson, E. B., Harris, G. S., and Detwiler, A. C. (1954). Paroxysmal fussing in infancy, sometimes called "colic." *Pediatrics, 14,* 421–434.

Some Babies Cry a Little, Some Cry a Lot

Aldrich, C. A., Sung, C., and Knop, C. (1945). The crying of newly born babies: Part II. The individual phase. *Journal of Pediatrics, 27,* 89–96.

Boon, W. H. (1982). The crying baby. *Journal of the Singapore Paediatric Society, 24,* 145–147.

Brazelton, T. B. (1962). Crying in infancy. *Pediatrics, 29,* 579–588.

Emde, R.N., Gaensbauer, T. J., and Harman, P. J. (1976). Emotional expression in infancy: A biobehavioral study. *Psychological Issues, 10,* 1–200.

Hunziker, U. A., and Barr, R. G. (1986). Increased carrying reduces infant crying: A randomized controlled trial. *Pediatrics, 77,* 641–648.

Illingworth, R. S. (1955). Crying in infants and children. *British Medical Journal, 1,* 75–78.

Lester, B. M., and Bookydis, C. F. Z. (eds.) (1985). *Infant crying.* New York: Plenum Press.

Lounsbuery, M. L., and Bates, J. E. (1982). The cries of infants of differing levels of perceived temperamental difficultness: Acoustic properties and effects on listeners. *Child Development*, *53*, 677–686.

Rebelsky, F., and Black, R. (1972). Crying in infancy. *Journal of Genetic Psychology*, *121*, 49–57.

Snow, M. E., Jacklin, C. N., and Maccoby, E. E. (1980). Crying episodes and sleep-wakefulness transitions in the first 26 months of life. *Infant Behavior and Development*, *3*, 387–394.

Zeskind, P. S., and Huntington, L. (1984). The effects of within-group and between-group methodologies in the study of perceptions of infant crying. *Child Development*, *55*, 1658–1665.

What Happens When Baby Does Not Stop Crying?

Carey, W. B. (1972). Clinical application of infant temperament measurements. *Journal of Pediatrics*, *81*, 823–828.

Carey, W. B. (1985). Temperament and increased weight gain in infants. *Journal of Developmental and Behavioral Pediatrics*, *3*, 128–131.

Carey, W. B., and McDevitt, S. C. (1978). Revision of the infant temperament questionnaire. *Pediatrics*, *61*, 735–739.

Collins, D. D., Scoggin, C. H., Zwillich, C. W., and Welf, J. U. (1978). Hereditary aspects of decreased hypoxic response. *Journal of Clinical Investigations*, *62*, 104–110.

Crockenberg, S. B., and Smith, P. (1982). Antecedents of mother-infant interaction and infant-irritability in the first three months of life. *Infant Behavior and Development*, *5*, 105–119.

DeVries, M. (1984). Temperament and infant mortality among the Masai of East Africa. *American Journal of Psychiatry*, *141*, 1189–1194.

Freedman, D. G. (1979). Ethnic differences in babies. *Human Nature*, *2*, 36–43.

Matheny, A. P., Wilson, R. S., Dolan, A. B., and Krantz, J. Z. (1985). Behavioral contrasts in twinships: Stability and patterns of differences in childhood. *Child Development*, *52*, 579–588.

Monnier, M., and Gaillard, J. M. (1980). Biochemical regulation of sleep. *Experientia*, *36*, 21–21.

O'Connor, L. H., and Feder, H. H. (1984). Estradiol and progesterone influence a serotonin mediated behavioral syndrome (myoclonus) in female guinea pigs. *Brain Research*, *293*, 119–125.

Schulz, H., Salzarulo, P., Fagioli, I., and Massetani, R. (1983). REM latency: Development in the first year of life. *Electroencephalography and Clinical Neurophysiology*, *56*, 316–322.

Shaver, B. A. (1974). Maternal personality and early adaptation as related to infantile colic. In P. M. Schereshefsky and L. J. Yarrow (eds.), *Psychological aspects of a first pregnancy and early postnatal adaptation* (209–215). New York: Raven Press.

Stenger, K. (1956). Therapy of spastic bronchitis. *Med Klin*, *51*, 1451–1455.

Sullivan, C. E., Murphy, E., Kozar, L. F., and Phillipson, E. A. (1979). Ventilatory responses to CO_2 and lung inflation in tonic versus phasic REM sleep. *Journal of Applied Physiology: Respiration, Environment and Exercise Physiology*, *47*, 1304–1310.

Tandon, P., Gupta, M. L., and Barthwal, J. P. (1983). Role of monoamine oxidase-B in medroxyprogesterone acetate (17-acetoxy-6 gamma-methyl-4-pregnene-4-3, 20-dione) induced changes in brain dopamine levels in rats. *Steroids*, *42*, 231–239.

Thomas, A., Chess, S., and Birch, H. G. (1968). *Temperament and behavior disorders in childhood*. New York: New York University Press.

Watanabe, K., Inokuma, K., and Nogoro, T. (1983). REM sleep prevents sudden infant death syndrome. *European Journal of Pediatrics*, *140*, 289–292.

Webb, W. B., and Campbell, S. S. (1983). Relationship in sleep characteristics in identical and fraternal twins. *Archives of General Psychiatry*, *40*, 1093–1095.

Weissbluth, M. (1981). Infantile colic and near-miss sudden infant death syndrome. *Medical Hypothesis*, 7, 1193–1199.

Weissbluth, M., Brouillette, R. T., Liu, K., and Hunt, C. E. (1982). Sleep apnea, sleep duration, and infant temperament. *Journal of Pediatrics*, *101*, 307–310.

Weissbluth, M., Christoffel, K. K., and Davis, A. T. (1984). Treatment of infantile colic with dicyclomine hydrochloride. *Journal of Pediatrics*, *104*, 951–955.

Weissbluth, M., and Green, O. C. (1984). Plasma progesterone concentration and infant termperament. *Journal of Developmental and Behavioral Pediatrics*, *5*, 251–253.

Weissbluth, M., Hunt, C., Brouillette, R. T., Hanson, D., David, R. J., and Stein, I. M. (1985). Respiratory patterns during sleep and temperament ratings in normal infants. *Journal of Pediatrics*, *106*, 688–690.

Brief Sleep and Night Waking
Dunst, C. J., and Lingerfelt, B. (1985). Maternal ratings of temperament and operant learning in 2- to 3-month-old infants. *Child Development*, *56*, 555–563.

Weissbluth, M. (1981). Sleep duration and infant temperament. *Journal of Pediatrics*, *99*, 817–819.

Weissbluth, M. (1984). *Crybabies*. New York: Arbor House.

Weissbluth, M. (1986). Infant colic. In S. S. Gellis, and B. M. Kagan (eds.), *Current pediatric therapy* (12th ed., 765–767). Philadelphia: W. B. Saunders.

Weissbluth, M., Davis, A. T., and Poncher, J. (1984). Night waking in 4- to 8-month-old infants. *Journal of Pediatrics*, *104*, 477–480.

Weissbluth, M., and Liu, K. (1983). Sleep patterns, attention span, and infant temperament. *Journal of Developmental and Behavioral Pediatrics*, *4*, 34–36.

Are Poor Sleep Habits Congenital?
Etzel, B. C., and Gewirtz, J. L. (1967). Experimental modification of caretaker-maintained high-rate operant crying in a 6- and 20-week old infant (Infans tyrannotearus): Ex-

tinction of crying with reinforcement of eye contact and smiling. *Journal of Experimental Child Psychology*, *5*, 503–517.

Richman, N., Douglas, J., Hunt, H., Lansdown, R., and Levere, R. (1985). Behavioral methods in the treatment of sleep disorders—A pilot study. *Journal of Child Psychology and Psychiatry*, *26*, 581–590.

Weissbluth, M. (1982). Modification of sleep schedule with reduction of night waking: A case report. *Sleep*, *5*, 262–266.

Williams, C. D. (1959). The elimination of tantrum behavior by extinction procedures. *Journal of Abnormal and Social Psychology*, *59*, 269.

Crabology and Momitis

Ogden, T. H. (1985). The mother, the infant and the matrix: Interpretations of aspects of the work of Donald Winnocott. *Contemporary Psychoanalysis*, *21*, 346–371.

Active Explorers

Karelitz, S., Fisichelli, V. R., Costa, J., Karelitz, R., and Rosenfeld, L. (1964). Relation of crying activity in early infancy to speech and intellectual development at age three years. *Child Development*, *35*, 769–777.

Chapter 5. Months 1 to 4

Etzel, B. C., and Gewirtz, J. L. (1967). Experimental modification of caretaker-maintained high-rate operant crying in a 6- and 20-week-old infant (Infans tyrannotearus): Extinction of crying with reinforcement of eye contact and smiling. *Journal of Experimental Child Psychology*, *5*, 303–317.

Fagan, J. W., Ohr, P. J., Fleckenstein, L. K., and Ribner, D. R. (1985). The effects of crying on long-term memory in infancy. *Child Development*, *56*, 1584–1592.

Leach, Penelope (1978). *Your baby and child from birth to five.* New York: Alfred A. Knopf.

Maziade, M., Boudreault, M., Cote, R., and Thivierage, J. (1986). Influence of gentle birth delivery procedures and other perinatal circumstances on infant temperament: Developmental and social implications. *Journal of Pediatrics*, *108*, 134–136.

Spock, Benjamin. (1983). *Baby and child care*. New York: Pocket Books.

Chapter 6. Months 4 to 12

Caren, S., and Searleman, A. (1985). Birth stress and self-reported sleep difficulty. *Sleep*, *8*, 222–226.

Douglas, J., and Richman, N. (1984). *My child won't sleep*. Hammondsworth, Middlesex, England: Penguin Books.

Hirschberg, J. C. (1957). Parental anxieties accompanying sleep disturbance in young children. *Bulletin of the Menninger Clinic*, *21*, 129–139.

Klastskin, E. H., Jackson, E. B., and Wilkin, L. C. (1956). The influence of degree of flexibility in maternal child care practices on early child behavior. *American Journal of Orthopsychiatry*, *26*, 79–93.

Mahler, M. S. (1972). On the first three subphases of the separation-individuation process. *International Journal of Psycho-Analysis*, 53, 333–338.

Thomas, A., and Chess, S. (1984). Genesis and evolution of behavioral disorders: From infancy to early adult life. *American Journal of Psychiatry*, *141*, 1–9.

Webb, W. B., and Agnew, H. W. (1974). Regularity in the control of the free-running sleep-wakefulness rhythm. *Aerospace Medicine*, *45*, 701–704.

Weissbluth, M. (1982). Modification of sleep schedule with reduction of night waking: A case report. *Sleep*, *5*, 262–266.

Winnicott, D. W. (1965). The capacity to be alone. In Winnicott, D. W., *The maturational processes and facilitating environment* (29–36). New York: International Universities Press.

Chapter 7. Months 12 to 36

Gutelius, M. E., and Kirsch, A. D. (1977). Controlled study of child health supervision: Behavioral results. *Pediatrics*, *60*, 294–304.

Howarth, E., and Hoffman, M. S. (1984). A multidimensional approach to the relationship between mood and weather. *British Journal of Psychology*, *75*, 5–23.

Largo, R. H., and Honziker, U. A. (1984). A developmental approach to the management of children with sleep disturbances in the first three years of life. *European Journal of Pediatrics*, *142*, 170–173.

Lozoff, B., Wolf, A. W., and Davis, N. S. (1985). Sleep problems seen in pediatric practice. *Pediatrics*, 75, 477–483.

Richman, N. (1981). A community survey of one- to two-year-olds with sleep disruptions. *Journal of the American Academy of Child Psychiatry*, *20*, 281–291.

Van Tassel, E. B. (1985). The relative influence of child and environmental characteristics on sleep disturbances in the first and second years of life. *Journal of Developmental and Behavioral Pediatrics*, *6*, 81–86.

Williams, C. D. (1959). Case report: The elimination of tantrum behavior by extinction procedures. *Journal of Abnormal and Social Psychology*, *59*, 269.

Chapter 8. Young Children: Years 3 to 6

Clarkson, S., Williams, S., and Silva, P. A. (1986). Sleep in middle childhood—A longitudinal study of sleep problems in a large sample of Dunedin children aged 5–9 years. *Australian Paediatric Journal*, *22*, 31–35.

Cullen, K. J. (1976). A 6-year controlled trial of prevention of children's behavior disorders. *Journal of Pediatrics*, *88*, 662–666.

Jones, D. P. H., and Verduyn, C. M. (1983). Behavioral management of sleep problems. *Archives of Diseases of Children*, *58*, 442–444.

Richman, N., Douglas, J., Hunt, H., Lansdown, R., and Levere, R. (1985). Behavioral methods in the treatment of sleep disorders—A pilot study. *Journal of Child Psychology and Psychiatry*, *26*, 581–590.

Wright, L., Woodcock, J., and Scott, R. (1970). Treatment of sleep disturbance in a young child by conditioning. *Southern Medical Journal*, *63*, 174–176.

Chapter 9. Older Children: Years 7 to 12 and Adolescence

Anders, T. E., Carskadon, M. A., Dement, W. C., and Harvey, K. (1978). Sleep habits of children and the identification of pathologically sleepy children. *Child Psychiatry and Human Development*, 9, 56–63.

Anderson, D. R. (1979). Treatment of insomnia in a 13-year-old boy by relaxation training and reduction of parental attention. *Journal of Behavioral Therapy and Experimental Psychiatry*, 10, 263–265.

Asnes, R. S., Sautulli, R., and Beuporad, J. R. (1981). Psychogenic chest pain in children. *Clinical Pediatrics*, 20, 788–792.

Backeland, F., and Lasky, R. (1966). Exercise and sleep patterns in college athletes. *Perceptual and Motor Skills*, 23, 1203–1207.

Bootzin, R. (1972). A stimulus control treatment for insomnia. *Proceedings of the American Psychological Association*, 7, 395–396.

Czeisler, C. A., Weitzman, E. D., Moore-Ede, M. C., Zimmerman, J. C., and Knaver, R. S. (1980). Human sleep: Its duration and organization depend on its circadian phases. *Science*, 210, 1264–1267.

Dollinger, S. J. (1985). Effects of a paradoxical intervention on a child's anxiety about sleep- and sports-related performance. *Perceptual and Motor Skills*, 61, 83–86.

Espie, C. A., & Lindsay, W. R. (1985). Paradoxical intention in the treatment of chronic insomnia. *Behavioral Research and Therapy*, 23, 703–709.

Hauri, P., and Fisher, J. (1986). Persistent psychophysiologic (learned) insomnia. *Sleep*, 9, 38–53.

Kirmil-Gray, K., Eagleston, J. R., Gibson, E., and Thoresen, C. E. (1985). Sleep disturbances in adolescents: Sleep quality, sleep habits, beliefs about sleep, and daytime functioning. *Journal of Youth and Adolescence*, 13, 375–384.

Nicassio, P. M., and Buchanan, D. C. (1981). Clinical application of behavior therapy for insomnia. *Comprehensive Psychiatry*, 22, 512–521.

Price, V. A., Coates, T. J., Thoresen, C. E., and Grinstead, O. A. (1978). Prevalence and correlates of poor sleep among adolescents. *American Journal of Diseases of Children, 132,* 582–586.

Delayed Sleep Phase Syndrome

Czeisler, C. A., Richardson, G. S., Coleman, R. M., Zimmerman, J. C., Moore-Ede, M. C., Dement, W. C., and Weitzman, E. D. (1981). Chronotherapy: Resetting the circadian clocks of patients with delayed sleep phase insomnia. *Sleep, 4,* 1–21.

Weitzman, E. D., Czeisler, C. A., Coleman, R. M., Spielman, A. J., Zimmerman, J. C., and Dement, W. C. (1981). Delayed sleep phase syndrome. A chronobiological disorder with sleep-onset insomnia. *Archives of General Psychiatry, 38,* 737–746.

Kleine-Levin Syndrome

Ferguson, B. G. (1986). Kleine-Levin Syndrome: A case report. *Journal of Child Psychological Psychiatry, 27,* 275–278.

Waller, D. A., Jarriel, S., Erman, M., and Emslie, G. (1984). Recognizing and managing the adolescent with Kleine-Levin syndrome. *Journal of Adolescent Health Care, 5,* 139–141.

Drugs and Diets to Help Us Sleep

Camfield, C. S., Chaplin, S., Doyle, A. B., Chapiro, S. H., Cummings, C., and Camfield, P. R. (1979). Side effects of phenobarbital in toddlers: Behavioral and cognitive aspects. *Journal of Pediatrics, 95,* 361–365.

Kahn, A., Mozin, M. J., Casimir, G., Montauk, L., and Blum, D. (1985). Insomnia and cow's milk allergy in infants. *Pediatrics, 76,* 880–884.

Kolata, G. (1982). Food affects human behavior. *Science, 218,* 1209–1210.

Norvenius, G., Widerlov, E., and Lonnerholm, G. (1979). Phenylpropanolamine and mental disturbances. *Lancet, 1,* 1367–1368.

Roehrs, T. A., Tietz, E. I., Zorick, F. J., and Roth, T. (1984). Daytime sleepiness and antihistamines. *Sleep*, 7, 137–141.

Russo, R. M., Gururaj, V. J., and Allen, E. J. (1976). The effectiveness of diphenhydramine HC1 in pediatric sleep disorders. *Journal of Clinical Pharmocology*, 16, 284–285.

Ryo, J. E. (1985). Effects of maternal caffeine consumption on heart rate and sleep time in breast-fed infants. *Developmental Pharmacology and Therapeutics*, 8, 355–363.

Schneider-Helmert, D., and Spinweber, C. L. (1986). Evaluation of L-tryptophay for treatment of insomnia. *Psychopharmacology*, 89, 1–7.

Spring, B., Maller, O., Wurtman, J., et al. (1982–1983). Effects of protein and carbohydrate meals on mood and performance: Interactions with sex and age. *Journal of Psychiatric Research*, 17, 155–167.

Yogman, M. W., and Zeizel, S. H. (1985). Nutrients, neurotransmitters and infant behavior. *American Journal of Clinical Nutrition*, 45, 352–360.

Chapter 10. Special Sleep Problems

Sleepwalking

Kales, A., Soldatos, C. R., Caldwell, A. B., Kales, J. D., Humphrey, F. J., Charney, D. S., and Schweitzer, P. K. (1980). Somnambulism: Clinical characteristics and personality patterns. *Archives of General Psychiatry*, 37, 1406–1410.

Klackenberg, G. (1982). Somnambulism in childhood—Prevalence, course, and behavioral correlations. *Acta Paediatrica Scandinavia*, 71, 495–499.

Sleeptalking

Reimao, R., and Lefevre, A. B., (1980). Prevalence of sleeptalking in childhood. *Brain Development*, 2, 353–357.

Night Terrors

Kales, J. D., Kales, A., Soldatos, C. R., Chamberlain, K., and Martin, E. D. (1979). Sleep walking and night terrors related to febrile illness. *American Journal of Psychiatry, 136*, 1214–1215.

Weissbluth, M. (1984). Is drug treatment of night terrors warranted? *American Journal of Diseases of Children, 138*, 1086.

Nightmares

Cason, H. (1935). The nightmare dream. *Psychological Monographs, 46* (5, Whole No. 209).

Cellucci, A. J., and Lawrence, P. S. (1978). Individual differences in self-reported sleep-variable correlations among nightmare sufferers. *Journal of Clinical Psychology, 34*, 721–725.

Head Banging and Body Rocking

Abe, K., Oda, N., and Amatomi, M. (1984). Natural history and predictive significance of head-banging, head-rolling and breathholding spells. *Developmental Medicine and Child Neurology, 26*, 644–648.

Bruxism

Reding, G. R., Rubright, W. C., and Zimmerman, S. O. (1966). Incidence of bruxism. *Journal of Dental Research, 45*, 1198–1204.

Reding, G. R., Zepelin, H., and Monroe, L. J. (1968). Personality study of nocturnal teeth grinders. *Perceptual and Motor Skills, 26*, 523–531.

Reding, G. R., Zepelin, H., Robinson, J. E., Smith, V. H., and Zimmerman, S. O. (1968). Sleep pattern of bruxism: A revision. *Psychophysiology, 4*, 396.

Narcolepsy

Yoss, R. E., and Daly, D. D. (1960). Narcolepsy in children. *Pediatrics, 77*, 1025–1033.

Poor Quality Breathing (Snoring and Allergies)

Anderson, O. W. (1951). The management of "infantile insomnia." *Journal of Pediatrics, 38*, 394-401.

Ballenger, W. L. (1914). *Diseases of the nose, throat and ear.* Philadelphia: Lea & Febiger.

Brouillette, R., Hansen, D., David, R., Klemka, L., Szatkowski, A., Fernbach, S., and Hunt, C. (1984). A diagnostic approach to suspected obstructive sleep apnea in children. *Journal of Pediatrics, 105*, 10-14.

Brown, S. L., and Stool, S. E. (1982). Behavioral manifestations of sleep apnea in children. *Sleep, 5*, 200-201.

Butte, W., Robertson, C., and Phelan, P. (1985). Snoring in children: Is it pathological? *Medical Journal of Australia, 143*, 335-336.

Flemming, B. M. (1925). A study of the sleep of young children. *Journal of the American Association of University Women, 19*, 25-28.

Guilleminault, C., and Dement, W. C. (1977). 235 cases of excessive daytime sleepiness. *Journal of Neurological Sciences, 31*, 13-27.

Guilleminault, C., Eldridge, F. L., Simmons, F. B., and Dement, W. C. (1976). Sleep apnea in eight children. *Pediatrics, 58*, 23-31.

Kahn, A., Mozin, J., and Casimir, G. (1985). Insomnia and cow's milk allergy in infants. *Pediatrics, 76*, 880-884.

Klein, G. L., Ziering, R. W., Girsh, L. S., and Miller, M. F. (1985). The allergic irritability syndrome: Four case reports and a position statement from the Neuroallergy Committee of the American College of Allergy. *Annals of Allergy, 55*, 22-24.

Kravath, R. E., Pollack, C. D., and Borowiecki, B. (1977). Hypoventilation during sleep in children who have lymphoid airway obstruction treated by nasopharyngeal tube and T and A. *Pediatrics, 59*, 865-871.

Lind, M. G., and Lundell, B. (1982). Tonsillar hyperplasia in children: A cause of obstructive sleep apneas, CO_2 retention, and retarded growth. *Archives of Otolaryngology, 108*, 650-654.

Mangat, D., Orr, W. C., and Smith, R. O. (1977). Sleep apnea, hypersomnolence, and upper airway obstruction secondary to adenotonsillar enlargement. *Archives of Otolaryngology, 103,* 383–386.

Mauer, K. W., Staats, B. A., and Olsen, K. D. (1983). Upper airway obstruction and disordered nocturnal breathing in children. *Mayo Clinic Proceedings, 58,* 349–353.

Weissbluth, M., Davis, A. T., and Poncher, J. (1984). Night waking in 4- to 8-month-old infants. *Journal of Pediatrics, 104,* 477–480.

Weissbluth, M., Davis, A. T., Poncher, J., and Reiff, J. (1983). Signs of airway obstruction during sleep and behavioral, developmental, and academic problems. *Journal of Developmental and Behavioral Pediatrics, 4,* 119–121.

Locating the Problem

Brouillette, R., and Thach, B. T. (1979). A neuromuscular mechanism maintaining extrathoracic airway patency. *Journal of Applied Physiology: Respiration, Environment, Exercise and Physiology, 46,* 772–779.

Brouillette, R., Fernbach, S. K., and Hunt, C. E. (1982). Obstructive sleep apnea in infants and children. *Journal of Pediatrics, 100,* 31–40.

Chokroverty, S. (1980). Phasic tongue movements in human rapid-eye-movement sleep. *Neurology, 30,* 665–668.

Felman, A. H., Loughlin, G. M., Leftridge, C. A., and Cassisi, N. J. (1979). Upper airway obstruction during sleep in children. *American Journal of Respiration, 133,* 213–216.

Haponik, E. F., Smith, P. L., Bohlman, M. E., Allen, R. P., Goldman, S. M., and Bleecker, E. R. (1983). Computerized tomography in obstructive sleep apnea: Correlation of airway size with physiology during sleep and wakefulness. *American Review of Respiratory Diseases, 127,* 221–226.

Remmers, J. E., deGroot, W. J., Sauerland, E. K., and Anch, A. M. (1978). Pathogenesis of upper airway occlusive during sleep. *Journal of Applied Physiology: Respiration, Environment, Exercise and Physiology, 44,* 931–938.

Wilkinson, A. R., McCormick, M. S., Freeland, A. P., and Pickering, D. (1981). Electrocardiographic signs of pulmonary hypertension in children who snore. *British Medical Journal*, *282*, 1579–1581.

Finding the Answers
McGeary, G. D. (1981). Help a snorer. *Journal of the American Medical Association*, *245*, 1729.
Simmons, F. B., Guilleminault, C., Dement, W. C., and Tilkian, A. G. (1977). Surgical management of airway obstruction during sleep. *Laryngoscope*, *87*, 326–338.

Enjoying the Cure
Guilleminault, C., Winkle, R., Korobkin, R., and Simmons, B. (1982). Children and nocturnal snoring: Evaluation of the effects of sleep-related respiratory resistive load and daytime functioning. *European Journal of Pediatrics*, *139*, 165–171.

Hyperactive Behavior
Busby, K., Firestone, P., and Pivik, R. T. (1981). Sleep patterns in hyperkinetic and normal children. *Sleep*, *4*, 366–384.
Conners, C. K. (1974). Rating scale for use in drug studies with children. *Psychopharmacology Bulletin* (Special Issue) 24.
Greenhill, L., Puig-Antich, J., Goetz, R., Hanlon, C., and Davies, M. (1983). Sleep architecture and REM sleep measures in prepubertal children with attention deficit disorder with hyperactivity. *Sleep*, *6*, 91–101.
Porrino, L. J., Rapoport, J. L., Behar, D., Sceery, W., Ismond, D. R., and Bunney, W. E. (1983). A naturalistic assessment of the motor activity of hyperactive boys. *Archives of General Psychiatry*, *40*, 681–687.
Simonds, J. F., and Parraga, H. (1984). Sleep behaviors and disorders in children and adolescents evaluated at psychiatric clinics. *Journal of Developmental and Behavioral Pediatrics*, *5*, 6–10.
Weissbluth, M. (1984). Sleep duration, temperament, and

Conners' ratings of 3-year-old children. *Journal of Developmental and Behavioral Pediatrics, 5,* 120–123.

Weissbluth, M., and Liu, K. (1983). Sleep patterns, attention span, and infant temperament. *Journal of Developmental and Behavioral Pediatrics, 4,* 34–36.

Chapter 11. Special Events and Concerns

Injuries

Carey, W. B. (1972). Clinical application of infant temperament measurements. *Journal of Pediatrics, 81,* 823–828.

Richman, N. A. (1981). A community survey of 1- to 2-year-olds with sleep disruptions. *Journal of the American Academy of Child Psychiatry, 20,* 281–291.

Weissbluth, M. (1981). Sleep duration and infant temperament. *Journal of Pediatrics, 5,* 817–819.

Weissbluth, M. (1984). Sleep duration, temperament, and Conners' ratings of 3-year-old children. *Journal of Developmental and Behavioral Pediatrics, 5,* 120–123.

Overweight

Carey, W. B. (1985). Temperament and increased weight gain in infants. *Journal of Developmental and Behavioral Pediatrics, 6,* 128–131.

deVries, M. W. (1984). Temperament and infant mortality among the Masai of East Africa. *American Journal of Psychiatry, 141,* 1189–1194.

Chapter 12. A Sleep Disorder: My Child?

Bettleheim, B. (1975). *The uses of enchantment.* New York: Random House.

Caplan, L. (1978). *Oneness to separateness.* Oak Park, Illinois: La Leche.

Dreikurs, R. (1964). *Children: The challenge.* New York: Hawthorne/Dutton.

Fraiberg, Selma H. (1959). *The Magic Years: Understanding and Handling the Problems of Early Childhood.* New York: Charles Scribner & Sons.

Winnicott, D. W. (1964). *The child, the family and the outside world.* New York: Penguin.

Chapter 13. The Pros and Cons of Other Approaches to Sleep Problems

Cuthbertson, J., and Schevill, S. (1985). *Helping your child sleep through the night.* New York: Doubleday.

Douglas, J., and Richman, N. (1984). *My child won't sleep.* Hammondsworth, Middlesex, England: Penguin Books.

Ferber, R. (1985). *Solve your child's sleep problems.* New York: Simon & Schuster.

McGarr, R. J., and Hovel, M. F. (1980). In search of the sandman: Shaping an infant to sleep. *Education and Treatment of Children, 3,* 173–182.

Index

A

Abnormal sleep schedule, 134–35
Adenoids, effect on sleeping, 208
Adolescents
sleep problems, 189–91
chronic mononucleosis, 192
delayed sleep phase syndrome, 191
drugs/diet to encourage sleep, 194–96
Kleine-Levin syndrome, 191
maintaining healthy sleep schedule, 194
relaxation techniques for falling asleep, 192–93
stimulus-control instructions, 193
Afternoon wakeful time, 122–23
Allergies, 207–8
allergic-irritability syndrome, 208
cow's milk allergy, 196
management of, 212

Anger
mothers, inability to express, 233
nondestructive anger, 243–44
Antihistamines, effect on sleep, 195
Anxiety, and difficulty falling asleep, 196
Attention deficit disorder, 214

B

Back snorers, cure for, 212
Ballenger, Dr. W.C., 205
Bed, graduating from crib to, 244
Bedtime/asleep, 123
Benadryl, effect on sleep, 195
Biofeedback, 192
Biological rhythms, 30–32
Body rocking, 202–3
Bootzin, Richard R., 193
Breastfeeding
and healthy sleep habits, 38–41
nursing to sleep, 129–30
solution to night waking, 156–57

About the Author

A pediatrician for 14 years, Marc Weissbluth, M.D. is also a leading researcher on sleep and children. He founded the Sleep Disorders Center at Chicago's Children's Memorial Hospital in 1982 and is presently its director. Dr. Weissbluth's first book, *Crybabies*, was published by Arbor House and Berkley. He frequently publishes articles on sleep and lectures extensively to parents groups. Dr. Weissbluth is the father of four children—and they are all good sleepers.